WATER AND SKY

YT.

NT.

BAKER L
-end
Aug. 19

Dubawnt R.

Kazan R.

BC.

L. ATHABASCA
-winter site-

Athabasca R.

JASPER
-start-
June 1985

AB.

SK.

MB.

Bozeman, MT.

WATER AND SKY

REFLECTIONS OF A NORTHERN YEAR

Alan S. Kesselheim

with drawings by
Marypat Zitzer

FULCRUM, INC.
GOLDEN, COLORADO

Library of Congress Cataloging-in-Publication Data

Kesselheim, Alan S., 1952 -
        Water and sky : reflections of a northern year / Alan S.
Kesselheim.
            p.   cm.
        ISBN 1-55591-046-7
        1. Canoes and canoeing—Canada, Northern. 2. Canada, Northern-
-Description and travel. I. Title.
GV776.15.C36K47   1989   89-7937
797.1'22'0971—dc20   CIP

Printed in the United States of America

10   9   8   7   6   5   4   3   2   1

Fulcrum, Inc.
Golden, Colorado

To Marypat
my partner

CONTENTS

PREFACE

As much as this is a story about crossing a continent by canoe, a story of fourteen adventurous months spent in northern wilderness, it is a tale about introspective journeying.

I traveled along twin, parallel paths. On one, a red, seventeen-and-one-half-foot canoe was my vessel. In it Marypat and I paddled nearly two thousand miles of Canadian waterways. For 416 days, we strove toward a goal, lived in and grew to cherish pristine country, accepted the environmental hardships that inevitably came our way, and adapted our lives to harmonize with our surroundings.

The second trail led into the wilderness of my mind and heart. It is a journey much more difficult to quantify or adequately describe, and has yet to reach its end. Profound but invisible landmarks stand along that pathway—lessons in friendship and love, benchmarks in physical and mental discipline, a deepening awareness of vulnerability, strength, and humility, appreciation for the value of silence, a reassessment of priorities. The circumstances of the physical expedition served as a means to embark on the personal odyssey. Each voyage enriched the other.

Unavoidably, what follows is my story. Marypat and I were almost never physically apart. Nearly every aspect of travel and daily routine demanded our concerted effort and attention. Our success is the product of that teamwork. And yet, we experienced separately. I cannot, except tangentially, illuminate Marypat's story. The insights she gained, the obstacles she overcame, the confidence she achieved, are hers. My view of them is dim and colored by my perceptions.

We began our travel tentatively, full of trepidation and anxiety. Physically and emotionally we were inadequately prepared for the scope and duration of the endeavor. But more than a year later, with the better part of a continent in our wake, and the confidence of achievement fortifying our self-esteem, we found ourselves struggling to cope with cultural re-entry, mourning the end of the trail.

By the final morning, when we beached our canoe for the last time at the Inuit settlement of Baker Lake, we had weathered the cyclical waxing and waning of northern seasons. Our bodies had become lean and strong. Prolonged periods of silence and reflection had lent our thoughts a crystalline clarity. We had become each other's most intimate friend. We had experienced a land so vast and powerful and wild that it surpassed any territory we had explored previously.

The seeds of the adventure were planted years before we ever set our canoe into the swift current of the Athabasca River. As best as I can reconstruct the scene, the initial suggestion came up during breakfast one spring morning in the desert. Marypat and I were camped in the canyon lands of Utah. Dawdling over the morning meal, while the second or third pot of coffee perked on top of the stove, we discussed some of our wilderness ambitions.

Between the two of us, we'd canoed the far north, explored southwestern deserts, pedaled thousands of miles on bike tours, skied and backpacked through the Rocky Mountains, and hiked the southern third of the Appalachian Trail. Somehow, that morning, we got on the subject of adopting a really extended challenge, a trip that would take us through a full cycle of seasons, cover a large chunk of geography, and bring to fulfillment the potential rewards of long wilderness immersion. Our common feeling was that while past excursions always had been satisfying, we invariably came to the end wishing the experience could be longer.

Over the months the topic kept resurfacing, pestering us. Without really committing ourselves, we began refining the plans. We identified the Canadian north as our geographic focus, decided on a canoe as our vehicle, considered a group of as many as six people then elected to travel on our own, and even sketched out some possible routes.

At some point it became clear that we had to call our own bluff or drop the idea. If we were in earnest, we had to set a date and work toward it. How the transition in our thinking came about remains largely a mystery to me. It certainly was arbitrary. One of us said something like, "What about the summer after next?" When we couldn't think of a good reason to reject it, the expedition suddenly had a departure date.

Then, for more than a year before we dipped a paddle into the Athabasca River, we prepared for our endeavor. That process itself proved as arduous and challenging as the goal we aimed for. It was a time fraught with stress and anxiety, full of drudgery and niggling details, and bereft of any exhilarating rewards. By the time the trip began, a kind of numbed exhaustion took the place of what should have been the heady fruition of months of work.

Our efforts consumed the time and energy of a half-time job. We wrote letters, ordered maps, ferreted out route descriptions, dehydrated hundreds of pounds of food, repaired equipment, and talked about our trip. We talked so often and for so long about our plans that I began to disbelieve them. I lost sight of the reality of the voyage behind the screen of words, and began to doubt the idea itself.

At several low points we were ready to drop the expedition completely. Money was a problem, the length of time outrageous, and the logistics overwhelming. For one reason or another, however, we kept at it. Each provided support when the other was at low ebb, or some fortuitous turn of events would buoy our spirits at a critical moment. Finally, I knew that I had talked too much to renege without having a damned good reason. Perhaps, as much as anything, I stuck with it out of a vain and stubborn refusal to be labeled a big talker who didn't deliver.

Despite all the work, despite my obsession with the goal, it was a shock to find myself, in early June of 1985, standing in our empty house, surrounded by expedition equipment, poised for departure. Our belongings filled a ten-foot-by-ten-foot storage shed. The small rental house we'd lived in was stripped of our things. The packs of food and equipment, our support framework for the next fourteen months, cluttered a corner of the living room.

Everything was done, the last item on the logistics list checked off, but I felt far from ready. Standing in the quiet bare house, waiting for a ride to a festive send-off dinner, I felt overweight and in poor shape, hassled by details, burdened with doubt. The pure unfettered vision of the journey had been lost in the pressure of chores and the obscuring fog of conversation.

That June afternoon I teetered timidly at the threshold of adventure. I could hardly conceptualize the superficial outline of what lay ahead, much less guess at its significance. The true test and eventual reward before me lay in the process of discovering the way, both the way across a vast wild land and the way into my veiled inner regions.

ACKNOWLEDGMENTS

Writing this book often resembled the process of taking the expedition it is about. I experienced similar highs and lows, daunting periods of trepidation and insecurity, times of complete mental and emotional immersion, even a moment or two of exhilaration. Beginning page one of the book evoked the same sense of awe and doubt that I felt sitting in the canoe on the first day of our journey. As I completed the final difficult paragraph, I found myself engulfed in a whirlpool of emotions that vividly reminded me of the internal conflict I experienced on Day Four-Hundred-Sixteen of the expedition as I climbed out of the canoe for the last time.

Neither the expedition nor the book became realities within a vacuum. Many people played integral roles in the success of both projects. My parents, Chelsea and Donn Kesselheim, have lived adventurous, creative lives during which reasonable risks have been seen as a critical part of growth and personal development. Without their example and encouragement, the expedition, and thus this book, might well never have been launched.

Marypat Zitzer infused the expedition with her exuberance, determination and joy. Her maps and illustrations are an essential and complementary part of this work. Beyond that, she willingly adapted her life in the many difficult ways necessary to allow the book to be written.

The editing acumen of my friend Marilyn Grant was instrumental in polishing and tightening the early manuscript drafts into a form acceptable for submission. The lightning typing fingers of Marjorie Smith transformed that manuscript into a tidy, professional package.

I thank Pat Frederick and the terrific crew at Fulcrum for their enthusiastic response to my story, and for shepherding the book through all the necessary, often tedious, frustrating, and time-consuming steps from manuscript to final product. Our interaction has been characterized by good humor, understanding, and sensitivity. Similarly, I thank David Walmark and the crew of Stoddart Publishing in Canada for seeing potential in my work and publishing it in the country across which I paddled.

The expedition logistics were faithfully tended to by Mark Cowett. Besides keeping us supplied with essential food and equipment, Mark sent books and magazines during the winter, kept us in touch with a network of friends, and lent his personal touch to our experience.

The following companies aided our efforts with equipment sponsorship: Bending Branches, Blackadar Boating, Blue Hole Canoe, Coleman, Dana Design, Delta Designs, The Great Outdoors, Gutmann, Harvest Maid, JLM Visuals, Medallion Knitware, Reliance, Rome Industries, Silva, Smokey Canyon, and Wigwam Mills.

Without the support, encouragement, and professional skill of these people, among many others, neither the expedition nor my written account of it would have been possible.

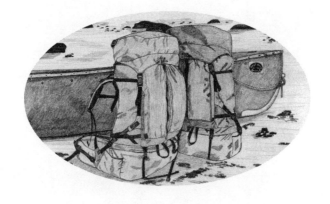

PART I

A PLACE TO BEGIN

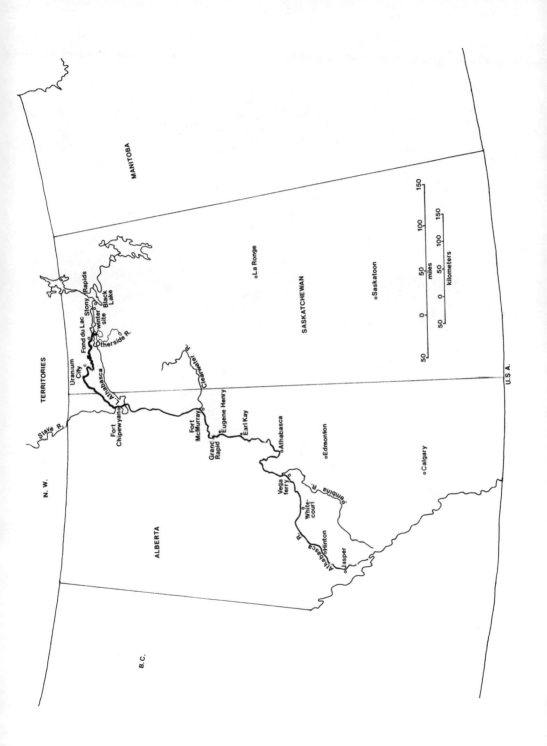

I approached the Athabasca River for the first time with the tension and diffidence of a frontier man meeting the train that carried his mail-order bride. It was not the kind of setting I had hoped for. Cold rain gusted out of lowering clouds and ran in frigid rivulets down the cuffs of my jacket. Dripping vegetation wetted my pant legs as I pushed along a narrow muddy trail to the river. The thick forest and dark slopes lent a forbidding sense of oppression to the mountainous scene. I felt confronted rather than welcomed.

The Athabasca would be my home for almost one thousand miles, my companion, my adversary, my only way out—an impassive force with which I had to negotiate terms. Like the lonely man meeting his mate, I had never seen the river and knew of its qualities only indirectly. Yet mine, like his, was a commitment not easily dropped should things prove difficult. I had set myself up for an adventure, done things to make it possible, romanticized about the experience, but felt, at this first encounter of the journey, as if the last thing I wanted was to begin.

I broke out of the woods onto a cobble beach. The Athabasca chuckled in front of me, flowing fast, a milky green from the slurry of rock ground under the inexorable weight of the icefields that feed the river. Wisps of mist and cloud tore apart on the black teeth of buttresses across from me. The grimy snouts of glaciers poked through the clouds, their fat tongues lolling down the valleys.

Even near its source, the Athabasca looked powerful, willful, cocky. The river appeared unconnected to the country it hurried through, as if pushing toward better things downstream. Below the steady chatter of current, I could hear the thudding and clicking of river rock being sorted—boulders and pebbles being jostled and sized, knocked against each other, rounded, ablated, and put in new order by an insensate but fussy hand. Upstream, the valley faded into fog and cloud and ice. Downstream, the river bed visibly tilted to aid the impatient current. I tried to imagine, without success, the challenges and rewards that lay that way.

It occurred to me that every river trip I could remember had begun in the rain. I recalled unloading canoes from a boxcar in northern Quebec, with sleety rain slanting out of the sky; changing a tire on another pre-departure night in a soggy Northwest Territory campground sited on clayey quicksand that sucked the car jack down as quickly as I ratcheted it up. Something in a cold rain at the beginning of a journey makes me feel puny and tentative—the whole thing is a crazy joke, so let's go home.

Minutes passed. Standing on the wet round river rock, with the rain like a clammy hand on my skin, I felt no communion with the Athabasca. I eyed the river as a stranger, unable to take its measure, without enough information to judge its character.

I returned along the sloppy trail to camp, where our red canoe lay strapped to the cartop, untested and looking a bit too virginal to inspire confidence. I watched Marypat trying to light a stove on the end of a picnic table that was sheltered by a small tarp tied incongruously to tree limbs and vehicle sideview mirrors. The family members who had traveled with us formed a disgruntled group under the sagging nylon protection.

Gear was stowed haphazardly in packs, car trunks, and back seats. Dinner, a one-pot conglomeration, took a good deal more time to prepare than it should have. With some difficulty and an assist from camp fuel, we finally managed to start a sputtering, wholly ornamental fire.

Later on, after dark, Marypat and I lay in our sleeping bags, listening to the drizzle against the tent and the wind rushing through the trees. We didn't talk. I knew she was thinking of the people we were leaving behind, the comfort of familiar patterns we were giving up, the gaping horizon of time and country that filled our future. I thought about the Athabasca River coursing by outside under the clouds, moving rocks, patiently wearing its channel, rising with rain and gathering runoff. The river I soon would begin to know.

I imagined the frontier man and his new bride riding home in the buckboard, daunted by the spaciousness, each shocked by the impetuous thing they had done, unable to find words to quicken the creaking miles.

2

I didn't expect to be ambushed by emotion at our departure, but when I look now at the pictures taken that morning, I can see tension in my facial muscles and in the thinness of my smile.

The weather had reversed itself. Puffy cumulus dotted a blue sky over sharp peaks and distant white snowfields. The Athabasca still appeared tricky and fast, still looked green and thickened with the flour of crushed rock, but a warm sun played on the waves and the current lapped benignly at the steep bank where we held our canoe.

Stage by stage we were jettisoning our material and cultural trappings, simplifying existence. First we had shed our home and most of our possessions. At the river's edge we left vehicles, more unnecessary supplies, and our human fraternity. There was the usual confusion of gear as we made the transition from car to canoe. Packs, sleeping bags, paddles, life vests, and duffles lay strewn next to the road in colorful disarray. It struck me that we had never had a trial boat packing. What an ignoble beginning it would be to have to reorganize the trip logistics on the riverbank because we couldn't fit everything into the canoe!

We had forty-five days of food and supplies for the first leg of the summer, enough to get us to Fort McMurray, Alberta, where we would pick up the next resupply at the post office. Although we packed as efficiently as possible, ruthlessly smashing food and equipment, our packs overflowed and would not accept our sleeping bags, which we jammed into plastic garbage bags and stowed under our seats. As each bulging parcel was manhandled into place, the canoe sank deeper into the water. Our gear protruded obscenely above the canoe gunwales.

Everything seemed to fit, finally, but the canoe rode alarmingly low in the cold river.

Before we climbed into the boat, the freeboard looked mighty marginal. After we stepped in, we were in danger of shipping water with the slightest unbalanced move. The small lapping waves near shore turned menacing, threatening to slop water over the gunwale. The spraydeck, a fabric cover with elastic skirts at the bow and stern seats, was our insurance against swamping in waves, but it didn't come close to fitting over the packed canoe. We contented ourselves with lashing everything securely to thwarts and fussing with the balance of weight. I found myself prolonging the process, retying the packs in place, searching for a water bottle, avoiding the fact that there was nothing left to do but start.

A small crowd of tourists gathered to watch our bumbling organization. It was as if a minor electric charge emanated from the scene, alerting people that something was happening. Tourists on the roads near Jasper are sensitive to sights anyway. Cars on the side of the road might mean a herd of elk, some snapshot opportunity. People in the background asked other bystanders what was going on.

It was when we said goodbye to the friends and family who had come with us that emotions caught me. I don't know why I didn't expect it. I had been so occupied with details, packing, getting through Customs, and the looming prospect of the journey, that I hadn't had time to think about it. When I hugged my brother, partner in earlier expeditions, in a bumping, male embrace, the force of our leave-taking welled up out of my chest and stung my eyes.

Other trips had been so brief by comparison. Marypat and I had always been safely ensconced in a group, part of a small canoe flotilla. The send-offs had been as boisterous and hearty as ship christenings. This time we were leaving for more than four hundred days, we were traveling alone, we were setting out with the intention of crossing the better part of a continent through some of the most intimidating wilderness left in the world. I barely managed to make it through the round of farewells and stumble down the rocky bank to the canoe without dissolving on the spot.

The Athabasca didn't allow us to linger over our parting. As soon as we each let go of our hold on shore, the current whisked us away, yanking us downstream. As we approached the first bend, I looked back at the people we were leaving behind. The small gallery of tourists were walking toward their cars, aiming for the next point of interest. We raised our paddles in salute, our boat rocking in the current, and slipped away around the bend.

For some time I didn't trust myself to speak. Marypat was silent as well, her small back before me in the bow. Besides, I was busy enough maintaining a wallowing equilibrium in the fast choppy water. Green waves slapped against the boat, splashing our packs. The wooden paddle felt new and awkward in my uncalloused hands. The heavy boat seemed lumbering and headstrong, testing my feeble strokes.

Day One. Day One out of over four hundred! It was too overwhelming to think about the trip in those terms.

It had been one thing to romanticize about more than a year in the north, about paddling alone through two thousand miles of wilderness, but now that we had crossed the threshold, the enormity of our endeavor brought me up short. Superficially, it was a simple itinerary. Two one-thousand-mile paddling summers, separated by a winter spent in northern Saskatchewan. Beginning in southwestern Alberta, we would trace a wobbly line north and east, through Alberta, across the top of Saskatchewan; and during the second summer, northeast again, into the Northwest Territories, through the deserted tundra Barrenlands, crossing several watershed divides, finishing our sojourn just below the Arctic Circle at Baker Lake.

We were assuming we could winter over at nearly 60° north latitude, a point well north of any roads, where settlements were few and far-flung. Although we had sent letters of inquiry to a fishing camp owner and several townspeople (letters that mostly went unanswered), we had been unable to nail down any contacts or housing leads. We hoped to arrive at the eastern end of Lake Athabasca by the end of August and have a month to work something out before winter descended.

I found myself questioning aspects of our plans. So many challenges were unknown, so many things untested. We had planned and prepared for three years, yet there were still so many gaps. When we had studied maps spread over our living room floor, the Athabasca River had been a tame blue line drawn through green country. Now it held our canoe as if it were a toy in its impetuous uncaring grasp. The possibility that we had totally overestimated our capabilities, that we were well out of our league, confronted me.

What about the heavy rapids lower on the Athabasca River? Would we be able to handle the whitewater? What about crossing two-hundred-mile Lake Athabasca at the end of the summer? Where would we stay for the winter? Was our untried equipment really adequate? Would the two of us get along, or would we succumb to acrimonious bitterness, like other couples I'd heard about on long wilderness trips? If our canoe hardly floated with forty-five days of supplies, what would it be like during the second summer of travel, when we'd have to carry fifty-five or sixty days of food and lug it across twenty or thirty tundra portages? Dozens of things that we'd let slide, hadn't found time to deal with, or had flippantly assumed we'd face when the time came suddenly loomed as major pitfalls, each one with the potential to deflate our ambitious and overblown scheme. Day One. What are we doing?

Several bends downstream, we paddled the cumbersome boat to a midriver sand bar and clambered out over the load. Still without speaking, we held each other, clumsily separated by the foam chestiness of our life vests. Jasper, Alberta, clogged with tourists, festooned with curio shops and restaurants, was visible just upriver. I could hear rumbles of summer traffic above the river noise. The human hum made our departure all the more poignant, reminding us of what we were leaving behind. The sunny skies and postcard mountains contrasted with our glum mood as we held on to each other, contemplating our future and the momentous separation we'd just finalized.

3

The first night out, we camped at a designated campsite on a sandy island, fifteen miles into our journey. Hours of warm daylight remained after we'd set up the tent under a huge spreading pine. Our untarnished canoe lay turned over, parked for the first time on a beach. Marypat burrowed into the tent to escape the sun and be alone with her melancholy.

I tried to initiate some kind of routine, wrote desultorily in my blank journal, unpacked cooking gear for dinner, collected sticks of firewood. The small island took only a few minutes to walk around. I made several laps, wilderness pacing. It's only the first day, I thought, stopping to look at the mountains upriver. In a month I'll look back in amazement at the days and miles gone in our wake. While my rational side asserted its reasonable patronizing voice, my emotional self wondered if I'd made a bad mistake. I wished there were more people along, company to buffer the shock of severed connections.

Marypat, even more susceptible to the emotional topography of transitions than I, lay in the tent mired in sadness, doing nothing. I could offer no more than comforting contact and soothing platitudes that sounded so predictable I stopped spouting them.

When the long day cooled we fixed dinner and ate near the river, leaning against the hull of our boat, oddly shy with each other. The wide river was calm in the evening stillness. Rock buttresses and wooded valleys were mirrored on its quiet flow. Marypat baked bannock for the next day's lunch and set the hot bread on the canoe to cool.

For the first few days, as the river pulled us too quickly away from the high mountains, the good weather held. Afternoon heat encouraged us to take short head-numbing baths in the icy water and wash bits of laundry to dry in the fierce mountain sun. I was conscious of trying to establish routines, enforcing a camp discipline, building a framework of chores and secure patterns to hang our days on. Basic maintenance becomes important during long trips. Laundry can wait on a ten-day run, but not for a sixty- or seventy-day expedition.

Our itinerary was based on a fifteen-mile-a-day average. On former trips, that had been a reasonable goal, taking into account wind and weather delays. On the upper Athabasca we could have paddled forty miles a day with minimal effort. Yet, to get too far ahead of our planned schedule would throw our resupply dates out of kilter. We had too much empty time, room to ponder the shock of our transition. We needed the challenge of whitewater, a stiff headwind, or a tough portage to occupy our attention. Instead, the heady river bore us downstream at a terrific pace, so that our miles were done without effort.

Fifteen miles and more slipped under the keel in a few quick hours, even without paddling steadily. We made camp with the sun still high, the day stretching on ahead. At lunch stops we napped and lingered. In the mornings we dawdled over breakfast. Our approaches to each other were tentative, appeasing, without the confidence lent by a familiar routine. Funny, how an established rut would have been a comfort. We were awash in unknowns. Would we be enough for each other as sole support, lone outlets for communication, human solace?

Marypat's tears seemed constant, the slightest imbalance causing them to brim over. My attentions were inadequate. What could I say? I had my own uncertainty to contend with. Day Two, I would think. Day Three. Like counting individual pebbles on a gravelly beach. Ridiculous. Because there was so little we could do for each other, we dealt with the separation from society internally.

What sniveling! I would chastise myself. This was a trip we had spent years readying ourselves for, saving for, slaving over, sacrificing for. Finally, here I was, on the water, in the clear mountain air, the river bottom whipping by, and all I could do was mourn my loss.

I thought of explorers and adventurers I admired: Shackelton spending years floating with his men on the Antarctic icepack after losing his ship; J. B. Tyrrell traveling the Canadian Barrens without maps of any consequence; Jed Smith surviving Indian massacres and crossing deserts without water; Sam Hearne walking across Canada; even Huck Finn striking out for "the territories." Had they spent time looking over their shoulders at what they'd left? How many of them had felt puny and vulnerable at the start of an adventure? Perhaps they all had had their moments, almost certainly they had, but I didn't remember those accounts.

Occasionally the Athabasca flowed under a highway bridge. Sometimes we'd see cars. Trains whistled by. We saw the human activity as if through a one-way mirror that rendered us invisible, untouchable, alien, moving in another dimension. The sense of a stretching umbilical cord was nearly physical.

As if we had just moved into a new house, we couldn't remember where things were. Every meal required repeated searches for ingredients. The little daily chores became matters of re-education. Starting a fire. Remembering recipes. Loading the boat. Reading the maps. Setting up the tent. I kept thinking, be patient, it'll come. But it felt so cumbersome, just the two of us trying to fill each day, trying to savor the journey, trying too hard.

Each morning we switched positions in the canoe. The stern person controlled the boat, dictated most route choices. The bow person read the maps, called out obstacles, provided the steady power. The two vantage points made for entirely unique experiences, required separate skills, and had essentially different perspectives.

In the stern—holding a straight course, setting up to go through waves, watching for downriver problems—I kept my eyes focused on the river. The responsibility of sterning on moving water made for tunnel vision. I studied Marypat's back, compact, straight-spined, muscular. Her brown hair was always neat, either braided or clipped back. I timed my paddling rhythm to hers, noting the characteristic pause on her return stroke, as if she counted a quick beat. By the end of our journey I would be able to interpret the subtle muscular motions in her back, to sense her moods and tensions in the set of her shoulders, to note the changes in timing the way most people read facial expressions. The boat stretched sleekly before me, arrowing forward, powered by our arms and the momentum of the river.

Paddling in the bow, I sometimes lost track of immediate progress and forgot that I was with another person. Unless we were in whitewater, I could watch the banks for game or study the mountains and sky. The steady unchanging paddling lulled me into a trance while hunks of Alberta went by, mountain ridges hogbacking away from the river, rocky banks slipping past, the blue dome overhead. The bow wave would plash quietly in concert with the river's murmur as the canoe scratched an ephemeral, self-healing scar through the water.

4

Jockeying with an unfamiliar river is like learning the ways of a new and formidable acquaintance. I am eager for a positive relationship, but aware that it is best not to relax my guard. The sense of lurking power and dire surprise—the impartial consequence for any lapse of attention—never wholly subsides. I play the role of a new kid in the schoolyard:

conservative, probing, gathering knowledge, looking for allies, hoping to find an unobtrusive niche before my vulnerable state is exposed.

Every river has a personality, a force of its own. The process of understanding that character is largely an intuitive one. I can pinpoint, in general terms, how I know a river will act the way it does—why, for instance, the standing waves develop where they do—but the dynamic teamwork with a flowing body of water is a thing learned through the fingertips. The thousands of daily judgment calls are made almost subconsciously, understood through the muscles of the arm, felt in the balance and motion of the boat, based on water minutiae as diverse as body language cues between humans.

Gradually, a file of subtle information gets cataloged in synapse and gray matter, snippets of knowledge, tools to help maintain equilibrium in a powerful medium: the way water pillows over a barely submerged rock, what power an eddy current will have, how deep a shoal will be when the water riffles over it in a certain way, where logjams tend to pile up, whether a certain-size upwelling whirlpool is something to avoid or a thing to plow through. Until the riverine signs and habits are ingested, a balance between skill and natural force achieved, the relationship is anxious and without grace.

The new boat added another factor of insecurity. It takes days before you're convinced that no traitorous intent lurks latently in the canoe's design, before you stop feeling for flaws and treachery. It will be months before the craft assumes a familiarity so complete that it seems an extension of your own body, before you can sense the water's language through the canoe bottom.

How much water does the fully loaded boat draw? What size waves can you go through before shipping water? Where is the weight best concentrated? How far can you lean before the boat becomes unstable? Does wind push you around on an open expanse? Is it better to ferry or pivot in whitewater? For days we experimented, learning the river and our craft—shipping water, bumping over shallows, getting caught by eddies, getting the angles wrong—upright but nervous.

Near its source, the Athabasca is a fast mountain river. The water rills over rocky shoals, runs with a kind of chattery newborn exuberance.

In several spots the river roars over falls and rapids, as if the grading crew hadn't yet gotten to smoothing things out near the top. It is active and splashing, quick and immature. The water is ice cold, befitting a river whose glacial source is still within sight.

Mountains of fantastic ruggedness crowd the valley: serrated ridges that are jagged as a wolf's jaw, dense steep-sided tributary valleys, rock layers upheaved, twisted, exposed, pressed against each other at impossible angles like broken bones. Snowfields and glaciers glitter in the distance on sunny days, as beneficent as heavy earthbound clouds. Coniferous forests clothe the valley floors and cover up the slopes like a ragged green cloak, giving way in the high reaches to naked granite peaks and jumbled frost-loosened boulders where the slow gnawing appetite of ice decays the upthrust bedrock.

During the first days, as we rode the current, the river bottom flashed under our canoe fast as blurred graffiti at a subway stop, dizzying and transfixing. The channel braids through sand bars and islands covered with rocks and willows, requiring frequent route choices. The river's speed forced quick decisions. Below Jasper the gradient is steady and the rapids minor, but eddies of surprising strength clutched at our often mishandled boat, choppy waves threatened to slap dollops of river into our wallowing craft, and surreptitious deadfall reached out dangerously from the banks.

On one gravelly shore we slipped by an alert confident coyote, tail full as a fox's brush, ears cupped toward us, thick gray coat, eyes quick but calm. Later on, coasting past a rounded knoll of bedrock that dropped into a deep eddy, we mirrored back the frank curiosity of a line of bighorn sheep silhouetted on the near skyline. We watched each other like wary mutual-admiration societies before returning to our occupations.

Two wide lake sections, like oblong gems on a thin necklace, bulge the Athabasca before it runs out of the mountains and enters the thick Alberta woods. The lakes are watery moonscapes, littered with weathered trees like shipwrecks, their arthritic branches the battered masts. The shallow expanses are veined with unpredictable capillary channels, etched through a shifting sandy foundation. The water suddenly slows, so that current is no longer any help in picking a route.

At the end of the lakes we left the mountains and entered dense northern forest. Our visual horizon narrowed dramatically, the river coursing through a green tunnel of vegetation. The relief we felt at being back on flowing river was tempered by the sudden loss of mountain scenery. Woods crowded the banks, shadowy and cloying, possessive of secrets. The river was already much larger, a load of silt mixing darkly with the milky slurry.

Even at its source the Athabasca isn't a clear river. Glimpses of the bottom come as through thick hazy glass. The water is fresh enough, and cold as a mid-winter blast of wind, but burdened from the start. First, by the grist of rock held in suspension by the agitation of hurrying water. Later, by diluted topsoil, irreducible grains of battered rock, forest detritus, an organic load mixed to a thin broth. Nothing toxic, though. I never hesitated to drink from the upper river, except to let the sediment settle so that the draught lost some of its texture.

Nothing toxic, until we passed Hinton, Alberta. The wind, from upstream on the afternoon we paddled by the pulp mill at Hinton, gave us no sensory warning. White smoke from a stack plumed downriver, a building or two loomed through the thinned-out woods, logging trucks in the distance groaned in low gear under loads of timber. By the time we recognized the insult spewed into the river from the pulp mill, we were in the midst of it.

I had expected visible sources of pollution: tainted effluence streaming from the end of corrugated pipe, rainbow-colored gullies stained by ingenious chemical combinations, blackened vegetation, chemical cesspools. But the waste is piped under the river level, pumped into the current subterraneously, deviously hidden from view.

One second we pulled ourselves through unsullied current, the next we were riding on coffee-colored blooms of industrial puke. I was surprised at the strength of my reaction, my outrage, my feeling of physical abuse. I hadn't gotten comfortable enough with the Athabasca to feel such affinity, yet I shared the affront with the river.

Pulp-mill stench belched at us in industrial-strength doses. We could not escape the spreading stains of excrement piling up continuously from the river bottom, permanently discoloring the water, at first a tannic brown, later a more diluted gray. I had known the Athabasca wouldn't be pristine wilderness, the way rivers of the far north are. We had set up our journey to get an honest cross-section of the continent. But I had expected the pulp-mill waste to be on the scale of a tributary stream, mingling and then quickly overcome by the larger flow of water—not this massive curse of filth. I caught myself studying the bottom of the canoe, expecting perhaps to discover cancerous holes eaten through the hull.

We never again drank water from the Athabasca River. Once past Hinton, we garnered our daily supply from springs and sidestreams. For more than seven hundred miles of tremendous flow, despite immense tracts of surrounding wilderness, I was never once tempted to dip my cup and drink. The stink followed us for miles. Days after we passed the mill, I thought I caught lingering whiffs of poisonous air on eddies of wind.

I half expected a dearth of wildlife after the pulp mill—oil-coated birds, fish belly-up in slack water—but it was not so. Flycatchers and thrush competed melodiously from the obscurity of vegetation. White-throated sparrows pierced the air with songs like the sharp clear lines of a Robert Frost poem. Fish puckered the water surface where they gulped flies. At night, beaver slapped and cavorted, sounding as if some energetic woodland nymph were throwing head-size rocks into the current.

Increasingly we adjusted to a river of magnitude and profligate strength. Upwelling blisters of water burst on the river surface like slow air bubbles in a can of paint. It was if the Athabasca had more exuberant energy than could be expressed, and the excess escaped in the only way open to it: upward. The canoe, paddled into these exhalations of power, took sudden half-turns and had to be fought back on course like a headstrong horse. Eddies behind rock points sometimes curled back with enough force to create sucking whirlpools. Cabin-size logjams were piled high on the upstream ends of islands and sand bars—gigantic flotsam foundered and accreted, anchored in silt, beaten by floods, manicured by the ceaseless murmuring current.

I wondered about the stories represented by the bits of dock, scraps of boat, pieces of house, and tremendous naked tree trunks. Each piece of the conglomerate had floated downstream—victim of flood, accident, carelessness—then lodged in the collage of local history, awaiting the next flood to carry it on or bury it more deeply.

We passed through several minor canyons, the river cutting through steep sandstone banks, forced by the rigidity of bedrock to discipline its course. Thus constricted, the water jostles and quickens its way along. I found myself both entranced and on guard, intrigued but wary. Once, the river pinched narrowly between jutting points of rock. Immense eddies whirled powerfully on each side. A thin corridor of choppy conflicted water pulsed between the greedy backwaters. Staying to the center path felt like balancing on a railroad track, our paddles braced on opposite sides like outriggers, our breath held, the river water indecisive and flustered as a spooked herd of elk.

5

Our routine slowly took shape. The days grew more purposeful and directed. We became more efficient, developed idiosyncratic habits, and our severance from society lost some of its raw acid taste.

Organizing gear in packs became a matter of consistent habit so that we no longer had to search aimlessly for lunch food or cooking utensils. The tent, our clothes, the hatchet, all found their niches, the pattern of packing reinforced each morning and evening. Under the deck, packs and duffles and ammo boxes were roped down, tethered to the canoe. The boat got sleeker and less unwieldy as we experimented with the fit and balance of the load. After four or five days, we actually stretched the spraydeck in place and managed to snap the protective cover over our supplies. That achievement was somehow disproportionately significant, as if before that we had lived precariously, flaunting a fatal weakness.

We camped on midriver islands or at tributary streams that provided clean water for cooking and drinking. The tent went up quickly, door faced away from the wind—sleeping pads, clothes bags, and reading material thrown inside—our nomadic home portable as a Bedouin's desert shelter.

Every two or three nights we drank a stingy cocktail from our meager alcoholic reserves. While sipping wilderness whiskey sours made from bourbon and lemonade crystals, we wrote river notes, keeping track of miles made, wildlife seen, weather experienced, quality of the river and landscape, ferocity of insects, size of the moon. Except for that ritual, we would soon have lost track of the date, holding on instead to whether it was Day Five or Day Six, whether we'd come eighteen miles or passed the Old Man River.

We made cooking fires from copious rafts of dry driftwood or toppled dead trees, setting the grill in sand or below high-water mark. Sitting on boulders or the ammo boxes that kept our cameras dry, we prepared meals from the supplies we'd dehydrated and packaged the preceding year. Our meals were surprisingly similar to those we ate at home. With a year's worth of dehydrated fruits, vegetables, meats, eggs, and sauces, we could make pizza, chili, quiche, omelets, curried vegetables. We baked desserts in a Dutch oven mounded over with hot coals, finished dinner with a cup of tea, filtered coffee in the mornings.

Both of us remained shy about striking off away from camp. The brooding forest accentuated our vulnerability, our mutual dependence, the unspoken need for company. A reticence about exploring that I'd never felt before in the wilderness kept me close to our tenuously established base. I kept checking to see where Marypat was, what she was doing, needing the assurance of her presence, her contentment.

I didn't perceive any direct danger. It was days before I loaded slugs into the twelve-gauge shotgun we brought along for bear protection. Each night I felt a little silly bringing the gun into the tent with us, like sleeping with a revolver under my pillow. But we clung to what known surroundings we had, established our tiny settlement, and stayed close as if within an invisible stockade.

The good weather of the first few days turned fickle. On overcast mornings we'd hurry through breakfast and break camp while everything was still dry, then load and cover the boat. With the deck buttoned up, my rain jacket on, and the spray skirt cinched around my waist, I was as self-contained and waterproof as a sea duck in mid-ocean. Having the deck snug around me made me feel more connected to the canoe, part of the whole unbroken entity. On those days I thought about a traditional Inuit hunter in a sea kayak—taut sealskin stretched over the boat frame, hooded sealskin parka attached seamlessly to the cockpit, wooden paddle biting the gray frothing waves—silent and watchfully impassive, dry and warm in the seething ocean.

Afternoon thundershowers sometimes caught us unawares, sneaking from behind or suddenly appearing over the valley sides like heavy black airships. More than once the rain was so torrential that we were forced to shore, where we waited, heads bowed, while warm rain lashed at our backs. I remember hiding in the lee of a steep dirt bank, hanging onto a grubby tree root that protruded from the dark earth, river sucking at the canoe, while rain as heavy as hail rattled in the forest like machine-gun fire.

I anticipated the first tests of fast water, worried about matching our skills with the river's power. The early whitewater wasn't even marked as rapids on our maps. Nonetheless, the Athabasca ripples with muscular strength. I dreaded the approaching encounters but hungered for them at the same time, like wanting the first hit in a contact sport to pin down my stomach butterflies.

On a gray overcast morning we crept up on a gooseneck in the river, marked on our maps for fast water, and scouted ahead. Then, life vests zipped up, kneeling in the boat, shouting strategy back and forth, we backpaddled into the current and slid downriver. Heavy waves bucked up the boat and slapped us down. Broken, flood-ravaged trees hung over the earthen banks. The run was as much a test for the canoe as it was for our skills. Conflicting chop hit us from the sides; a quick slug of wave washed over the spraydeck. Marypat backpaddled smoothly through the rollers, pointing ahead to barely submerged obstacles. I could feel the boat through my knees and hips, responding to the river, to our strokes. We rode out the fast water as the sun came out, pulled into a sandy island for lunch, and lay back on our life vests after eating, soaking in sun and relishing the early sense of teamwork.

A week out, we pitched camp on a small island, our tent on a ledge of sand and rock a few feet above the river, the canoe beached nearby. During the night, a steady hard rain beat at the nylon umbrella over our heads. When dawn moodily illuminated the day, we peered out the door at the thick clouds riding across the valley, socked in, it seemed, for the duration. We stayed inside, assailed by the blustering watery sheets pummeling the tent, watching nervously for signs of a breach in our shelter.

We lost track of time. As we lay in our damp bags, reading books and periodically peering through the screen door, exclaiming in amazement at the unrelenting length of the storm, the day passed. Each of us made short forays outside to tighten tent guylines, check the boat, and feel through packs under the protective tarp for snack food. What had seemed an attractive campsite in sunlight turned into a gritty, sodden prison under the storm's onslaught. Night came with the rain unabated.

Cocooned in the dark, having slept too much already, I listened for the rising river running just beyond the door. The surging passage of water changed in pitch, varied in volume, and I imagined a dark liquid hand seeping under the tent floor, making advances on our canoe, carrying off trees and boats on the cresting flood. Marypat hunched down inside her sleeping bag, hood pulled around her head. I assumed she lay awake, but we'd already exhausted our conversation topics and she didn't need my depressing worries.

When another underwater dawn arrived, I was on my knees at the tent door to check the river. It had risen. A silty brown flow the consistency of milkshake ran by the low island at a perceptibly higher level than on the previous day. Rain still poured from the sky, no break in sight. I couldn't tolerate the thought of another day in the tent. The prospect of miserable traveling conditions was preferable to another anxious day of confinement and inactivity.

We discussed strategy. First, a few handfuls of cold cereal in the tent. Then carefully stuff the sleeping bags in waterproof sacks, organize our loose gear for a quick rush to the packs, strike the tent, and hustle everything to the boat before snapping the spraydeck over it all. Things went roughly as planned, but the disorganized heap of gear in the canoe was dismally soggy and coated with sand. We weren't much better, squelching in wet shoes, shivering.

The thick river hissed against the canoe hull. Large submerged tree limbs turned slowly in the roiling current, like drowning people lifting an arm out of the water before being sucked back under. Trunks and stumps bobbed up unexpectedly from the murky depths; styrofoam coolers, bits of rope, wood planks added to the forest flotsam. We paddled hard to warm up, rain still slashing, cold trickles running down under our sleeves, the clouds unrelenting.

I developed an excruciatingly vivid, debilitating fantasy. I imagined coming round a bend and seeing a small log cabin on the riverbank, smoke sifting out of a stovepipe. A man in wool pants and a checked shirt sees us coming, steps onto the porch, and hails us over. We come. He ushers us into his tiny wood-heated house, where a tea kettle steams on the stove, and closes the door on the storm. He wonders if we might like a tot of rye to chase out the chill.

No cabin appeared. Instead, we paddled under a high bridge just as a pickup truck drove over. I could see a white face turned toward us from the confines of a warm dry cab; a man on his way to work, startled at the sight of people canoeing on the flood-swollen Athabasca in the rain.

Twenty miles downstream, chilled to the core, we pulled to shore, this time choosing a thickly wooded mainland site within which to find shelter. I desperately wanted a fire. After stringing the bedraggled tarp between trees to cover our packs, I explored the woods for reasonably dry kindling. After thirty-six hours of hard rain, dry twigs were rare indeed. Eventually, I came upon some large spruce, the kind of conifer that makes a roomy circular umbrella with its lower branches. Inside these minute havens, close against the tree trunks, I found small handfuls of dry dead twigs. Collecting several piles, I carefully put them in a plastic bag and placed the treasure inside my shirt. For larger kindling, I found dead standing trees, big around as my wrist, and sawed them down.

Under our meager shelter, we cut up the wood and split the small sticks with our hatchet, exposing slivers of the dry core. When the rain slackened, I arranged my pile of prickly twigs, struck a match on the protected underside of a rock, and gingerly pushed the flame into the stack with trembling numb fingers. The little pile of spruce smoked and hissed with tiny vehemence, took an agonizing time to send up tentative candle flickers, but finally took. We kneeled in front of the struggling fire, and coaxed it with little finger prods, fed in slivers of branch, gave encouraging breaths. It caught. Slowly we added bigger sticks.

One match after a thirty-six-hour rain! We chortled at each other with self-congratulatory glee, rubbed and clapped our cold wrinkled hands together, and dove into the packs for hot drink supplies. We hadn't eaten properly for nearly two days. I had an almost insatiable appetite for hot food and drink. Two cups of coffee, one cup of cocoa, two Cup O' Soups, and three large helpings of gooey macaroni and cheese later, I was a restored man.

The clouds thinned enough to give us a feel for the sun, and we were startled to find that it was still early in the day. We had assumed it was late afternoon, but the sun glowed through clouds straight overhead. Our riverbank camp, with the muddy flooding torrent in front of it, gradually assumed the look of a gypsy gathering. Clothes, tarps, packs, cooking gear were strewn everywhere. We hopped around laying clothes out to dry, adding wood to the fire, setting up the tent, putting on dry long underwear, rifling the packs for more food, anxiously checking the sky for signs of relapse.

The next day was Marypat's birthday. Early bright sun warmed the tent and coaxed me out. Over rehydrated scrambled eggs and warm biscuits, I shared small gifts with my partner. We drank coffee while our boots finished drying in the sun. No present I could have brought along would have rivaled in magnificence the advent of a warm clear day and the satisfaction of knowing everything we owned was dry and safe.

The engorged river assumed a new order of volume and obscured power. Once in the canoe, tearing downstream in the company of assorted victims of the storm, we were sobered by the burgeoning strength of the flow. Logjams required more elaborate maneuvering, fresh snags lurked just below the muddy surface, eddy currents sucked like huge drains and whirled motley collections of trapped debris in dizzy monotony.

Even the side streams were viscous with flood. We settled for the day's water on a tiny tributary a few shades less brown than the Athabasca, and hoped the main sediment load would thin by the time we had to drink it.

Just below Whitecourt, Alberta, past a highway bridge, we stopped for lunch at a boat launch and picnic area. The wood picnic table was a major luxury after sitting on stumps or rocks or ammo cans. In the sunshine at the deserted park, we took advantage of the flat table surface to catch up in our journals. Briefly, we discussed hitching into town, but decided, for no clear reason, against it. We brushed by humanity, never meeting anyone, visiting like shy night animals, and went on our way.

6

Sometimes we'd drift for hours, letting the current do the work, watching for obstacles, looking for game. Beaver and muskrat sleekly furrowed the backwaters, deer browsed the banks, geese lathered the river with their wings at our approach, finally lifting heavily off the water, broadcasting their disgust with loud honks. Great blue herons stalked the shallows with stiff deliberation, looking gaunt and predatory, motionless and watchful for the flash of movement that would trigger their terrible lightning jabs.

On shore the mud was pocked with sign: goose prints like three lines in a child's stick drawing; the webbed compromise of beaver, animal of land and water; dainty cloven deer print; heavy oblong cleft of moose; dog pad of coyote; round pug of cat. We left our less subtle marks: flattened circle where we bedded down, tread of boot and sneaker, dribbles of dropped food, narrow scar where the canoe bow rode into the soft shore.

One cool misty dawn, still near the mountains, I felt a thudding reverberation through the ground. Out the window of the tent I saw a cow elk and spindly legged calf, surprised by our camp, thunder across a foggy clearing and into the woods.

Only rarely did we concentrate on stealth. Drifting along, watching the banks, developing an eye for the brown shade of deer or the quick movement at the edge of vision, we'd try to coast by wildlife at a canoe length, but seldom succeeded. Deer on the banks would jerk their heads up as we passed, only thirty feet away, nostrils flaring for scent, ears cupped for news, and then pound into the brush on pogo-stick legs. More often we were quiet because we were occupied. When an animal appeared, going about its business, we reacted to each other with equal measures of startled disorientation. How many such meetings must occur between furtive creatures?

At a sand-bar lunch stop, intent on the process of getting cheese slab on cracker and then to mouth, I was jolted to my senses by a tremendous thrashing in the river. A cow moose had swum to within a dozen feet of us, realized only as she arrived that her halfway point was occupied, and was making undignified haste to continue on her way. Again at mealtime, an early breakfast just downriver from Five Mile Island, I looked up from my enamel coffee cup at a coyote trotting in preoccupied silence along its game trail, no more than twenty feet away. My movement alerted the gray animal, and it performed a comic double take before scrambling off into the forest as if chased by a pack of baying hounds.

In a larger group someone is always making noise. Absolute quiet exists only when everyone sleeps. No wonder close animal sightings are rare. Our own encounters made me realize how dense the wildlife is and how much more we missed by our lack of wilderness astuteness.

Game trails wound sinuously through the woods behind the tent, crammed with overlapping prints, punctuated by assorted piles of dung: massive mound of bear, mouse-bone matrix of coyote, hairy owl pellet. Waking at night, probing with unhoned ears, I'd listen to the decorous movements of wild things. The small scufflings, snap of twig, quiet brush against guyline, magnified in my imagination to accompany beasts all out of proportion in size and ferocity to those actually about.

During the repeated searches for drinking water at clear tributary streams, we'd nose the canoe into waterways from another world. The Athabasca flows fat and arrogant with volume, so wide that there was never any escape from rain or sun, so dominant that the bordering country went unnoticed. In the thin sidestreams, however, banks overhang the water and threaten to close out the sky altogether. Some screened backwaters offered delicious relief, like entering a cool adobe hacienda from a day hot as the inside of a kiln. Others I found menacing, with unspoken threat dangling like anacondas from the close underbrush. I filled the jug and returned gladly to the open, liquidly conversant Athabasca.

The mud at water's edge held the deeply embedded foreprints of front-weighted animals bent to drink—deer print up to the joint in clay, wide scarring claws of bear, tiny pad of fox. Otter and beaver slides slick with use led into the water from dens in the earth banks. Lingering northern pike undulated in the slow water, weather vanes to the current, pointing upstream with predatory intent. Warbler and towhee and thrush flashed through the foliage and sang subdued notes, as if conscious of the sanctuary nature of the cool enclave.

I waited in daily dread for the minuscule northern wildlife, for the inevitable depredations of the insect world. No northern trip had ever begun as bug-free as this. We paddled shirtless, sometimes in shorts, only rarely broke out one of the repellent bottles. I am used to seeing the northern world through the green haze of netting, to synchronizing bites of food with quick lifts of the headnet, to feeling the plastic of my writing pen melt under the caress of my DEET-coated fingers.

We tried not to talk about the general dearth of insects; perhaps, by exclaiming, our good fortune would be jinxed. Once in a while we hit a bad pocket of mosquitoes or discovered a few black flies in the afternoon. I would assume that our period of grace was over, that the battle for sanity and unpunished flesh would commence. Not so. Days went by and the bugs grew no worse. I gave quiet thanks for another twenty-four-hour space of relief, and hoped respectfully that the cycle would be repeated on the morrow.

7

No watches came with us into the wilderness. The arbitrary metro-nomic ticking of time increments had no connection to our endeavor. Whether we rose at five or nine in the morning made no difference. Whether we took fifteen minutes or two hours at lunch had no bearing. What time darkness fell or dawn cracked over the earth was not a concern.

We measured our days, but used different gauges. Our work day was finished when fifteen miles of river bottom had passed under the canoe. Anything over that was gravy, average padding. Rest days and weather delays amounted to mileage debt. With seven or eight miles gone, we could think about lunch. At some point in the morning and afternoon when our bodies asked for fuel, we stopped and had a quick snack.

Since miles substituted for minutes and hours, the maps were always at hand, protected in plastic bags, held in view of the bow person. Large bends in the river, tributary streams, islands, bridges passed in our wake. These were our signposts, calculated with the meticulous care of astro-nauts positioning for re-entry. At lunch, we spread the creased, pencil-marked sheets on our knees and leaned against each other in studious posture.

I can look at the same map day after day, the same square of country, and continue to find new things of interest. Tight spots that might mean tricky current, the close contour lines that signify steep valley sides, marshy areas prone to insect concentrations, islands for possible camp-sites, major sidestreams for water, the rich mystery of place names. Mellowdale, Christmas Creek, Meekwap Lake, Freedom, Swan Hills, Heavysound Creek, Middle Whirlpool River, Yellowjacket Rapids. We added a microscopic grain of history as we passed, anointed worthy sites with our own names, and grew more adept at imagining the shape and quality of land from two-dimensional information.

At lunch and again at night, the day's navigator measured exact progress for the river notes—exact as measurements can be made by laying a piece of string or blade of grass along our route for scale, or following the contortions of water with a slippery map wheel. The charts, fairly precisely, revealed our position in the larger world and often dictated whether we felt content or restless at the end of the day.

My paddling rhythm settled into a recurrent daily pattern. Early in the morning, breakfast and coffee in my gut, I worked myself into the harness like a mule positioning in the traces for a day of plowing. I'd hitch here and there in my seat, searching for a posture that wouldn't produce backache, getting a position that made for efficient paddling, minimiz-ing extra motion. Like a night watchman, I mentally went the rounds, making sure all was in order—load lashed down, maps handy, water jug available, rain gear in accessible pack pocket, spraydeck over gear or close at hand. Then I'd sniff out the mood of the river, watch to see from which direction the clouds moved, test the wind, line up the day. Under way, I set goals for myself: five miles before I'd switch paddling sides, three long bends before taking a break, nine miles before lunch, shoot for a distant island or confluence for camp.

The quest for good drinking water niggled at us like any neglected chore until we put it behind us for the day. Sometimes only one or two likely opportunities appeared in twenty miles. Tributaries we counted on were dry or so overgrown that we missed them altogether. Others offered water as muddy as the Athabasca or iron-stained to a deep orange tint. We checked lush greenery in hopes of springs, some days searching until late afternoon before finding a fresh trickle to replenish the jug. The five-gallon container bulging with clear water in the bottom of the canoe was like savings in a retirement fund.

The miles kept coming easily. We gained days on our itinerary even as we dawdled. On hot afternoons when the bugs were light, we took chilling dips in the silty river and wind-dried our white skin. We followed temptations to explore interesting shoreline; found poplar stands clear-cut by ambitious beaver, whole groves toppled like pick-up-sticks by patient single-minded gnawing; and inspected the survey-straight, awkwardly reclaimed cuts opened for oil and gas pipelines, arteries pulsing with raw fuel from the Tar Sands. Photographic impulses were indulged, whole chunks of afternoon spent angling for a close-up shot of a family of geese.

By mid-afternoon, muscles loosened or numbed through use, the rhythm of locomotion assumed an unthinking beat. Our blades entered the water at the same moment, feathered back at the end of every stroke, arcing a spray of drops on each side of the canoe, and sliced anew into the river in tandem. Miles passed between spoken words. Our efforts stayed in thoughtless synch, a choreography of movement practiced thousands of times a day—but we faded away from each other mentally, lulled by the dancing river, encouraged by paddling mantra.

I found myself savoring past events. Reminded of a childhood fishing trip with my grandfather, I reconstructed all that I could: bits of conversation, the feel of the dropline as I let the hook down after flounder, the way the swells outside of the breakwater rocked the white-and-red skiff, my grandfather's nonchalant expertise at impaling hairy writhing sandworms on hooks, the smell of outboard fumes, and the salty awkwardness of my Mae West life jacket.

I spent the better part of several afternoons mentally turning over my motivations for the expedition. For months before we began paddling, I had been preoccupied by the question of purpose and provocation. My grandmother had written me a letter, the usual newsy affair, but at the end, almost as a postscript, she had asked, "What is the purpose of this journey? Or is it simply an escape?"

It needled me, that question. I realized that, in a sense, the expedition was a form of withdrawal. I wished to distance myself from aspects of society—random machine-gun attacks in fast-food restaurants, the fickle horror of terrorism, common perversity, systematic befouling of the environmental nest. But that was tangential cerebral stuff, cocktail party conversation.

I justified the worth of my occupation by matching it against others: stockbroking, for instance, or being tethered to a word processor in a crowded newspaper office. I recognized that tack as weaselly, pompous.

Then there were the catch phrases: clarity of mind, self-reliance, the mystery and power of wild places, simplification, living the cycle of seasons. Not that some didn't have their place, even a profound importance—but I still didn't feel that I'd pushed myself to the precipice of self-examination and confronted the meat of the issue.

I *was* escaping from things. I was fleeing my compulsive tendencies to eat too much, to anesthetize myself by drinking too much beer. Some things I honestly didn't like about myself. There was room for improvement, and I hoped the wilderness would provide avenues for catharsis. But also I was seeking relief from a sort of insidious boredom. I wanted a release from the dulling influence of routine existence. Get up. Go to work. Come home. Have a beer. Eat. Do dishes. Read a book. Go to bed. Start again. That kind of boredom. I was addicted to the drug of adventure. I fed spiritually off the heightened awareness, the tingling sense of aliveness that comes with traveling in quiet style through big, powerful, spacious environments.

Though it still ignored looming conflicts and contradictions, this assessment nibbled at a bit of the core and got me past the self-imposed blocks to understanding why it was I bothered. With the river uncoiling before the bow, miles clicking by, the days blending together, I shed some of the internal pressure to question. Not that it no longer mattered, but the drive to justify paled in the light of present circumstance.

From absorbed afternoon wanderings, I'd wake again to the wide river, notice the building thunderheads, listen to a vulgar bunch of ravens raising a ruckus, see the fin of fish whirl out of a warm shallows near shore, feel the numb fatigue in my shoulders.

Since the big storm, I'd grown philosophic about the weather. Wind and rain and sun each waxed and waned in turn. We were here for the long haul. We took what came and knew we'd still be around when it changed again. We'd been tested, knew we could cope, accepted what was served, and adapted.

8

The valley of the Athabasca lies cloaked by forest, a wobbly stripe of untamed terrain, but in places settlement and human encroachment pull up abruptly at the brink. We saw hardly anyone—a motorboat or two, a distant house, a vehicle treading across a bridge—but I could feel the humming air of human industry in the distance. The maps showed railroad outposts, old clumps of buildings, cleared land, pipelines just out of view. We avoided the cultivated gauntlet as if sneaking down an abandoned alleyway.

Two weeks out from Jasper I noticed on the map the legend, "Vega ferry." Tilled fields rolled right to the edge of the river in a few spots, bucolic views of haystacks and alfalfa stubble interspersed with the usual muddy banks and rustling brush. I recognized an edge of subdued anticipation as we pulled ourselves around the last long bends before the ferry. Would the map be right? Would the ferry still operate? After two weeks of quiet, a thin rustic veneer coated on, I was ready to visit if the mood seemed right.

We saw the ferry from well upstream, halfway across the river. The engine throbbed over the rippling current, the noise arriving on impulses of breeze. A blue-and-white barge with Alberta pennants on a wire, it rode a thick cable like an amphibious trolley, backwards and forwards, gobbling vehicles in one end and disgorging them out the other. Our little boat sliced the river toward the thundering ruckus. Contrasting with four-wheel-drive and dirt bike, the racket and exhaust of recreating humanity, we arrived as if out of a James Fenimore Cooper stage set. Natty Bumppo and Associates.

We eddied in against shore as the metal ferry scraped to a rising stop on the dirt road and dropped its hydraulic tongue. The operator let a chain down to the deck so the jeep could jounce on its way. He was a big, loose-jointed man, with deeply creased hands and a broad face. His bluejeans rode halfway down his hips, so that his belt served a functional rather than ornamental purpose. The sleeves on his dark workshirt were rolled to his elbows. A faded green billcap shaded a set of blue eyes, sent a shadow over his weathered face.

He hooked the chain back up and shuffled toward the closet-size engine house. I hurried up the bank.

"Is there a good place to camp nearby?" I called from twenty feet, thinking he might know a nice gravelly beach, a favorite fishing hole.

"Right up there." He pointed to the far bank, the dirt scarp high enough that I couldn't see what lay behind it.

"Water and everything?"

"Sure," and he got set to roar back across.

We aimed the canoe at an upstream angle and paddled hard so as not to lose ground in the churned water and fumes behind the big boat.

The campground was a shock. Lawn grass, stand-up metal fire grates, vans and trucks and recreational vehicles tucked into their spots, people playing radios, the smell of lighter fluid and briquettes. We portaged up the hill, set our no-wheel vehicle on a site, dumped out our five gallons of cloudy water in favor of a well supply, and ate dinner at a picnic table. It seemed odd, a little disorienting, not to have to scout a tent site, not to sink our grill into the dirt and build a fire underneath.

Later on, for an hour or so, we rode the ferry with Garth, the boat's affable operator. He'd run the ferry for fifteen years, averaging forty-five cars a day. He lived in Vega, had all his life. He and his wife ran the farm his parents had homesteaded. When he took his hat off to wipe a hand over his balding head, he revealed shocking white skin beneath, his face as two-toned as a dyed Easter egg. He wanted to talk River.

Garth wondered if we were ready for the Grand Rapid, said he'd read about plenty of people who'd drowned or lost boats down there, but never heard of anyone making it. Not that it couldn't be done, mind you, but he hadn't been notified. He remembered some German guys who acted like they knew pretty much everything, and went down there only to lose their boat and damn near drown in the deal. His advice was to take a bus from Athabasca to Fort McMurray and skip the rapids. But if we did run the river, and if we made it through, he wanted a picture, at least a postcard.

Garth's friend John came on the boat for a few laps, the air cool and the bugs out. Marypat and I became deckhands, dropping the chain to let cars out and hooking it back up, squinting at the swirling river while we leaned against the railing. John spoke with the heavy German underlay of first-generation immigrant, despite having lived in Vega since he was ten. He came then with his mother, following after his father, who had set up on a bit of land and built a cabin. They had arrived in winter, at night, by sleigh, and he remembered the little candle glow at the window like a lighthouse in the black cold night. He never really gave any thought to leaving, he said. Oh, he'd been up to Peace River once.

Garth regarded the Athabasca with the skeptical familiarity of long acquaintance. He pointed a thick finger to the spot, halfway up a stairway and a solid fifteen feet above the present level of the river, where the '71 flood had crested. Most years the ferry ran from May 1 to November 1, although he'd dodged ice nearly to Christmas some years and started up as early as April once or twice.

The two men tried to come up with news surprises. "Did you know Reagan has cancer?" No, we didn't, but that was all they could produce. Garth chuckled, his teeth spaced by large gaps. "You know, there were some people homesteading back in the bush early in the century, who didn't know World War I had begun until eight months after it was declared!" I doubted we'd escape the advent of World War III, even in the bush.

Around ten o'clock, John offered us a truck tour of the countryside. Garth called his wife and told her we might stop in. There was talk of a dance at the Vega town hall. Marypat and I stowed our things away and hopped into the pickup truck, leaving, for the first time, our nomadic home and the river we were riding.

Topping out of the valley, we drove across thoroughly settled land, cleared fields, grain silos, crops in plowed ground, farmhouses with kitchen lights on. John pointed out some of the original homesteading log cabins, now made diminutive by all the clear acreage around them. He knew all the farms by name, a few were run by relatives. We stopped at his place, an expanded operation since the homesteading days, boasting large metal equipment sheds with the bulk of tractors and wheat drills inside, a clutter of outbuildings, substantial farmhouse. His wife Dorothy joined us in the cab, a cheerful stocky woman with red cheeks and skin pale as biscuit dough. She had grown up on a farm close by and married John before she was twenty.

Vega hardly rated municipal billing. Town took up a corner, occupied by the post office, a tiny store, and the town hall, surrounded that night by farm trucks and pickups parked for the dance. We never did go dancing. Instead we sat talking in Garth's kitchen, his wife Martha serving up coffee with unstinting vigor. Garth didn't get off work until midnight. At one in the morning he had a lunch that consisted of a healthily stuffed beef sandwich and a solid wedge of homemade pie, sent down with the inevitable tide of coffee. Martha kept encouraging us to come for Sunday dinner on the next day, even offered us their shower if we wanted.

We wavered, didn't know if we'd go on in the morning or not, wouldn't commit one way or the other. At two in the morning, John and Dorothy drove us back to the river. "Best to check on your stuff. You never know what nuts will be rampaging about after the dance!"

From the benchland above the valley, the sun, still glowing under the horizon, was soon to come up. Mist wafted off the river and the grass in the campground was wet with dew. We crawled into the tent, jazzed with caffeine, and lay just within earshot of the Athabasca, a reminder of what we would eventually return to.

Some sort of dedication ceremony was to take place in the campground on Sunday. By mid-morning the population had increased dramatically. People in church dress milled around in the warm sun. We decided to take Martha up on her dinner offer and called her from a phone in the trailer Garth used when on duty. She sent someone after us, reiterating the availability of a shower, making me wonder just how grubby we appeared.

The house was full of family. Daughters, sons-in-law, aunts, little children with a giggly magnetic attraction to Garth. He played the bellowy gruff grandfather, but was given away by the gleam in his crackling blue eyes, eyes permanently squeezed by the glint of sun on water.

While I waited for my turn under the shower nozzle, I watched an inning of the Cleveland Indians–Toronto Blue Jays game and made conversation with a son-in-law. In the kitchen there were sounds of platters being loaded, potatoes being mashed; oven doors let out billows of scent. My salivary glands slavered with anticipation.

Dinner was the fantasy stuff of a glutton. We were used to one-course meals and were unprepared for the massive farm-style onslaught. Unprepared but willing. Garth admonished us to compete vigorously or we wouldn't get our share. "All's fair as long as your feet don't leave the floor!"

There were fifteen or twenty at the table, confronted with a staggering array of goose, turkey, five or six salads, easily that many vegetables, homemade bread, dressing and gravy, stuffed cabbage. The platters were refilled as soon as they emptied. Every Sunday! I thought as I waylaid a passing dish of potatoes. Good God! Pies, cakes, and fruit followed the main meal like the second wave of an attack force.

It was late afternoon before we arrived back at the river. Garth was operating the ferry again, wearing the same uniform, running manic recreators to their trails.

Standing in river mud halfway up to our calves, we loaded the canoe. Campers gathered around, some taking pictures. Marypat and I glanced at each other and laughed. We said goodbye to Garth with little ceremony. "Send a picture," he reminded us. Strangers waved us off like celebrities as we eased out of the muddy berth. Garth, halfway across the river, his blue-and-white ferry riling water, raised a wide hand as we made the first bend.

As if returning to office routine after a refreshing but frenetic vacation, we settled back to our occupation in the canoe. The river looked wide as the Mississippi, broad enough for long diagonal tacks to economize distance on the bends. The events of the last day gave us some mile-eating conversation, the warm sun massaging our working backs. A pair of loons popped to the surface like periscopes, called to each other, and plopped back under when we approached, unpredictable as U-boats in the murky water.

I felt the strength of Marypat's paddling stroke. She stopped momentarily to adjust the ammo box in front of her, got her feet comfortable, and I heard her chuckle.

"What's funny?"

"Could you believe all that food?"

"Not exactly nuts and dried fruit, was it?"

"I don't think I'll eat for a week."

9

Twilight settled on the river like mist. Heat dissipated from the calm air almost visibly. We didn't really plan on traveling all night on the current, but we didn't stop either.

For the most part we drifted, letting the cool silence descend on us, looking and listening. A buck whitetail, his coat a rusted gold in the low light, worked his way across a steep dirt scarp. Small avalanches of gravel and sand rattled to the water's edge as he crossed. He stopped to yank at tufts of dry grass, pulled on a leafy branch above him. For a long moment he tensed when he caught wind of us, clear eyes wide, ears straight up, leg muscles quivering. He watched us all the way past, refusing to spook, tight but controlled.

The sun glowed at the edge of the forest, the hot red color contrasting with the cooling temperature. We put on jackets. Two beaver sent small V's of water through an eddy. The canoe loomed up on them, silent and sleek in the river, until they humped up and slapped down their tails with ferocious alarm. We could see their competent bodies for a moment below the surface, furry web-footed streaks of aquatic economy. Another deer parted the alder at a sidestream, noticed us and immediately drew back, as if shutting a curtain before it.

Gradually we began to hear the river more than see it. Near shore the water sucked and gurgled at the banks, piled over submerged logs with a subdued cascade of sound. Islands bulked out of the gray air, the river forced around them as at the prow of an ocean liner. A cream-colored full moon rose through the forest at our backs, sending a shimmering path of cold light down the river. Mosquitoes converged out of the darkness with greater fury than we'd yet experienced. We tried paddling fast, thinking we'd shake them loose, but failed. A family of beaver plopped and slithered one after another into the river. We could sense urgency in their rush, but couldn't see them. A startled loon sent out a loud sudden cry as we went past.

A skin of cloud moved up on the moon, adding to the darkness. I noticed a heavy overcast line in the sky that hadn't been there before. A flock of ducks flew up the river, their wings whistling close overhead, their flight a muffled whooshing concert of muscle and bone.

The band of cloud advanced across the sky, almost completely shutting off the moon's light. I thought I might have seen the pale white haze of northern lights where the late sun had been. We grew tired. Marypat sat in the bottom of the boat and rested her head on the webbed seat, like a schoolgirl napping at her desk. I paddled quietly to take the edge of chill away.

Off to the left, in complete darkness, I heard the sounds of a large animal getting into the river. Rustle of willows, splash of big hooves/paws, rippling water around large body. "Marypat. Listen!" We drifted silently, our ears obtuse antennae, our vision limited to five feet. We heard the distinct sound of heavy breathing, working lungs pulling air through large nostrils. Water surged as if someone were doing the breast-stroke toward us. The breathing continued, steady, paced for endurance, unperturbed. Close by.

"Hey!" I shot an echoey word out like a weapon in the darkness. The noises stopped. Completely. I imagined a bear or moose—seven feet away? ten? twenty-five?—holding its breath, treading water in tense consternation, rudely interrupted by intruders. We paddled away, heading further into the black night. More noises in the deep woods, beaver in the river. Under the cloak of darkness, the sounds that had been enchanting in moonlight turned sinister.

It began to rain lightly, the clouds quilted across the sky. Even right up against shore, we couldn't make out possible campsites. The brush seemed impenetrable. We watched for the confluence of the Pembina River, trusting ourselves to distinguish only major landmarks. The sun that had seemed to drop away briefly on clear nights was taking its sweet time about returning. We felt our way along shore as if reading Braille.

Suddenly the bank fell away: the Pembina. Either that or a huge backwater. We found a small clearing on shore, pulled the boat onto a slick clayey footing. A soggy unappealing camp, but a wonderful discovery in the black drizzly night. We felt for and pulled out essentials—tent, sleeping bags, ground sheet—and left the boat loaded, two-thirds in the river, covered with deck, tied to the willows. The rain didn't dampen the humming enthusiasm of mosquitoes. We erected the tent blindfolded, under insect attack, our clothes clammy, shoes heavy with wet clay, and then dove in.

I woke to a misty dawn, feeling as if I had closed my eyes only moments before. In retrospect the spooky night paddle took on a ludicrous aspect—until I remembered the close sounds of a large animal breathing in the river.

10

We lived in the wilds, but passed signs of settlement almost daily. A motorboat rumbled up to our camp one morning. "How's the fishing?" the driver called, throttling back the engine. He assumed that anyone traveling the river would certainly be fishing. "Don't know," we answered. He gave us a look like we must have been of some shady persuasion, vegetarians probably, and roared off, leaving his fumes behind. Minutes later, just upstream, a moose swam the river and shook off on the far side before stepping deliberately into the bush.

We passed a sawmill just off the river, piles of chips and plume of smoke out of a rusty burner visible through the trees. Near the town of Hondo, Marypat walked across the lawn of a riverside home with our water jug to ask for a fill-up. An older couple asked where we'd come from, where we were headed, did we know about the Grand Rapid? Several highway bridges spanned the river, the water piling branches and junk against the abutments.

Yet we rarely talked with anyone. No one else camped on the Athabasca. Humanity went by in a different dimension, without connecting. Serenaded by the white-throated sparrow, we kept sneaking up on deer, searching out water, collecting firewood, putting in our miles in the company of the wary furtive life of the northern forest.

July days were blisteringly hot. We soaked bandanas in the river and wore them on our heads like sheiks. Skin peeled from our noses, lips cracked, our arms and faces grew brown while the rest of our bodies stayed pale. If we paddled shirtless or wore shorts, the rays burned our skin red and painful. At camps in the evening we soaked in the cold river like hippos at a watering hole.

Good camps were sometimes difficult to find. Big conifers often signified spacious forest floor, room for the tent, but the ground wasn't always level. Islands might have sandy spits or gravelly shore, but just as easily they could drop sheer into the water, thickets of tall willow right to the lip. Imposing mud banks, difficult to tote our packs over, lined entire sections of the river. We went miles some days, checking and discarding spots, forever seeing a likely place one bend down, growing cantankerous with each other over the process.

"Christ, Marypat, what's wrong with this spot? It's the best thing we've seen for miles!"

"Look at that grove of trees down there." She jabbed a finger at the forest. "No, no, not the poplar, that tall bunch of spruce. I'll bet it's nicer than this. I don't want to slide around in the mud."

We marked our camps with a little letter "c" on the maps, concrete daily symbols of progress. The memories of overnight homes ran together—pine groves with thick beds of needles, tall riverside grass we had to force down to set up the tent, the sand beach where our tent almost blew away in a terrific wind gust, open meadows with morning mist like damp smoke in the air.

Once we camped in a tiny, secret alcove, a sanctuary. We'd been looking for a place to stop for some time. Marypat thought that a small opening in the bush looked like a possibility, but it was up a steep mud bank, cloistered by dense woods. We scouted. Over the lip of the shore, at the base of a spruce, we found an old camp, a place that looked abandoned but special, as if the same person returned every few years to be alone and quiet, to watch the river. A slab of sandstone formed a base for the fire, behind the spruce. A billy can hung by a thin wire from a branch stub. A green stick, anchored in the ground, leaned over the fireplace. The little clearing was hidden from the river, like a hunting blind, the air shady and still.

We set the tent in a hollow, a well-used game trail running behind it, and moved about with special care, tempted to whisper, as if we were using someone's home. I woke late in the night and went outside. The moon rode over the far valley like a golden round of cheddar. Small warm breezes ran up the river. The forest murmured with life.

With a growing string of camps in our wake, we approached one of the last towns of the summer. Athabasca sits at the bottom of a deep southerly curve in the river. When commerce still utilized the upper waterway, the settlement was called Athabasca Landing, jump-off point for steamboats, supply source, a town tied to the water. Steamboats ran down to the head of Grand Rapid, where goods were transferred over a short tramway to hardy wooden scows. The smaller boats, controlled with a prodigious sweep oar, ran the long wild stretch of whitewater to Fort McMurray.

The river traffic is gone now, the commercial buzz shifted away. The settlement of Pelican Portage, once a lusty halfway point to Grand Rapid, is a dilapidated heap of fallen buildings, a modern archaeological site. The difficult river has been abandoned, supplies now moved by highway and rail. The old days are remembered only by wizened, stubble-faced men in the dark bars of Athabasca who tell stories of flood years and waves that would devour boats.

We too would collect ourselves in town for a day, and then jump off in the old style, heading into the most challenging stretch of whitewater on the entire river, an eighty-mile run through an inaccessible gorge, accentuated by a steady sharp drop in the huge river. The two hundred miles of deep wilderness between Athabasca and Fort McMurray constituted the most intimidating obstacle of the journey so far.

I wondered if we would find the same sort of welcome generosity in Athabasca that had greeted us at the Vega ferry. What spontaneous friendships might unfold? The prospect of another social chapter in our journey was intriguing, but I remained preoccupied with thoughts of what lay ahead. It felt too soon to emerge from the wilderness for another bout with society. Increasingly, the water and woods had hold of us, our commitment becoming a way of living.

Grain elevators and a sprawl of buildings our distant goal, we battled a headwind down the last long stretch of river to the town, gusts and current fighting us for control of the canoe. The clouds had played powerfully across the sky all day. In the morning, leaden cumulus with heavy streaks of rain descending from them had marched threateningly upriver. The sky turned a tornado gray. The clouds overhead became shockingly turbulent, looking as if giant fists had punched into them, kneading and agitating the angry black masses. Rain fell out of trap doors in clouds all around us, bore down on us, but never struck. By afternoon the sky was predominantly blue, but dazzling white thunderheads towered in the wings. A campground perched conveniently above the river at the edge of town. We lugged our belongings up a bank reinforced with concrete and rebar, mined with broken glass and jagged bits of rusty metal, to deposit our load on another grassy, fire-grated site, picnic table chained to the ground.

The campground was just off the main drag. Stores were convenient and we hoped to find a laundromat, but the cars and trucks, tourists and cruisers, the industry and cacophony of town made us cringe. For the first time, I felt the effects of culture shock. Crossing the busy street flustered me. The inside of a Safeway store, where I wandered in search of fresh fruit and vegetables, hummed with cold artificial air, smelled of syrup, old produce, and meat. I remembered the rules of the game: line up, push across paper money, leave with your goods.

Late in the day Marypat went off in search of the laundromat while I jotted the day's notes in a journal, distracted by the muttering exhaust of teenagers' hot rods taking rumbling tours through the campground. Looking up, I noticed a native woman making her determined though erratic way toward me. I bent over my notes in a pose of studious concentration, but to no effect.

Carol, as she introduced herself, had singled me out from fifty yards away and was not to be rebuked by anything so mild as body language. She sat across from me at the picnic table, liquid brown eyes studying my face myopically, and put forth a strong bony hand for me to shake. Her plastic shopping bag slumped over next to her. She set about telling me, at length, what she was doing.

Since she mixed native and English phrases with slurred indiscretion, I grasped only a fragmentary picture. The essential information was that she was hitchhiking back to the native reserve after spending the day in town. Carol was an avid shaker of hands and toucher of arms. She had muscular male hands with pronounced arthritic knuckles and tendons that stood out under her leathery skin. Her grip was strong.

My guest extracted a crumpled cigarette from a pack of Players and lit up with a shaky two-handed technique. She sent me a gummy smile, exhaling a shot of smoke across the table. Addressing me formally, Carol began with a loud "Sir!" fired off like a starter's pistol. In the course of thirty minutes or more, she repeated in varying forms her town experience and her strategy for getting home to Calling Lake.

Marypat finally returned from her foray, and was dexterously incorporated into Carol's hand-shaking, arm-patting circle. She received a detailed but no more coherent reiteration of our entire conversation to the moment. Only partly listening, I noticed a small gathering of drunken natives just up the riverbank from us. One member of the group was puking on the grass, hunched over, hands on knees, like a shortstop waiting for the pitch, while another five or six men reclined on the ground under some large poplars.

Marypat and I turned blunt with Carol, as she showed no sign of moving on until requested to. Eventually she gathered up her bag, crammed her last few cigarettes into a pocket, and stood up. She gave Marypat an enthusiastic embrace before navigating her way toward me. I prepared myself for her hug, managing to turn the attack into an awkward tango. Then Carol made her slow, wavering way back to the road, stopping four or five times to wave at us or shout some slurred question that sounded like a command because of the strident force in her voice.

In a stone pavilion just down the hill from our tent, two natives were arguing loudly, shouting curses and exchanging a mixture of abusive English and Cree. A stocky man with a Scots accent arrived to collect a camping fee from us, visiting for a moment. He asked if we were ready for the Grand Rapid. When I said we were planning to portage the big falls, he nodded as if we'd passed the quiz, and tucked his receipt book into his belt, heading off in the twilight toward the next campers.

Marypat and I turned to the minimal protection of our tent, both thinking that we'd much prefer the alarming night sounds along a nearby game trail to the uncertainties of weekend urban camping.

We spent one more day in Athabasca, staying only because it seemed worth doing our laundry and running some errands. A thrift store provided us with a re-supply of reading material, we talked ourselves into a regrettable fast-food meal, and I tracked down the mounted police office to check in. Well before the end of the day, I was eager for the river, motivated for an early start.

At dawn the river noise encouraged me out of the tent into the cool air. A man and his two young daughters watched us pack, observing without comment while we settled everything in place, tied the load down with efficient speed, and climbed into the familiar canoe. The little girls waved to us as we slipped from town. The man stood watching, his hands on his daughters' shoulders, but he didn't wave. Jealous? Distracted? Contemplative? We held up our paddles once, happy to leave, and looked ahead to the next stretch of the wide flowing Athabasca.

PART II

NEW CHALLENGE—NEW FEAR

The river defined our lives. Water surrounded us always. The fluid movement under the canoe, at first alarming and unpredictable, had become as comfortable to us as the sway of ocean swells to a sailor. We measured our progress in sinuous miles, bathed in cool silt-laden eddies, and listened to the rush and swirl and slow erosion of the river until it infused the rhythm of our thoughts. The changing character of the Athabasca dictated our moods, varied our pace, became an emotional barometer.

Water even infiltrated my dreams. Camped one night on a gravel bench, the river flowing below the tent, I dreamed I was swimming in the ocean, the waves warm, my strokes tireless. The beach receded, but I felt no anxiety. Far out, I sensed another presence nearby, like a faint turbulence underneath me, and a whale surfaced just out of my reach. At first I was frightened, but the huge animal accepted me, almost seemed to communicate a welcome. I reached out and felt the rubbery flank, and was surprised by the yielding warmth of the skin.

In the evenings Marypat and I read to each other from a Robertson Davies novel. While one of us cooked dinner over the fire, the other read a chapter. Later on, the evening air cool and still, we'd read in the tent, lying next to each other in sleeping bags, our murmurs a kind of territorial substantiation. Sometimes packs of coyotes yipped and caroled in the distance, the sounds pregnant with evocations of home—

dawn on the high plains, or a full-moon night in the desert.

Abandoned cabins, barely more than log shacks, perched on the riverbanks or hunkered in the brush at sidestreams. The trappers drawn to the busy Athabasca in the steamboat days have since left. Only a few solitary men still work the river for pelts. Most of the cabins are low-roofed, dirt-floored, tiny affairs succumbing to the infiltration of decay and the attacks of weather. The country had the feel of a western town forsaken by the railroad, hovered over by ephemeral ghosts of more active times.

We held ourselves back from making too many miles in a day, already well ahead of our resupply schedule. With good current, we sometimes floated entire afternoons, reading books in the canoe, watching the sky, talking about the rapids downstream, wondering about the men who'd lived along the river.

At Pelican Portage we stayed inside a cabin maintained by the province; a front porch overlooked the river and the ruined settlement beyond it. During the late afternoon we poked through the buildings, littered with fragments of the recent past: Empress jam tins, jars of syrup, cast-iron machinery parts like mastodon bones, a pair of tattered wool pants left on a nail, worn-out shoes, even the frame of an antique car rusting in a thicket of blackberry bushes. At one time the halfway stop had supported a permanent population, offering hotel rooms and a bar to river travelers. Mosquitoes clouded around our heads.

That evening, as a pot of chili simmered on the grill, several jet boats arrived across the river, their motors an affront to the peaceful air. They carried a boisterous gang of men set to spend the night in a cabin there. Loud shouts, foul language, even a shot or two from a brandished pistol cracked through the air. We watched as if from spectator stands as our neighbors swilled whiskey and took their boats on reckless full-throttle spins down the river. After dinner, with darkness settling around us and the drunken crowd across the way gearing up for an extended binge, we retired into the cabin and barricaded ourselves against the clamor.

The inside air felt stale and trapped, filled with suspended dust, stifling after our weeks outside. The bunk bed sagged into a deep valley under my weight. I listened to the muffled intrusions of drunken revelry, thought about the wild river that lay ahead, and tried to sleep. Persistent mosquitoes hummed around my ears. I heard mice scrabbling across the floor, scampering along the loosely chinked logs, and wished we had paddled on by instead of stopping. In the morning we ate our breakfast on the wooden porch, drank our coffee in the warming air, and departed downstream. Our neighbors were out of sight, probably comatose, their bodies working up retributory hangovers.

Just as we were becoming comfortable with the river, confident in our intuitive understanding of its habits, secure in our ability, the Athabasca grew difficult and threatening. The valley sides steepened, funneling the current into a tighter channel. I hung back mentally, reluctant to meet the new level of challenge ahead, but the river seemed eager to carry us forward, running with a revitalized spirit and strength, gathering momentum.

Huge boulders, rolled down from steep slopes or thumped downstream by unimaginable floodtides, punctuated the riverbed with greater frequency. As on the upper river, fast water quickened over rock shoals, welled up with slick expressions of watery force, the bed visibly falling away downstream. But the swollen volume of water made the magnitude of the river dynamics far more intimidating than they had been in the mountains.

The first few rapids were simple runs, with wide chutes and obvious route choices. Pelican Rapids, Stony Rapids, early intimations of things to come, warm-up exercises before the main event. Even the mild water kicked up treacherous standing waves, created raft-size holes behind big rocks, boasted filaments of current powerful enough to mock our steering strokes. We ran the river girded for whitewater—deck snapped on, life vests snug—kneeling on the bottom of the boat so we felt the new power through our hips, the canoe swinging and plunging beneath us.

We watched for Earl Kay's cabin on the shoreline. Ever since Athabasca, people had talked of Earl, saying he knew the rapids better than anyone around. I wanted to meet this solitary man, to square up properly for the bad water. We knew only roughly where his cabin was supposed to be. The forest grew thickly to the river's edge. I looked for a boat, a trail, hints of a clearing.

The afternoon was sultry, verging on rain. We heard an approaching boat from upstream and recognized one of the visiting craft of the previous evening. The fast boat sluiced downriver, spreading the cocky skirts of big wake behind it. We watched, paddles resting across the gunwales, waiting for the intruder to pass. Four men, gray faces—either still drunk or debilitated by hangover—throttled down as they came abreast, their fumes catching up with them. "You all right?" the driver asked, as if he was concerned for our safety. I waved them by, thinking, Good God! They're worried about us? In time, our pace with the river came back, the quiet returned.

We never saw Earl's cabin from the canoe, but spotted a wooden skiff on a mudflat at a curve in the river. Our friends with the jet boat had tied up along a steep bank of river cobble, where the current ran fresh and strong against their boat. Only close inspection revealed a faint trail leading away into the forest. We turned in behind the big boat, grabbing a boulder to hold our place.

2

I've never gotten over feeling as if I'm swimming away from a life raft when I leave my canoe in current. What would we do if it got away from us? Walk? I cinched the bow line around a three-hundred-pound boulder and stacked a few fifty-pounders on the rope for good measure, before we followed the path up the bank.

Entering Earl's clearing was like happening onto a deer yard—sudden opening, the area trampled free of vegetation right down to the dirt. Small low cabin, several outbuildings, substantial stack of cordwood, a bird feeder. Bird feeder?

We stood at the screen door and got a meshed view of a male gathering, a bevy of men scattered around the dark room.

"You've got visitors, Earl," one said. General turning.

"Come in, come in!" like admonishing foolish people standing out in the rain to get the hell out of the storm. No one got up. A partially drained bottle of vodka stood on the table in the clouded light that came through the window. One member of the jet boat crew was well into the glacial process of flowing out of a stuffed armchair, his upper body lying mostly on the seat cushion. Another had found his base level and sprawled as if dead on the floor.

We shook hands with the two visitors still able to remain seated and transport glass to mouth. Dan and Scott. We shook Earl's rough hand too and found seats at the small table. The inside air was close, encumbered with the smell of sweat and vodka and cigarettes. Behind the table a calendar two years out of date hung on the wall. A *Farmer's Almanac* from the previous year lay on the windowsill. A wind-up clock ticked on a shelf above the wood-burning stove.

I studied Earl Kay. A bristling head of peppery hair cut short, as if to get it out of the way. Mouth plagued with a molar desertion problem. A day or two of beard growth grayed his cheeks. A lean narrow man with hard arms and quick hands. His frost blue eyes had the sharp squinty look of someone used to seeing life in its unrefined state.

Earl was still sober. Not that this signaled any reticence on his part to drill a bottle when it came his way, but the others had a long head start on him. Besides, I had the feeling that, even juiced up, Earl was pretty reserved. He didn't seem like the kind of person who would relinquish control willingly. He had a good open laugh and a quick way of jumping on a subject. He didn't talk like an introvert who'd forgotten how, but more like someone with plenty of time to think and who didn't get much outlet for expression.

"So, you're going down the river. You know about the Grand Rapid?" I'd already heard the question so many times that I almost laughed, but I cared to hear what Earl might have to say.

"The Grand is the easy one," he continued. "It's a portage. But below the Grand is some bad water. I know. I've capsized in every rapid!" He laughed and sipped a little watered-down vodka. "I've seen that river from the bottom up!"

He must have run those rapids hundreds of times in his mind, figuring out his mistakes. He needed no map to conjure up clear pictures. There are over a dozen rapids worth talking about and we covered every one, even taking notes—what to watch for, which side of the river to stick to. For some of the descriptions, Earl penciled out a diagram of the rapid and sketched in a route with arrows.

"Now, as you're coming up to Crooked Rapid," he explained, hands gesturing, "you'll see the river take a hard right bend. You want to be on the inside of the turn. Don't, whatever you do, go around the outside. The river runs smack into a wall and there's no getting away from it!"

Earl got up and navigated his way through human limbs to a curtained-off back room. In a minute he returned with some much-handled snapshots of the Grand Rapid. Men up to their waists in water, lining an eighteen-foot Prospector canoe loaded like a mule taking a year's supplies to the desert; huge sandstone boulders stood in the background with the frozen dance of whitewater frothing through them.

Mainly, we wanted to mine Earl for information on the rapids, but the conversation had a habit of getting out of the corral. Dan and Scott, despite their lack of expertise, were determined not to be left out. The talk surged around like loud surf. Scott would vociferously defend his positions with, "Don't tell me I don't know about . . . !" or, "I've seen 'em. Don't tell me!"

At more or less the same time, Dan would be tugging my sleeve like a kid at a candy counter, capturing my attention. His soliloquies invariably began with the statement, "I come from the Peace River country . . ." From there, he'd launch into some canoeing tale or a story about a charging moose or a defense of carrying guns in the wilderness. After an hour or so, and maybe twenty repetitions of, "I'm from the Peace River country," Earl shouted, "We know that! You said you're from the Peace River already, about nineteen times!"

Around the topic of whitewater we talked wolves, trapping, bugs, floods, bear, moose, river traffic, and politics. I was amazed at Earl's grasp of political issues. He listened to the radio and had plenty to say. But politics wasn't what I cared to hear about.

In the background, the two fallen players would send out a moan from time to time, or let loose with an incoherent spate of gibberish, as if some point of discussion had penetrated their fogged consciousness and piqued a response. I kept expecting the chairbound member to realize his quest for the floor, but he seemed to defy gravity, only his head and shoulders supported by the chair cushion.

"How long have you been in the bush, Earl?" I asked, steering the conversation away from another charging moose story.

"I guess I'm the old man of the river now." Earl sipped his drink. "I'm fifty-seven years old and have trapped alone here for twenty-eight years."

Christ, twenty-eight years out here! Not that it's all that crazy. People spend longer than that as drones in a secretarial pool or camera-department managers in a shopping mall. Which is more surprising? Still, to cut yourself away from the larger body of society and impose an isolation like this . . . twenty-eight years . . . I imagine the seasons slip by like they do anywhere, and you suddenly realize that life has largely flowed on past.

But think of all the little difficult things he must have come up against alone that would be debilitating of will. Sickness. Getting lost in the bush. Having your boat motor conk out sixty miles from anywhere. Teeth that ache and then fall out of your head. Frantic animals in traps biting you as you move in to kill. Stuff that makes you feel the press of wild space around you, makes you listen to the echoes of your own scurrying.

What would make someone do that? He would have been twenty-nine years old then, 1957 or so. No war to escape. Too young to have been completely fed up with the drudgery of self-support. Running from trouble? Wronged in love? I didn't think either would provide the staying power to overcome the tough times. Not for twenty-eight years. Probably he just jumped at the adventure of it, a strong young buck lured by the solitary independence of the life. Out he came, staked out a line, and got going at the work. Then maybe he was too stubborn to ever give it up. Now, what else would he do?

Earl had a succinct way of summing up a position, especially on wilderness matters. The power of his experience lent his statements a certain conversation-stopping weight. Nothing sententious, but pithy summations that generally moved things along to another topic.

On bears: "I've been attacked by bears six times. If a bear is good and runs away like he should, he lives. If he doesn't, he dies."

On trapping: "Ninety-nine percent of trapping is hard work. The other one percent is luck." Or, "Three years out of twenty you make good money. The other seventeen, you starve."

On seasons: "Winter is the best time up here. The summer is hot and humid and the bugs are bad."

On people: "The river's deserted now. It used to be full of traffic. Lots of trappers came out to the bush when times were hard. Now there's just a few of us."

"Well, what do you mostly trap?" I asked Earl, fumbling for a way into his occupation.

"Mixed fur," he replied tersely.

Mixed fur, I found, is trapper's lingo for anything unlucky enough to step into a set or stick a furry neck into a snare. Marten, lynx, fox, beaver, weasel, rabbit, squirrel, wolf, whatever.

He bemoaned the effects of supply and demand on his trade. "When marten are plentiful, you can't sell 'em for anything. When they're worth money, you can't find any."

I confessed surprise at the appearance of squirrels on his list of furbearers. "In a good year I average about two thousand squirrels," he continued, deadpan. "Squirrels bring two fifty apiece. You figure out the money." Earl put the economics in perspective.

Squirrels seemed more a target for suburban kids with slingshots than worthy quarry for a full-time trapper. I imagined killing, skinning, and preparing two thousand of those little suckers.

Outside, blue jays pecked away at seed on the feeder, their wings making bruise-colored flashes in the gray light. On most days the birds were Earl's only company, the silence layered like bandage wrappings around his cabin.

The summers must get long. After you cut your wood and tidy up your traps and repair a few things, the months would stretch like an endless hot day—time in which thoughts and doubts would grow and you'd feel yourself rattling around in your pitiful little box. What would you do all those days?

"Squirrels are the easiest animals to tame," Earl was asserting. "In three days you can have one semi-trained."

Small amusements. I could see Earl enticing those gray chatterboxes with a trail of bread crumbs, playing games to speed the summer by. How many of his trained menagerie, I wondered, later ended up in a snare, kicking and dying in the cold quiet woods.

I couldn't help finding Earl's occupation distasteful. I respect the life he's hewed out and admire his willingness to cut close to the bone of experience. But I dislike the means of sustenance: learning the ways of animals, knowing their signs and habits so that he can better lift the fur from their backs, fur that in perfumed state graces the shoulders of fashion.

How many women, when they snuggle into their coats, think of cracking the skull of a fox with the blunt side of an ax to save a bullet, and then ripping the pale naked body out of its covering in dusky winter light? Hadn't we evolved beyond the use of pelts to cover our nakedness? That furs have been elevated to luxury, status-symbol level, like owning a Porsche, made the industry even more heinous in my eyes.

It was time to go. Dan and Scott, never articulate, were well on their way to joining their subdued friends. I worried about the canoe, fretting like an anxious horse in the current.

Earl told us to stop at his neighbor's cabin, twenty miles downstream, just below House River. "Eugene and I are the last ones on the river. Ask him to tell you about the last time he ran the rapids!" He gave us a final bit of advice about the river, a rough benediction: "Just have a look at that water before you run it. Don't get in a hurry."

We left the little clearing and stood again above the strong river. Earl's place was swallowed up in the bush. I breathed the clean air, turned so the breeze washed across my face, thought about camping in the next few miles.

3

Sign of bear steadily increased, or else we became more proficient at noticing it. Scouting our camp on a muddy gravel bar, barefoot to keep her shoes clean, Marypat stooped suddenly to study the ground. She had walked right past a fresh bear track without seeing it and, on the return trip, noticed her footprint side by side with the obvious, disconcertingly human-looking track of bear. Naked, nearly akin imprints.

"Geez, at first glance, I thought it was mine," she laughed and looked into the forest. We decided on another campsite across the river.

The next morning, just entering a stretch of fast water, we spotted the first bears of the summer, black lumps in the willows along shore. A sow and two cubs—silent, watchful, unalarmed. The sow's brown face turned in time with our passing. With the fluid unthinking stealth so menacing in bears, she trotted into the thicker growth, checking once with a turn of her alert face to see that her cubs followed. We passed in the same silence, watchful in our own right, two species circling, avoiding confrontation.

I no longer felt silly having the loaded shotgun in our tent at night. It didn't occur to me that I would actually have to use the weapon, but it was a distinct comfort. Sometimes before sleeping I'd visualize the steps required to fire the gun. Lift it from the case. Slip off the safety. Pump a round into the chamber. Sight and shoot, gun butt tight against my shoulder. I had never been a hunter, never killed a large animal, but the shotgun was a comfort.

Rains on hot July days arrived as magnificent thunderstorms. Clouds like titanic skyscrapers, brutally black from underneath, lit to snowfield brilliance at a distance; they opened like the bay doors on a fire-fighting bomber. The day after we left Earl's, we were eating lunch when a storm hit. We sat in the boat, bent over to shade our small piles of food, passing plastic-protected morsels back and forth to each other, using our paddles like long-handled serving platters. Raindrops struck the river so hard that erupting columns of water rose an inch or two into the air.

By the end of lunch, the towering cloud had moved down the valley, dragging its sheet of rain. Warm sun sent steam off the rocks, dried our backs. We stripped off rain gear to stay cool, adapting to the abrupt change.

We didn't find Eugene's cabin at House River. Instead, we discovered a fresh pipeline scar blasted through the forest, caterpillars and work-camp trailers and bulldozers lined up in the mud on one side of the river. The other pipelines we had seen had all been completed, reclaimed, planted incongruously with grass, like a front-nine fairway in the middle of the bush. The new line was an open wound, freshly cut, raw, still oozing, unbandaged. Floating buoys strained in the current, marking the lay of pipe. The deserted camp had the air of a military bivouac during a truce that no one believes will last.

If it weren't for Eugene's skiff, pulled up on shore, we would have missed his cabin completely. Like Earl's, his den sits back from the river, obscured, hidden in the woods, built by a man who, having chosen reclusivity, feels no ambivalence. A rough rope secured the wooden skiff to a tree well back from the Athabasca. Several ten-gallon fuel drums clustered on a weathered wooden pallet. A trail led through mud and thigh-high grass to climb steeply into the forest.

At the top, in a cleared opening, five or six sled dogs slept in the sun, chained to metal stakes, each with a small shelter. Flies crawled at the corners of their eyes, their ears twitched with constant nervous tics. They lay deflated by the heat. I expected a ferocious lathering explosion at our arrival and hesitated at the edge of the bucolic clearing, reluctant to set off the alarm; but when we walked out of the forest, the dogs just raised their heads and watched. One let off a moaning howl, mournful as a train whistle in the quiet hours of night.

We walked the border of an impressive garden toward a tiny log cabin—peas, lettuce, potatoes, rhubarb, horseradish. A well-worn wooden toboggan lay almost completely camouflaged in tall grass. Hulks of defunct snowmobiles squatted like rusting tractors in a farmyard. The screen door on the cabin squeaked open, emitting a lanky, unkempt, grizzled man, shrugging into the arms of a tattered workshirt, tucking shirttails into baggy pants, an extra foot of belt hanging limp from the end of the buckle.

"Hello," our voices timid in the strange clearing.

"Hello," Eugene spoke to the ground, finishing the clumsy job of dressing for unexpected company. "You're the first I've seen all summer!" He settled a pair of glasses straight and shook my hand with a grip startlingly soft and shy, face held as if avoiding bright light. "Come into the cabin. Too many bugs out here." He turned back to the door, muttering a distracted continuation that I missed.

His place was minuscule—a box, ten feet by twelve perhaps, two windows and a door, stove against the front wall, bed against the back, rough shelves and a sort of closet along one side, small square table in the middle of the floor. It was hot inside. "Boiling some clothes," Eugene laughed, a dry sound. He stirred a simmering pot full of trousers and shirts in soapy circles with a thick stick. "I'll make some tea." A partially eaten plate of food rested like a still life on the table. Eugene moved piles out of the way—clothes, snowmobile manuals, a worn pair of Cree-style snowshoes.

Marypat and I sat on a bench facing the bunk, where Eugene hunched over, knees under his arms. "I was wondering if anyone would be paddling downriver this summer."

"Earl told us to stop in." I stripped off an outer shirt layer. "He said to ask you about your trip."

"He did, eh?" Eugene lurched out of his seat to tend to the tea. "Earl's been down it a few times and had his problems too. He always has people with him, though. I went alone, just once. Never been back. Never will go back. Lost my nerve for that kind of water."

He handed us mugs of black tea. Mine said, in red letters, Edmonton Is For Lovers. "I had the same idea as you. Go all the way down the river to the big lake. I planned to spend the summer down there, fishing off of islands, eating berries, getting out of the bush. Relaxing." Eugene's mouth sometimes worked without any sound coming out, as if he were exercising it, reacquainting himself with the mechanics of speech.

"Cripes, that was a trip. Bad water! I lined the Grand, though. Nobody thought I could do it, but I took four hundred feet of rope and lined the boat all the way down the right side of the Grand. It was the only rapid I didn't have trouble with. Every other one I capsized in, sometimes more than once. Even so, I almost made it. I don't know the names of all those rapids, didn't have a map with me. I just heard the big water coming and got ready for a ride.

"It's those ledges that surprise you. You can't see them until they're right in front of you. Some of them are so close together you can't tell if you're hearing the noise from the last one or the next one." Telling the story, Eugene escaped some of his shyness, met our eyes, let out diffident chuckles.

"I found out later that the rapid I lost my canoe in is called Big Cascade. I went right over the middle of it. The boat got jammed under a ledge and I had the rope wrapped around my arm. The water kept pounding me under and I couldn't get loose of the rope. Every twenty seconds or so the river let me up for air. Got so I didn't know when I was upside down or rightside up. I finally grabbed the framework of the canoe and climbed up it to the top of the ledge. The water was so shallow on top that I could walk right across to shore. I lost everything. My shoes had come off, my shirt was torn up, both pant legs had big rips up them. No matches, no map, no shoes, nothing." Eugene got up to pour more lukewarm tea, as if his story were finished.

"How did you get out?" Marypat insisted.

"Walked." As if it was so obviously the only choice it required no mention.

"Took me three days to get to Fort McMurray. The bugs were the worst part of it. They about chewed me completely away. Walked right into town. Luckily I had some money in my pocket, so I got a hotel room and had the owner go get me some clothes at the Salvation Army. That was enough fast water for me. I came back home and never tried again."

Answering our questions, he filled in the picture of his life in the bush. He'd lived alone for seventeen years, had come out because city life and menial labor jobs were driving him crazy. His lease cost him ten dollars a year and gave him access to more land than he could ever trap. "Never have covered my whole line," he said. "More than one man can do."

Where Earl trapped nearly every fur-bearing animal available, Eugene stuck to fox, marten, and fisher. "They're the best money and the least trouble. If I tried to snare as many squirrels as Earl does, I'd still be skinning the little shits." Eugene squinted at us, as if fighting the sun. "You have to be quick with a marten in your trap. They'll chew off their leg to get free faster than you could believe. Lots of times I've found a trap with just part of a leg left in it."

Earl confidently called himself a jack-of-all-trades, had a power plant, a welder, several snowmobiles, could fix anything he cared to. But Eugene still used dogs and an old toboggan, wore snowshoes in the bush. He had no power, talked about building on to his house, but probably never would. "I'm getting too old now. I'm used to this." He looked around his little room. He complained that snowmobiles never worked when he needed them most, couldn't be fixed, got chewed up by bears when he was away in the summer. "Cripes, I'd just have to haul more gas if I had all that stuff. It already costs me two hundred bucks a trip just to get to town."

We went down the trail to the riverbank to set up our camp and have dinner, saying we'd be back later for a visit.

"If you see a bear down there, shoot him and I'll use the meat to feed the dogs," Eugene called from his doorway.

We returned in the cool thin light of evening, carrying a pan of hot blueberry biscuits. One of Eugene's dogs skittered around us playfully, shy as his owner. The cool air triggered the mosquitoes' attack impulses. "The bugs have been bad these last weeks," Eugene said, closing the screen door and shooing away the dog. "Some days I don't come out of the cabin before ten or eleven. Can't stand them getting behind my glasses. I couldn't live in this country if I didn't have bug dope and mosquito coils."

Eugene never lit a lantern. The light in his cabin gradually faded, so that his features grew indistinct across the room. We drank more tea and ate biscuits, the incense of a burning coil wafting about the room. He didn't believe we'd last out the winter. "Never do it," he said, as if assessing an athlete's chances of breaking some formidable record. He was skeptical about our plans to canoe the rivers of the far north as well.

"You looking for mineral?" His face sparked with interest. "You should! Take a book and a hammer and be on the lookout. Cripes, there's mineral all over that country. Never been explored. That's what I should have done, gone up prospecting for mineral." He shook his head and mumbled something to himself. "We all go a little crazy out here, living alone year after year, never talking to anyone. You kind of forget that there are other people in the world."

It was dark when we walked past the dogs down to the tent. Mosquitoes beat lightly against our faces as we followed the path and hurried to get behind the tent screen. We'd meet the next challenge in the morning. The Grand. The rapid lay eight or ten miles downriver. I strained to catch the distant murmur of battering water in the still air, but heard only the hum of the insect world, the ticking of tiny bodies against the tent. In the last camp before the bad water, we lay our sleeping bags together and found a silent solidarity in physical contact.

4

I woke with a familiar inner tension working on my stomach, a morning dread reminiscent of Monday school days in second grade, when a spelling bee was scheduled. I had felt the same on other trips, and remembered other mornings shadowed by the specter of unknown obstacles: the first day of ocean paddling on Hudson Bay; starting up against the eighty-mile stretch of fast water on the Rat River above the Arctic Circle; reaching the first falls on the Moisie River in Quebec. Reworking difficult trips, picturing the Grand Rapid, I delayed, wondering absurdly if perhaps we shouldn't cancel our plans. I lay in my bag until the sun was well up, making the tent uncomfortably hot.

What about explorers who dealt with major unknowns every turn in a trip? I tried to buck myself up. John Wesley Powell must have awakened each day in the Grand Canyon with the same tightening knot of dread. What would he find? Would he be up to the challenge? Would today bring to fruition the complete disaster he had so narrowly averted many times in the past?

By the time we were ready to go, the day was hot and a brisk wind blew up the river canyon, roughening the current. Eugene came down the path to wave us off, telling us on the way about a German canoeist who had stopped by a few years back and then had lost his boat and belongings in the rapid. He had to walk back to Eugene's cabin and stay until a ride out came along. I thought bleakly about struggling back up the river, left with only our clothes, defeated by the Athabasca.

He gave us a final shove off the mudflat and stood by his skiff to watch us leave. We had to fight the wind right away. By the time we had the canoe in control and I looked back, Eugene was walking up his path, head bent down for the climb.

For once the headwind was a welcome nuisance, an ally in procrastination. We stayed near the right shore, even eight miles before the portage. The river seemed to pool, like a reservoir that has to gather volume before breaching a dam, wide and swollen, brooding with threat. The valley grew more and more canyonlike, lowering us inside dark forested walls, the renewed vigor of water cutting a deeper bed. We talked hardly at all. In the bow, I counted river bends on the map to the rapid.

Still three miles upstream, I heard the first whisper of the Grand. It was more a sensation of vibration than actual sound, a tremble of shock, hint of concussed air. The pace of the river quickened, swirling past rounded boulders that humped up from beneath the surface. We clung to the shore with the tenacity of an elderly person gripping a banister. The wind no longer delayed our accelerating approach.

At a mile, the sound of chaotic water was an approaching thunder, a grumbling shiver in the air. Logjams big as barges piled up in the channel, colossal victims of flood. The river sucked through the gnarled branches. Much as I wished to stay near shore, I was careful to give the forest wreckage a wide berth, lest our red canoe become another toothpick of river debris.

I could see the large island around which the river splits. The old steamships used to back up at the top of the island and transfer their load down a tramway to the smaller boats waiting in the churning eddies below. Mist made up of vaporized river hung in the air, making prisms out of sunlight. Ahead, the riverbed fell away abruptly, white waves and huge boulders just visible along the descent.

Portage trails are invariably so damn close to the edge of disaster. We made our way cautiously along shore toward the steep gully up which the trail ascends, well into the early fast water of the fall. Capsize in the wrong spot and you'd get the whole wild ride. We were forced into the main channel to avoid long tongues of debris and shallow rock gardens. Just a paddle length out from the boat, current leapt toward the rapid, hurrying over and around the sandstone boulders.

Dozens of round sandstone concretions, oval in shape, the size of Stonehenge blocks, bulged out from the overhanging banks, slowly being extruded like geologic eggs to replace their predecessors, beaten to sand by the river. Round boulders, some neatly cleaved in half, littered the shore like gigantic cannonballs.

We scouted each little advance toward the portage, cautious as thieves, surrounded by watery explosions. Where we could run the canoe, we paddled little chutes and caught eddies near shore, our strokes sharp and abrupt. In places we lined the boat around tight corners and lowered it over shallow ledges, jockeying with bow and stern lines like the traces on a team of horses, seeing our craft safely around each difficult point. Where neither paddling finesse nor lining skill was feasible, we waded the canoe through water up to our hips, slogging the muddy river, feeling the tugs and swirling conflict of current like a live thing about our legs.

It seemed hours before we rested on a warm sandstone shelf at the base of the portage trail, our canoe berthed in a fat eddy beneath a boulder twice the boat's size. We took baths in the relative peace of the backwater while the main flow churned and smashed through the rocks in front of us. The proximity of battle focused our attention, forced us to heed.

Now that we had arrived, had safely found our way to the trail, I drank in the tumult around us. Our boat was tucked away as if in a garage, floating serenely just a few feet away from forces that would destroy it in seconds. I stood on a boulder in the channel, feeling the vibrations of impact through my feet, studying passages through the jumbled rocks, thinking about Eugene walking his boat on a leash through the powerful maze. It felt like standing on the edge of a cliff, nonchalant proximity to certain death. A wild joy quickened my pulse.

The portage trail works straight up a gully for a quarter-mile, hardly winding in the climb, pushing up through underbrush to a bench several hundred yards above the Athabasca, where it levels off in a pretty meadow. It was the first real carry of the summer, the first time we were forced to portage in some five hundred miles. Over thirty days into our food supplies, our packs were significantly unburdened, but we realized how easy the summer had been to that point when we began lugging loads up to the meadow.

Toiling up the steep trail under the eighty-pound canoe, negotiating fallen branches, slipping in mud, the wooden center yoke painful on my neck, I confirmed the decision to take our time on the carry and camp in the meadow, leaving the balance of the mile-and-a-half portage for morning. It was the farthest we'd camped from the water since the start. The river had always been within a hundred yards of us, its presence somehow magnetic. Without realizing it, we had tethered ourselves to the Athabasca, more and more a known force, an impartial companion.

The river was nearby, the rapid a constant pounding roar below us—but out of sight of it I felt liberated, stimulated by the change. The meadow had the air of camps I'd known in western mountains, our tent on the edge of the clearing, shaded by a large pine, the ground covered with long needles and fallen cones. A grove of poplar bordered the upper slope of the clearing, a large lone spruce grew in the middle of the meadow. I almost expected the looming shapes of granite peaks on the far skyline. The sleek canoe, overturned in dry grass, looked as out of place as an ocean liner in the desert.

I leaned against the boat to write notes, wilderness cocktail in my enamel cup, split-pea soup simmering on the grill, the smell of pine in the clear air. In stark contrast to the trepidation at dawn, I felt a satisfaction and ease. I remembered all those do-you-know-about-the-Grand-Rapid people, all the calamitous tales, my own doubts. I could say now that I did know about the rapid. We hadn't been sucked into its grasp, hadn't lost our boat or capsized. The rapids below waited, but we'd weathered the first encounter, made our way with care and confidence, no longer had to anticipate shadowy unknowns enthusiastically embellished by strangers.

The next morning I got up early and kindled a blaze from a small still-hot ember left from the evening cook fire. Marypat lingered in her bag while I drank coffee and planned our portage loads. A pair of siskins chased each other around a sunny branch of the pine, and a nuthatch called from the poplars up the hill. The meadow lay in cool shadow, dew on the grass, drops of water hanging from the petals of Indian paintbrush and outlining the intricacy of a spider's weaving.

We decided to take only the canoe and some loose gear on the first carry, sort of a scouting trip, and left the tent still up in the clearing, our packs stacked against the trunk of a pine. Looping a life vest around my neck for shoulder padding against the center thwart, I started out, following Marypat's feet leading off in front of the bow. As soon as we entered the brush, mosquitoes swarmed around our heads, landed on our unprotected hands and faces, collected under the boat. The trail led along the edge of the chasm, the rapids a roar below us but screened from sight by the dense underbrush.

Sweat ran down my face within minutes. Deadfall and gullies crossed the trail frequently. One muddy washout required a detour into the forest, where the seventeen-and-a-half-foot canoe became as cumbersome as a grand piano on a winding staircase. The boat hopped around on my shoulders when I jumped gullies or stepped off fallen trees, wrenched me off balance when I slipped. On a steep descent, we were forced to slide the canoe under overgrown vegetation through a fog of insects, and follow it through in monkeylike crouches or scooting along like limbo contestants. For over a mile the path stayed in the woods, a surprisingly exhausting obstacle course. I had thought the initial steep climb from the river would be the toughest part, but found myself wondering when the trail would finally lead back out to the Athabasca.

When it did we returned to a world of watery intensity. The portage ended on a rocky shore, littered with massive driftwood at high-water mark, bordered by a narrow beach. Mist rode the air like light rain. The sound pummeled us, much more engulfing at the bottom of the rapid than at the top. I tried to imagine the river boats loading goods in the heavy water below the island, but couldn't manage it. Downstream the rapids continued without break, blending immediately into the Little Grand Rapid, less severe, but still formidable. The water at the edge of the beach lapped and jostled against the shore, agitated from the ride, heady with the force of the fall, milling in anticipation of the next rush forward.

I caught myself looking downstream, already antsy to know what lay ahead. It looked like a choice between picking a zigzag path through a field of boulders or taking our chances down a main chute with large waves. The rapid continued out of sight, too extended to read from the top. We left the canoe on shore with paddles and loose gear, abandoning our craft alongside the riotous water while we returned for the next load.

Bear sign along the trail motivated us to make noise; we sang and whistled and talked inanely, the antithesis of our stalking style in the canoe. By the time we'd retraced the route, moving logs and establishing detours as we went, we were primed with an accurate appraisal of the portage's difficulty.

We sang our way back into the meadow, losing mosquitoes in the hot sunshine. Our portable home was where we had left it, sleeping bags still laid out inside. But even from a distance I picked up something wrong, something changed. There was something different about the fire pit.

With the sudden somberness of returning vacationers discovering their burgled home, I crouched over the ashes. They were scooped up strangely, arranged in a way we hadn't left them. "Marypat, something's been here." The tent was as it had been, but we saw that our packs by the pine were tipped over and spread around. "Is that how we left those packs?" Our sluggish acceptance of fact was as much a denial that this could happen to us, out here, as the slow focusing of comprehension. Our lunch pack was ripped open, the zipper torn apart, the contents devoured. An ammo can lay several feet away, as if flung aside. The bottom of a pack with cheese inside was chewed into, obvious tooth marks through the heavy cloth, a seam ripped open, the fabric still moist with saliva.

We straightened up and looked at each other. "Damn, I can't believe it!"

Turning, we saw the bear coming toward us, twenty-five feet away.

5

"Hey, bear! Hey!! Ya! Ya! Wooha!!" If pots and pans had been handy, we would have been clanging away like village idiots. The bear stopped, took a small hop away on his front legs, a kind of disconcerted double take, but held his ground. Marypat, still yelling, started scrambling up the lower branches of a small pine. The gun, I was thinking. The damn gun is still in the tent!

Our tent stood directly between the bear and us. I have to get the gun! The bear watched us: heavy black fur, contrasting brown face, making no noise, no movement, brown impassive eyes observing. I stepped forward. Marypat's shouts behind me faded, as if a zoomed-in camera lens cut out all but the confrontation. My eyes held the bear's. With no thoughts of what to do if the bear charged, no contingency plans, I visualized the exact placement of the gun in our shelter, the movements I'd have to make to reach it. Where did we leave the zipper on the front door? Was it in the near corner or would I have to reach to the far side of the tent?

I kept moving, slowly advancing toward the gun, the animal. The bear hadn't moved once. When I reached the side of the tent, the bear stood ten feet away. Our eyes locked, the eye of the hurricane. I felt as if I could reach out and touch the animal, the way I might offer my hand to an unfamiliar dog. I bent down and felt around for the zipper. It wasn't in the near corner. My fingers felt up the track. Where is it?! Halfway up the side, I fumbled onto the hanging key that would open the door, yanked it down. I felt inside for the open gun case, had my eager hand on the shotgun, my eyes on the bear, found a grip, slid the weapon out into the sunlight.

Remember the steps. Safety off. Pump a round into the chamber. The sounds metallic and menacing, the action of the pump a movie scene noise. I aimed over the bear's head. BLAM! The gun kicked, the bear recoiled as if hit, ran off downhill into the woods, disappeared. Jacked up with adrenaline, I levered another round in. BLAM! Leaves and twigs flew off trees, the echo like shock waves. BLAM!

Marypat was out of the tree. We moved together, tense, fumbling for each other, the gun hot in my hand, our heads turning, turning, wishing we had a wall to back up against, a side we could leave unguarded. "Okay, we have to try to carry the rest in one trip." I started piling things together abstractedly. "I don't want to leave anything behind."

"One trip! I don't think we can, Al. We didn't take enough the first time."

"We have to try." I moved into the clearing. "Start organizing while I keep a watch for the bear. Consolidate as best as you can."

I walked away from the pines, into the open, the gun loaded with slugs. I noticed clouds moving in, but the meadow was still in warm sunlight. I circled and circled, listening, watching, periodically shouting out, "Hey, bear! Hey, bear!" The scene seemed out of a corny western, protecting the homestead from lurking Indians, waiting for the next attack, not knowing where it would come from. We scared him off, I rationalized. He won't be back.

Marypat had the tent down, sleeping bags stuffed. I heard her pulling gear from packs. "How's it coming?" I called. "Okay, getting there." I kept circling, watching the borders. Then I saw the bear again. Brown face, black body, standing at the edge of the poplar forty yards away, studying our camp. Aiming into the woods, I fired. BLAM!! The bear ran off, using the trees for a screen, loping into the gully below our tent site. Marypat stopped to watch, then went back to packing.

"If he comes back, I'm aiming for him! Enough is enough. Hey, bear! Hey, bear!"

Marypat finally finished. The load looked only marginally possible. Our three packs were combined into two, sleeping bags strapped to the outside, pots tied on, zippers and pockets straining. The heavy duffle was stuffed with the things that wouldn't fit in the packs. We'd carry it between us. Somehow, we had to manage two ammo cans and the shotgun. Picturing the trail ahead, I was dubious, but felt we had no choice. Anything left behind would almost certainly be ransacked by the bear.

We stood by the pile of equipment, mentally figuring the load. Marypat put insect repellent on her hands and face, then took the gun from me while I did the same. "Al, there he is!!"

The bear had crept up on our camp, using the single tree to hide behind, and again approached from thirty feet. Marypat handed me the gun as the black animal moved around the tree and started toward us. So quiet. We didn't once hear him come up on us. Even in a meadow, he could get so close before we saw him!

For the first time, I aimed to kill. Head on, I sighted for the chest, firing a bit low to account for any rise in the bullet. BLAM!! The slug plowed into the dirt. The bear bunched up and whirled, sprinting uphill with incredible speed. I shot after the retreating back, firing up the slope, knowing I had missed.

"Goddammit! I missed him!" We both started picking up packs.

"I can't believe he keeps coming back, Al!" Marypat looked like an overloaded Sherpa under her pack; massive, shapeless mound with two stubby legs at the bottom. "Let's get out of here!"

I was hoisting my own burden, checking around us, only letting go of the gun for a second. We each grabbed a handle on the duffle, piled on the ammo cans, and staggered away from the meadow, looking over our shoulders as we went.

Instead of the two reasonable carries I had prepared myself for, we stumbled along under ridiculous weight, forced to walk side by side on the narrow trail to manage the duffle, our emotions close to panic. The vegetation was so thick that the bear could have been on us without any warning. Okay, just keep moving. Think about how long the trail is, how heavy the load is, how bad the bugs are, just don't think of the quiet bear. I looked behind us, listening for noise in the brush. "Hey, bear!" We kept moving, tripping over logs, stopping to rest briefly when exhausted. Our hands free on the short breaks, we killed the mosquitoes that otherwise went unmolested. The washout gully took tremendous effort to cross. Fighting the slippery bank with our loads, I pictured the bear appearing behind us, the brown face above us. Pace yourself. Keep moving. Don't think, just get to the end.

Without enough wind to talk, we toiled onward, pointing out obstacles to each other or blurting out, "Gotta stop for a second." My spine felt compressed by weight, my arms ached from the awkward load between us. I thought about strapping the gun to my pack, freeing my hand. The bear won't follow us, I told myself. We really frightened him with those last shots. But I kept the shotgun in my grasp, checking to make sure the safety was on, the weapon suddenly invaluable.

My sweat stank. Is it panic coming out my pores? "Let's keep moving, Marypat. Slow and steady, we're getting there." As I recognized spots near the end of the trail, some of my panic subsided. We were more than a mile from our camp. A light rain was beginning to fall. I couldn't imagine the bear chasing us across the portage. "Almost there, MP, almost there." Marypat had to hunch over almost double to carry her huge load.

The trail left the woods, opening onto the beach and the pounding river, our canoe on the rocks. "We made it!" The rain started falling harder. We dropped the gear in a heap, covered it over, and pulled on our rain suits to wait out the storm.

Exhausted but immensely relieved, we sat with our legs under the overturned canoe, shotgun just in reach, and faced the Athabasca. "I think we're okay." I began absently cleaning the muddy waterline off the canoe with my finger. "We've come over a mile from camp. The rain will be covering our scent. It seemed like the bear was pretty convinced by that last shot. He really ran off fast."

Even as I verbalized our case, I looked behind us at the dark silent woods, at the end of the trail like a doorway into the forest. I didn't like having my back to the trail, but to change positions would give the lie to my rationalizations. I noticed Marypat turning to look behind us every few seconds. I cleaned dirt off the wet boat with nervous energy. "That bear must have liked those garlic biscuits!" I managed a laugh. "He ate them plastic bag and all! Probably figured we had more around somewhere and couldn't stand the thought of letting them get away."

The passage of time increased my feeling of ease. If the bear was going to follow us, he'd have been here by now. I looked behind us less frequently, thought more and more about how to navigate the rapids. We relived the confrontation incredulously. "I've never seen a bear so persistent! He must have really laid claim to our stuff to be so stubborn." I could see blue sky at the edges of the storm clouds. When the rain ended we could pack up and leave this place behind.

"Al, there he is again!!" The fear in Marypat's voice had me on my feet as if prodded with an electric shock, unthinkingly moving around behind the canoe to use it for cover. "I don't see him, Marypat! Where is he?" I'd forgotten the gun in my surprise, and Marypat was scrabbling under the boat with her hand, had the gun out, backed toward me. "He's right there!" I was looking at the edge of the woods, expecting the mute face in the screen of trees, but Marypat pointed to the side, on the beach.

Christ, right there! The bear ran down near the water, ten feet away, swiveled his head toward us, scenting for information. Marypat tossed me the gun.

For the fourth time I raised the shotgun toward our tormentor. The bear's scenting face turned our way. I didn't have to think through the steps of firing, didn't consciously consider my aim. Rain had wetted the bear's fur, making it look smaller than before. The intensity of my focus blotted out the crescendo of river, the rain drizzling out of the sky, everything but the bear. Instead of hearing the blast of the gun, I felt the solid kick in my shoulder and saw a bloom of crimson burst out in the black fur, just behind the shoulder.

The bear whirled away, stumbling this time, and started off at a run. I pumped another round in, still concentrating terrifically, sighted, and saw another blotch appear on the bear's haunch. Still running, into the driftwood. Pump again. Fire. I thought I saw the fur crease across the top of the skull, just as it disappeared over the driftwood toward the thicket of alder.

"Al! Stop! You hit him three times!" Marypat had backed away from the firing line, her hands pulling nervously at her rain jacket.

The bear was gone again. Dead? Mortally wounded? I was sure I'd made solid hits, but could the animal be alive and close by? I was ready to believe anything. We retreated, backing up to the very end of a gravel spit, the river one step behind us, finally graced with a point from which we could observe all approaches. After reloading, I held the hot gun, acrid with the smell of explosion, under my rain gear.

"Jesus! He followed us! He actually followed us all the way across!" I had a knot of tension in my back the size of a softball. "I think I killed him." My voice had an adrenaline quiver to it. "I hit right where I aimed. I saw blood where it hit." We kept watching the woods, the silent woods.

"I saw all three hit." Marypat was shivering, her body hunchbacked with the strain, her eyes moving up and down the beach.

The rain slackened so that I could take the shotgun from under my jacket. "We should look for blood. We have to know what happened." I was imagining the wounded animal at the edge of the alder, imagining our coming upon him, the black lunging shape making a death stand. We waited while the rain ended and the cloud moved slowly up the valley.

Ready to defend ourselves, we tentatively worked toward where we last saw the bear, following the path of its flight. Blood on a rock, a dark red spot, and further on, another patch. I neared the alder, gun up, safety off, round in the chamber, ready to flee. Stepping to the top of a large river-beaten tree trunk slippery with rain, I looked around. There he was, twenty feet away.

Even at a distance, I could tell the bear was dead. The black fur looked like a rug thrown down in the pile of wood, without shape, without energy. "I see him, Marypat. I think he's dead." Circling around, gun still aimed, ready for surprise, the knot in my back clenched like a fist, I moved in. I could see the eyes, like display eyes at a museum, glass eyes. A spew of blood flowed out of the bear's mouth, shockingly red against the black body. "Be careful, Al!" Marypat stood at a distance. I picked up a round rock and tossed it at the bear, hitting the animal's chest with a hollow thunk. "He's dead. He's dead."

Only then did I realize that I was shaking, shivering with the collapse of adrenaline supply, releasing the spring that had wound more tightly with each episode of the afternoon. I noticed small details: the thickly padded paws, heavy claws, yellowed teeth, bloody chest wound, the way a stick of driftwood poked up under the slack fur. Curiously, I was tempted to unhook the bear's hide from the stick, as if to relieve some discomfort.

We snapped pictures of the dead bear, my hands shaking the camera. When Marypat wanted a shot of me next to the corpse, I was repulsed by the idea. The last thing I felt was triumph. To be pictured like a game hunter, posed by his kill, seemed obscene. I had wanted to kill the bear. It had been the only thing in my mind at the last, and I felt relieved to be rid of the animal, but I harbored no glee, no elation. We had been caught in a circumstantial accident, a rare wilderness confrontation. I wanted no credit for the kill, felt sadness at the loss of life, was left only with an urgency to move on, away from the scene.

We ran Little Grand Rapid in a kind of distracted state of shock. Scouting ahead, clambering over the grainy, iron-colored boulders, I kept glancing into the forest, half expecting another dramatic chapter. We snuck much of the whitewater close to shore, running a contorted course through side channels, staying away from the main flow of water, avoiding excitement. At the bottom of the rapids we began looking for a camp, wishing there were some islands, but having to find a spot on shore instead. We selected a narrow beach backed up against a steep sandbank, a site that seemed somewhat inaccessible from the woods.

The gun came out of the canoe first, and stayed close by as we set up the tent, moved gear, and collected firewood. I found an old pile of bear dung, dry and whitened with age, down the shore a bit. The sign, even ancient sign, sent a chill through me, focusing the image of bear in my mind.

That night, Marypat and I sharing the comfort of physical closeness, contact more reassuring than words, I felt the way many small animals must feel for the whole of their existence. For the first time I saw myself as an object of prey. We read a book chapter out loud, re-establishing routine, sending our voices into the night. The swift river pulsed by our camp. I listened for sounds in the woods and kept replaying images of the bear I'd killed. The nightmare flight across the portage, the brown eyes at ten feet, the alert swiveling head, the stealth and natural cunning so frightening in a large animal.

We were up at dawn, shotgun in hand as we emerged from the tent. The pile of equipment lay undisturbed, tarp tucked around the packs like a drop cloth over furniture. I found no fresh tracks in the sand, no sign of visitors. Sitting with my back to the river, I wrote up the bear encounter in my journal during breakfast, already finding the incident incredible.

We set out downriver in our laden canoe, the craft a safe, maneuverable island. Around the first bend, a quarter-mile from camp, we came upon a large black bear. The ball of emotions I'd tamped down with rationalizations rioted back up in my throat. The bear seemed lazy and insouciant, ambling along the verge of the river. We coasted by at twenty feet, paddles dripping in the water.

I said something and the bear turned quickly to study us. That same brown face, confident sharp glance, new menace. As we floated by on the back of the current, the bear gave us a last look and lay down in the thick grass like a huge satiated mastiff before a fire.

6

The deep canyon walls created a sense of confinement, accentuating the fragility of our boat, the degree of our vulnerability. The farther we progressed into the remote wild section of river, the fewer options for retreat remained. Anticipation of whitewater, combined with the new anxiety of bear encounters, produced a level of nervous strain neither of us had experienced before.

Bear began to appear as if on cue. We'd pick a stretch of beach to land on, and just then, a black sow with two cubs would break out of the bush. A day would go by without our seeing a bear and we would hope we'd passed out of their area. Five minutes later, one of us would discern the rounded black shape mauling a blackberry bush for fruit on a steep slope.

When we pulled up to shore for lunch, we'd invariably find bear sign, the square, padded, grotesquely humanlike print in the mud. I got so I could make out a bear track at twenty yards. Time after time that tightening in my chest, the feeling that I couldn't quite breathe deeply enough, would fasten on me as I walked up to be sure. If tracks weren't visible, it was the unmistakable, seed-filled mound of bear turd.

We ate standing up, the canoe a jump away, quickly dispatching dried fruit and nuts and slices of cheese as perfunctorily as refilling a gas tank. Neither of us fooled the other with small talk. Our heads turned to cover the shoreline like timed searchlights over a prison yard. One day we lunched on top of a midstream boulder. The river eddied smoothly below the rock, a massive striated egg of sandstone. I tied the bow line to my ankle and we actually napped after eating, our heads pillowed on life vests.

None of the bear acted frightened of us. Even with the boat twenty or thirty feet away, they'd lock onto us with a gaze of complacent dominance and make sure we continued on our way, standing their ground. Before the confrontation, bears had been a rare wilderness sight but one I enjoyed catching a glimpse of. A sense of threat accompanied each encounter, but it was a vague danger, the way you think about a car wreck before you're in one. Afterward, the sight of a bear darkened the day like black thunderheads.

Not a single island offered itself for a campsite for most of the eighty-mile stretch of fast river. It was as if the forceful current, arrogant with power, bulldozed any stubborn obstacle. We chose camps after searching the mud for sign, abandoning those with fresh bear tracks or dung, seeking out locations that would offer little enticement for ursine curiosity.

"Well, I found goose, wolf, and moose tracks, but no bear," I'd announce after a tracking foray. "What do you think? Should we camp?" Feeling foolish and paranoid, I nonetheless continued to be nervous whenever my back was to the woods. I'd force myself to sit facing the river, but then would notice Marypat's blue eyes roving the shoreline and studying the vegetation, her face tight.

At night the gun case lay zipped open alongside my leg like a splint. A shell rested in the chamber, ready for the tap of the hammer. The bear was the only animal I'd ever killed, yet the gun seemed as essential as insulin to a diabetic. If I woke in the gray pall of night, the small twig snaps in the forest or the slap of a beaver tail in the river instantly brought the bear face to mind, furred muzzle sniffing for me.

Rapids offered a welcome diversion from our preoccupation with bear. Whitewater was a danger we had expected, a force we were prepared for. Caught up in the concentration of picking a route, negotiating waves, riding to the bottom of a run, I forgot the fretful anxiety of choosing camps, the edgy lunch stops, the tentative trips up brushy sidestreams for water.

The Athabasca has such volume and breadth that a narrow route in a larger rapid appears deceptively diminutive, easy to underestimate. Once into the run, I realized again and again that I'd misjudged the size and strength of the water. What had seemed from shore like two-foot waves turned into a conflicted roller coaster with four-foot crests, often with side current beating against the canoe gunwales. Even inching along against the shoreline, ferry maneuvers and eddy turns required all of our strength and ability. The current sucked and whirled and fell downstream with the unthinking weight and momentum of a runaway freight train.

Sections between rapids were pretty and serene. The current hurried along, but without effort, through heavily forested valley and steep-walled canyon that dropped sheer to the water. In the sun, feeling the steady river beneath the boat, it seemed almost inconceivable that dangerous water loomed ahead. But then the next rapids would announce themselves with a distant grumbling murmur. Turning a corner, I'd see the river pitch away downstream, the uneven profile of water the result of rock and wave and ledge. I found myself dropping to my knees in the boat in anticipation of action, wanting to paddle for shore. White spray tossed by the waves flashed in the sunlight.

Well above the start of fast water, we'd choose a shore to scout from, commit to one side of the river. On a bend, we tended to take the inside of the curve, opting for somewhat slower current. Once decided on a course, there was little chance of changing our minds. To cross the wide strong Athabasca close to the head of a rapid would be courting disaster.

Some rapids were miles long. Others ran continuously, one into the next, so that we'd be fixed in watery athletics for a dozen miles at a stretch. We scouted section by section, sometimes taking most of an afternoon to run a few miles, debating the merits and dangers of a passage, strategizing from the tops of boulders, making sure we both knew the intricacies of a plan.

At the boat, before kneeling, before tightening the life vest and spray skirt, we'd review. "Okay, we start out down the center tongue. Just missing the big sleeper." We'd stand together, gesturing a mime of our intended route. "Then we backferry over near shore, outside that white rock but inside the biggest waves. On the corner, we'll catch the eddy behind the point of rocks and scout ahead from there. Right?" Stepping into the canoe, taking up paddles, holding our place, one of us would clarify a point. "Now the sleeper we want to be outside of isn't the one with the big curler wave behind it, is it? It's that one next to the ledge."

In the water, talking our way through a rapid helped us maintain our equanimity. "Okay, slow us down, slow up." Marypat's conversation from the stern was a pacifying litany. I'd backpaddle through the rolling waves, slowing the boat to the speed of the river so we wouldn't slam into the next crest, my paddle levering in the water as if against a solid force. "There's the chute we want. Stay close to the dark rock. Draw a little." Leaning out over the gunwale, I dug my paddle into the water and pulled in toward the boat, bringing the bow closer to the target. "Okay. Good. Now, backpaddle!" Our voices communicated the level of urgency for each move. "Ya! We're through! Let's ferry into the eddy."

It was never possible to read all the intricacies of a rapid from shore. A chute that looked entirely benign at a distance turned into a serious ledge drop close up, the current twisting through rocks like a corkscrew. "We can't make it, Marypat! We have to get outside. Let's sideslip now!" Paddles dove into the river—the heavy boat too slow, our feeble strength nothing against the casual muscle of the Athabasca—and the canoe would broach frighteningly through a wave trough or skim the rounded shoulder of a ledge, tipping a gunwale underwater.

By then the entire route would be changed, forcing us to ad-lib the rest of the way, shouting instructions and strategies, setting our knees against the sides of the boat for stability, sensing the language of the river with our eyes and legs and arms. "No, Al, we're too close now, we have to go over the ledge!" "Okay, let's get some momentum and then brace as we drop!" Our voices tiny in the roar.

In Boiler Rapid we declined to scout from shore, cocky and ebullient with early successes, succumbing to laziness, reading the run by standing up in the canoe, picking a route through waves in the center channel. When it was too late to retreat, we both saw how badly we'd misjudged the waves. The canoe bucked alarmingly, suddenly possessed with wild energy. The bow repeatedly submarined, dollops of water filling the skirts, side waves rocking us with a wicked wallowing motion that we absorbed in our knees and hips. "Keep straight, Marypat. Give me a draw. Good. Now, I'll brace. Give us some power!" Another wave, more cold river in our laps. I could feel water in the bottom of the boat, sloshing around my knees. "We need to get to shore. Let's work to the side of the channel!" I kept thinking of Earl Kay's last words, telling us not to hurry, to look at the rapids before running them. So stupid! We should always scout!

"I'm taking on water, Al!" The pile-up of waves, the slapping side current, lasted eternally. When we tried slowing, the canoe rolled and tipped in the trough, water grabbing at the hull. When we powered ahead, half the boat went under in each wave. Finally, the worst of the rapid behind us, we pulled for the rocky shore, giddy with our foolish luck. "God, were we stupid!" Marypat laughed with the relief of not capsizing and swimming the rest of the rapid. She emptied the last water from the skirt and turned in her seat to look at me. "Hey, let's camp here. We've got our miles in. I've had enough whitewater for the day. We'll finish Boiler in the morning."

Another gravel bar campsite, the heavy water rumbling in front of us, the wide flood plain providing ample view of any approaching danger. Waiting for dinner to cook, we sat on round boulders by our fire, our camp in the sand that would be river bottom at flood stage. Pale smoke from the burning driftwood lined out toward the forest, drawn straight by a slight wind.

A white-tailed deer stepped across the rocks on its way to the river, but tensed partway there, alarm in fiber and sinew, ears like radar, nose flaring. It sensed our presence, but wasn't sure what it meant. Were we a threat? For a long time the deer stood, statuesque, immobilized by indecision.

I wanted the deer to stand at the edge of the wild water, vulnerable and untroubled, front hooves in a shallow eddy, bending its neck to drink. Instead, it trotted away to the shadow of some willows, stopped, took in another draught of wafting breeze, walked into the thickets.

The roar of the water precluded any possibility of listening for small noises outside the tent, so I didn't bother trying and slept better than I had since the bear drama. Early in the morning mist rolled off the river like ocean fog, melting away when the sun climbed above the lip of the valley. We began the day by scouting the rapid ahead, chastened by our lesson, our respect recharged.

Crooked Rapid marked the end of the rock-choked whitewater and the start of ledge drops. The river made a hairpin bend in a hard gray layer of limestone, dropping over a set of resistant steps, sending the full power and volume of its flow slamming into the outside corner. We hung along the inside, just out from smooth rock walkways on flat layers of limestone. Across the way, the Athabasca flung its fluid, unfathomable weight against the hard rock, an impartial violence. Around the sharp turn, layered rock walls bent in a graceful arcing curve, smooth as an engineered racetrack. Compared to the near catastrophe in Boiler Rapid, our navigation this time was a twilight paddle on a calm lake, an enchantment.

At the bottom of the fast water, we found the first island since Grand Rapid, a barren sand bar, no more than two feet above the level of the river, devoid of vegetation. Perfect. We had to scour the entire surface to find enough driftwood for our small fire, but I felt utterly safe. The site had literally nothing to offer a bear. I refused to consider the possibility that a bear might be so motivated to investigate us that it would swim to the sand bar. Relief from the nervous paranoia of forest camps and shorebound stops infused our evening with the giddiness of gangsters in an impregnable hideout.

By morning it was drizzling. The thought of rising river level prodded us out of the tent. Munching a breakfast of cold cereal, we quickly packed our gear so as to minimize the coating of gritty rain-soaked sand. The island was markedly less appealing in a rainstorm than in the sun, and my eagerness to depart was sharpened by a preoccupation with the nearby danger of Cascade Rapid, waiting just a few miles downstream.

As Eugene had said, the ledge rapids give little warning of their location. If you don't anticipate them, aren't armed with maps, they suddenly crop up just ahead, too close to escape. By the time you see the funny break in the river horizon, there is little to do but hope for a forgiving ride. We ran Little Cascade on the far left, the ledge a jagged line of limestone spanning the river, rock visible just beneath the boat in the chute we chose, a sharp tooth snatching at my paddle as we shot by. Nothing to it, cushioned suspension.

I was so used to the long, convoluted struggle through riverbed mined with boulders, offering new difficulties in frantic, exhausting progression, that the quick drop seemed cheap, as if we'd gotten off too easily. But I heard Big Cascade just ahead, thought about Eugene blithely paddling down the center of the Athabasca, fresh with enthusiasm from the run of the Little Cascade, unaware of the mortal conflict a few strokes ahead.

We planned to portage the rapid, and scouted along an old mudslide on the left for the best way. Wet grass soaked our shoes and pant legs. The river fell over a five- or six-foot ledge, a sharp deadly plunge. We tried to figure where Eugene might have gone over. Nowhere in the center looked even remotely doable. Right below our feet, though, it seemed we might sneak past the main drop and continue downstream over some small shallow ledges.

Kneeling in the canoe, not believing we could escape without a carry, we slid along with the bank so close that it got in the way of our paddles. At a bend, we wanted to stay near shore, but the strong current pulled us partway into a whirlpool so powerful it looked like a suctioning sink drain. Marypat was straining backward with the strength of her desperate strokes, little paddle fighting against the river, the bow hanging in the balance, already into the vortex. My own backpaddling efforts twisted me almost forty-five degrees in the stern, hanging over the side for more effective purchase, my face looking straight down into the green river.

Grudgingly, the whirling water gave up its hold. We guided our canoe to a backwater, sat up in our seats to recover. Every time I felt confident in the river, I was taught a lesson, a smart slap to the ego.

By afternoon the sun beat back the clouds and we stripped to T-shirts. Even the bear we'd seen laboring up a steep sandy hillside muted our satisfaction but momentarily. Only a few rapids remained. We'd done the worst of it without mishap. Marypat wondered who we'd get mail from in Fort McMurray, what the city would be like.

I could smell Tar Sands petroleum deposits in the air, the sun warming the sand banks, the smell like a hot asphalt parking lot. We'd heard stories of natural gas springs, streams that would blaze at the drop of a match. Higher on the river, we passed by such spots, fuel oozing from the earth, mosquitoes inexplicably attracted in droves. Earl Kay had known a man who piped free natural gas to his cabin simply by trapping the escaping fuel. He'd even laid pipes through his vegetable garden that he fired up on cold nights to keep his tomatoes from freezing.

"Do you hear that, Al?"

I listened. Our canoe was midriver. We coasted along without life jackets, enjoying the sun and the break between rapids. "I hear water, but it must be the river going over a boulder or something."

"It sounds bigger than that. Maybe we should get closer to shore." Hint of fear in her voice.

"But there's no rapid on the map. Nobody mentioned a problem here. It's miles before the next marked rapid. Even the small whitewater has been on the maps."

"I'd just feel better near shore."

We began across the current, the unmistakable rumble of water in the air.

"Damn, there's a ledge. Right ahead!"

"What? It can't be!"

Shore was still a quarter-mile away. We could see the break in the smooth river, another ledge, unmarked on the maps, just downstream.

"Let's turn around and paddle against the current, angle for shore!" I began turning the canoe.

"No way, Al. It's too far."

The lip of the ledge was visible ahead of the bow, our backpaddling efforts bringing the drop into focus in slow motion. Nothing to be done. We had to go over.

"Is there a chute?" I yelled out, noticing again Marypat's life jacket tossed on top of our load.

"Over there." Marypat pointed to an indent in the ledge to our left, a thick filament of river funneling through it. We were sucked toward the lip, sideslipping frantically for the goal.

"When we get there, power into it and then brace!" My voice high and sharp. With surprising equanimity, I observed that we at least had calm river to swim to shore in. I wondered briefly which side we should make for. The drop was right there, the bow wavering like an arrow shaft in the current, our strokes no longer holding us back. "Okay. Power and brace!"

We go, have no choice, the boat leaping into the air, bow diving, river in our laps . . . but upright, upright!

I so expected to capsize that I had to visually check the canoe, look back at the three- or four-foot fall behind us. "Holy shit! How could they not mark that on the map?!"

"I don't know, but let's get over by shore." Marypat was already zipping into her life vest.

Feeling entirely deceived, we paddled in silence toward the final marked rapid. Once there, we scouted the series of ledges from land. Given the lessons of the day, I should have advocated caution, but instead found myself lobbying for a run down the center. "If we get in the current at the very top of the eddy and then draw to the left, we should be able to hit the ledge just right and ride out the waves." Marypat's look as much as said, "Haven't you learned yet?" but my foolhardy enthusiasm swayed her. We decided to try it.

Back to the boat. Into the eddy, a big rotating pool kept in motion by the rush of the main current. Entering the fast flow, we leaned out over the gunwale, literally drawing the canoe sideways with our strokes, slipping across the top of the choppy river, but being drawn ahead as well. Then the ledge, the final stairstep in a descent that began eighty miles upstream, the last plunge of bow into river, wash of water down the deck.

"Great!" I was yelling.

"Yahooee!" Marypat whooped, pumping her paddle overhead in victory.

7

We prepared for Fort McMurray like farm kids going to the city for the first time. Using periodic rain showers for our excuse, we laid over a day on another island camp. As it was, we were a solid week ahead of resupply schedule. Between storms we took baths, heated water to wash our hair, sorted through clothes to find the least grubby ensemble, made lists of errands, argued excitedly over whom to call first on the telephone.

I'm capable of nearly intolerable fits of anxious agitation if some unknown lies just out of view. I pace and fidget and effectively drive Marypat to distraction. She is much more accomplished at enjoying the present than I, allowing the future to arrive in good time. The usual result is that we compromise, she dilly-dallying and I compulsively packing up, so that by the time we leave, we're testy with each other and neither feels satisfied.

At least the morning weather was clear and warm. Spiffed up for our urban encounter, exasperated over our conflicting styles of departure, we paddled the few remaining miles of river into town, rounding a bend in front of a long highway bridge. Nestled in the confluence of the Clearwater and Athabasca rivers, Fort McMurray was bigger than I had expected: apartment buildings, office towers, tracts of suburban housing, the smell of fast food and diesel exhaust, hum and honk of traffic. Where will we stay? I found myself intimidated. Who will watch our gear while we do errands? How will we get around?

I pondered logistics on the way up a steep bank to the roadway, Marypat waiting in the boat. At the top, trucks blasted by and the city looked formidable. No place to camp, not a good spot to stop. Perhaps we could find a more hospitable berth if we paddled up the Clearwater. I returned with the scouting report and we continued.

Just past the bridge, an old guy in loose black pants and dark workshirt sat on a decrepit sofa rooted in six inches of silt, fishing an eddy pool, red-and-white bobber shivering with tiny excitements. What is this? Mississippi? He pointed up the Clearwater in response to our query about a good place to dock up, but didn't bother speaking.

We arrived at a small riverside park and pulled up next to some motorboats at a piling. A bright yellow-and-red float plane rode in the muddy water next to our canoe like a gaudy water insect. Some boys were engaged in sand construction down the beach. Cars and bicycles crunched along the gravel roadway. Resting the paddle across my thighs, I thought back over the last week, the watery tumult, the dead bear in the driftwood, our isolated vulnerable camps, the tracks of wolf and bear and moose the only signs of traffic.

As so often happens, problems almost immediately began taking care of themselves. A woman on her lunch hour offered to drive us to the post office. A pilot in an office overlooking the water agreed to watch the boat while we were gone. "Can't be held responsible if something happens, mind you, but I'll keep an eye on it."

Thirty minutes in the immigration building was sufficient to extend our visa to the projected end of our journey, still more than a year distant. Within an hour we had collected a stack of letters at the post office and parked ourselves in molded plastic seats at a sandwich shop in the Peter Pond Shopping Center to pore over the mail from home. Peter Pond, the intrepid fur trader, would have appreciated the scene. The two of us were distinctly unkempt by urban standards—canvas pants stained with the grit of wilderness living, my chin grizzled with a month's beard, the air around us no doubt fragrant. The nylon and polyester crowd jockeyed with shopping bags and succumbed to the ambiance of piped-in muzak, giving us a pretty generous berth and some surprised glances.

Our heavy boxes of food, fuel for the next month, waited for us at the post office. Everything had arrived, but the containers looked as if they'd been drop-kicked the entire way by postal workers who took offense at the bulk and weight of our supplies. We decided to let a cab portage us and our load back to the park.

Mid-afternoon, we rediscovered and assembled the food and equipment we had sent ourselves, spreading a disorganized mess across half an acre of park grass. Our collapsed stuffsacks began filling up alarmingly, reminding us what packing had been like at the start of the summer. Rice, noodles, spice refills, hot drinks, beans, flour, cake mixes, dehydrated fruit and vegetables, lemonade; writing pads, new books, pens and pencils, the next set of maps, film. Each item found its way to a well-known niche in our packs.

At the height of the disorganization, the two of us standing in the midst of what looked like bomb wreckage, the pilot who'd watched our canoe came over to observe this curious phase of our town visit: Alan Woods, his handshake firm. It turned out that Alan had grown up on Lake Athabasca, more specifically, in Uranium City, where his father had worked in the mine for twenty-eight years, up until the boom went flat and the remote, prosperous town shriveled to a collection of empty buildings. He was a mother lode of information about the lake, communities along the shore, the difficulty of winter, names of contacts.

"Look," he said, staving off the next volley of questions, "come over for dinner tonight. I've got a bunch of walleye fillets from a flight north."

Our ungainly load finally stashed, everything stowed away in the office of our new friend, we had time to ourselves while Alan piloted sightseers overhead. A few blocks away we found a bar and went in for a beer. Complete darkness, air-conditioned cave, one or two customers. Above the bar a color television ran constant music videos, groups I'd never heard of before, a mesmerizing production of fantasy, violence, and bizarre imagery that I found myself unable to ignore. We lasted for only one beer—but long enough for a profound sense of dislocation to develop.

Alan Woods was a gust of wind straight from the north. His easy, straightforward hospitality and enthusiasm for wild places reminded us of other northerners who had befriended us. At his home, a trailer he shared with a partner, we frittered away the evening with talk of the lake, life in Uranium City, places where we might try to winter over. With exhilarating rapidity, Alan rattled off the names of lakes, rivers, old Indian trails, campsites, and towns in his quiet voice.

Everyone in the north says walleye fillets are the best eating fish. If Alan's were a typical example, I am in complete agreement. Belly full of walleye and beer, mind thundering along with new ideas and evocative place names, I lay awake half the short night with thoughts of the near future.

Within a day we were both ready to leave again. By the time we'd taken Alan out for a pizza lunch, spent what seemed an outrageous sum of money from our small savings, and called our families to relate the first installment of our adventures, we realized that there was nothing left to do, that our home wasn't in town but back on the river. That in fact we were impatient to go.

Alan saw us off, standing next to his plane while we slowly furrowed around the bend, the canoe again cumbersome and riding low. Out of the Clearwater, back to the familiar green Athabasca, late afternoon light on the forest, the retreating sounds of the city beating at our backs. The old feeling of disconnectedness from society quickly returned, and I welcomed it.

*   *

Although almost two hundred miles of river remained, my attention focused beyond, to Lake Athabasca, the next sizeable challenge: two-hundred-fifty miles of open-water paddling. Alan Woods's stories provided grist for the millstones of my imagination. As muddy miles of river went under our keel, I fantasized clean water, bedrock islands, calm mornings, loons calling at twilight.

Except for the insulating depth of wilderness, the lower Athabasca might as well have been the Mississippi. Barge traffic still plies the waterway and channel markers lean downstream like inflatable pop-up toys. The river flowed green-brown with silt, hundreds of yards across, the only obstructions shifting sand bars on which even the canoe sometimes grounded.

The short tentacles of road leading out from Fort McMurray reach purposefully to sawmills or strip-mining operations, and then end. A day or two out from the city, we passed under the final bridge of our journey, the last manmade span in fifteen hundred miles, the end of pavement for more than a year.

We no longer needed to hold ourselves back. In fact, it would be handy to have extra days for crossing the lake, a cushion of time to absorb windbound delays. We paddled more steadily than we had all summer, regularly logging twenty-five to thirty-five miles in a day, putting fifteen miles behind us before lunch, taking the river in gulps, stretching out our muscles. Goal oriented, I'd calculate days to the lake on the maps at night. "We could be there as early as August first, Marypat, if we don't get held up by weather." As usual, I played the role of anticipator, Marypat less eager for the future.

Even away from strip mines, the air near Fort McMurray was laced with petroleum. Oil and tar permeated the ground. Sections of bank looked like rough, lumpy old roadways, black tar in thick layers. On hot days the surface turned soft, making molded imprints of our bare feet, blackening their bottoms.

A day downriver from town, we passed the immense strip-mining plant that is in large measure responsible for the economic well-being of Fort McMurray and the province of Alberta. From far upstream we saw the miles-long ridge of sand piled up next to the operation, unnaturally manicured by heavy equipment. Paddling closer, the smell of gas and oil an invisible cloud in the air, we came into view of the buildings and machinery. Black stacks poked up against the sky, spouting orange, heat-shimmering flames. Machinery the size of houses labored with be-hemoth strength in the sand, mining the surface for fuel that sustains the human antpile.

The Athabasca eddies right in front of the spectacle and provides water for the lubrication of the plant. I imagined myself as an extra-terrestrial, and felt our craft utterly foreign. We were speechless, eyes riveted on the humming, grinding, ponderous process going on a few hundred yards away. I studied the scene through binoculars, as if scrutinizing alien territory. For miles downriver the clang and rumble followed us. When we stopped for lunch—eating at the base of a limestone cliff made almost entirely of fossilized sea creatures—the smell seemed to seep insidiously into the taste of our food.

We began paddling past native clusters of habitation. At Fort McKay settlement housing squatted on the riverbank, little clapboard houses patched with whatever was at hand: plywood, tar paper, shingles, plastic, old boards slapped onto the buildings like appliqué. Exteriors were painted a shocking array of pinks, greens, oranges, and yellows, as if a barge had supplied an assortment of colors, one can of each. Dogs howled at us from the ends of chains. Native boats, all powered by outboards, lined the muddy shore. I could hear an electric guitar whanging away in accompaniment to the fretful, abstracted mourning of canines.

A group of native men worked at unloading a high-sided wooden boat. One of them straightened up to watch us approach. "Where you come from?" His voice at conversational pitch was audible at midriver.

"Jasper."

"Where are you going?"

The steady current was already taking us by so that we looked back over our shoulders. Marypat stopped paddling to answer, resting her paddle across the gunwales. "Stony Rapids this summer."

"Baker Lake next summer," I added.

The man watched us in silence, the whole group of them standing up, arms loose, looking at the canoe. "Holy shit!" the muttered reply clear across the water. Then, louder, "Be careful!"

*   *

Sidestreams became less frequent, making our daily water collection more of a chore. Muddy banks sucked us down to our knees in dark goo when we had to get out of the canoe. The river was finally losing its grasp on the heavier sediment, the glacial scrapings and sandstone grains and bits of limestone ledge ending their travel, silting in the channel, bottomless as quicksand.

Perhaps it was only a matter of forceful longing, but I caught ephemeral hints of the far north in the look of the sky or the quality of a breeze. A clarity in the air, the way clouds were arranged, the fragrance of spruce bog would lift my spirits, invigorate me. "It feels like we're getting north, Marypat. There's something about today that reminds me of the north, makes me want to paddle around the bend." The next coil of river would destroy the mood, the slow heavy Athabasca lethargically unwinding, the big lake still days and miles away.

The current no longer had the power to render us immune from headwinds. Blasting up the broad straightaways, winds confronting the current kicked up a rough chop. We measured our progress against channel markers or distant islands, tried to stay against a lee shore, every mile a battle.

Once we were stymied altogether. Hours of hard paddling had netted only a few miles. Wind was a steadily howling torment, the river humped up in two-foot rollers, the valley a wind tunnel no matter which way we turned. Exhausted, we stopped on a sand point for lunch and had to stand up in order to escape the blowing grit. If anything, the wind increased while we ate, forcing us to haul the canoe higher onto the beach to keep it from taking on water in the slapping waves. Continuing on seemed foolishly hardheaded. Our first windbound camp.

We began searching for a good tent site, quartering over the sand and mud, looking for a spot a bit out of the wind. Well back from the river, I came across unmistakable human footprints, the smooth sole of workboots. Alongside, a drag mark indented the sand in a wide shallow rut. I followed, back toward the river. The steps ended abruptly at a recent fire pit, the blackened remains of a deer head lying among the charred wood and confusion of footprints. Cracked bones and bits of hide were already partially covered by drifting sand, like the scene of a prehistoric picnic. Mixed in, even fresher than the fire, the tracks of a large bear, long claw marks deep incisions in the mud.

8

Sharp paranoia over bears, held in hovering abeyance since Fort McMurray, sneaked back into our minds like a sickness. We fought downstream from the deer kill, struggling against the wind for another few miles, finding a denuded sand bar for camp. Wood proved so scarce on the island that we had to paddle to shore to find more, along a forest edge littered with bear sign.

In the late evening—the orange sun slanting toward the horizon, the wind spent and the river smooth—we saw a large bear on the near shore along which we had collected wood. It padded up the sand, heavy loose fur rolling with the ponderous gait. The bear stopped at clumps of willow, half of the black body disappearing while it foraged. When it came to our tracks, the bear looked over at us, face inquisitive, nose lifted toward our camp. Twilight deepened and the bear stayed on the close shore, sometimes entering the edge of the forest, but always returning to the sand, moving a few steps farther to the next bunch of willow.

We watched in the echoey silence until it became too dusky to pick the bear out from the vegetation. After building up our fire, we went to the tent and tried to sleep. For hours I listened to the night settle, turned over to see Marypat equally restless. We slept the sleep of refugees who expect the hammer of the secret police on the door at any hour, and rose with the first lightening of the sky.

That morning, following the current as it swept around a bend close to a sharp dirt bank, I glanced into the cool forest and looked into the brown eyes of a bear, twelve feet away. Mute as stone, black as river mud, watching us pass. In the afternoon we saw another familiar black shape and again provoked no alarm by our proximity. If bears moved off as we approached, it was with an unperturbed rolling shuffle. Sighting a bear had become so commonplace that it required no exclamation. Marypat or I would point the animal out and stop paddling, drifting by in our safe vehicle, knowing we'd have to leave the canoe at day's end.

Fatigued by another long stretch of river after little sleep, we beached the boat on a wide sandy delta and went into our campsite selection routine. Moose seemed to be the dominant users of the area, their pancake-size hoof divots in the sand, but I found little comfort in

the superficial lack of bear sign. Feeling as I had at the bottom of the
Grand Rapid portage, camped with our backs against the river, I kept
watching the still woods, no longer feigning a lack of concern.

The same tense drama developed that night. We stood brushing our
teeth in the thickening twilight, when a large black bear padded
purposefully out of the bush toward the water, one hundred yards
downstream. The noose of fear tightened around my neck, my breathing
difficulty returned. Toothbrush in one hand, shotgun in the other, I
watched the heavy bear progress to the river. He seemed preoccupied,
inattentive, his feet slipping in the mud, routinized as a commuter
making his way to the familiar bus stop.

Suddenly, he noticed us—smelled our fire, our food, our sweat,
sensed something—and began to run in a shambling laborious gallop
toward the Athabasca. At the river's edge he turned toward us, hesitated,
and then waded in.

We were elated. Finally, a bear that ran from us! He swam the wide
current, black head holding his own in the flow. I remembered the
steadily breathing animal in the river on the dark night near the Vega
ferry crossing, the unperturbed exertion. On the far shore he climbed up
the slippery bank, flung a haze of spray into the air with a heavy shake
of fur, and melted into the woods. "Well, at least he seemed a little
frightened." Marypat bent over for the water bottle to finish rinsing her
mouth. I turned from the river and saw a second bear, coming our way
from upstream.

"Goddammit, there's another one." My voice lacked the urgency of
surprise, events of the past weeks flooding over my threshold for alarm.
If the first bear was a picture of ursine consternation, the second was a
portrait of unflappability. He foraged in the willows unconcerned,
hardly deeming us worthy of a glance. It was nearly dark. "Do you think
we should move camp?" I checked the gun while I watched the bear.

"I don't know, Al. It's late, and with our luck we'd just move into
another bear's feeding grounds. They're so thick here!"

We heaped punky driftwood onto our fire to create a smokey
deterrent. The bear browsed along, sometimes lifting up on his hind legs
to reach into a higher clump of willow, broad back disdainfully turned
to us. Almost even with our camp, the bear began following a tongue of

thick vegetation up a slope, shaking the brush as he moved. After a minute we lost sight of him altogether.

I was tired of our meek quaking existence. My hand gripped the ridged pump action along the gun barrel and I levered a cylindrical slug into the chamber, the movement smooth, the sounds harsh. Snugging the butt into my shoulder, aiming into the enigmatic forest, I shattered the still night with a lethal blast of frustration.

Tremendous reaction when I had expected none. A crashing racket, shaking trees, snapping branches. It sounded like someone was driving a dump truck at full speed through the woods.

"Good God! What the hell is that?" I slammed another round into the chamber, the spent cartridge flipping onto the ground. We moved closer together, and I pointed the gun toward the sound. The thudding, thrashing tumult lasted and lasted. We couldn't tell if the noise was retreating or coming our way. Thoroughly rattled, I found wholly credible the possibility that some rabid beast would come thundering out of the forest in a full-speed charge.

The noise eventually diminished, finally fading away, leaving the sounds of the tranquil river in the calm twilight. "It had to have been a startled moose," I tried to make sense of the outburst. "No bear would make such a ruckus."

We went to bed. For the second night running, I lay awake, rehearsing the act of defending ourselves, listening to Marypat's fitful rustling, turning to meet her open eyes. Off again at dawn, we sighted the first bear of the day within half a mile of camp.

The lush spread of wilderness radiated from the edges of the river. The mysterious vastness that I have always found so exhilarating struck me as sinister, hostile. I felt trapped by it, oppressed by my own reaction, embittered by the realization that I had been stripped of a freedom I had always taken for granted.

The lake became a kind of obsession for me, a mental balm. I ached for the change of scene, clear water, an escape from mud. Bears seemed so attracted to the riverbanks. Perhaps a different environment would at least render them less visible. I could anesthetize my fear if it weren't visually reinforced so frequently.

The river slowed and meandered in the final twenty-five miles, as if

all purposeful energy had been expended, procrastinating before reaching its destination. In the delta, river water wandered about, the current
hardly discernible, whole channels silting in within a year's time. Our
map was woefully inadequate for interpreting a way through the maze.
The surrounding land was a sea of muck and grass and weed. Where there
was a bit of elevation rising above the level of mire, alder thickets were
so dense they required a machete to penetrate.

Determined to make Lake Athabasca in one long paddle from our
last camp, we decided not to follow the marked barge channel, but to
take a shortcut along smaller, still substantial waterways through the
delta. We concocted rambling conversations to make the slow miles go
by. For a good chunk of morning we reconstructed a history of family
bicycles, complete with auxiliary features. "Did you ever put baseball
cards in your spokes as a kind of obnoxious speedometer?" I'd remember.
"Yeah, but what about those plastic streamers that you could attach to
the handlebar grips?" Marypat responded from the stern.

In the bow, I kept track of the small bends, the little tributary
streams. Up ahead I saw a brown fuzzy patch, not the color of mud, not
the right shape for vegetation. Marypat picked it out as well. The brown
patch slowly resolved, like an image focusing through a camera lens. The
beautiful rusty bear methodically mauled a willow shrub, working the
bush over with the absorbed intensity of a fisherman tying a knot in
eight-pound test line.

At twenty feet the bear still hadn't scented us. Our conversation
didn't alarm it. Finally the brown circular face turned toward us, the bush
forgotten. It still shocked me to see something that big disappear with
such complete stealth and speed. Gone. No sound. We ate lunch in the
boat, rationalizing that it was too muddy to get out on shore, but we both
knew why we stayed in the canoe.

It became clear that we were either not where we thought we were
or that the map was completely inaccurate. Bends didn't correlate with
those on the charts, tributaries went unmarked or were misplaced.
Channel forks confronted us with route choices we made by studying the
weeds to see where the slight current flowed. Around us mudflats and
marsh grass and stagnant water created a mecca for sandpipers and

mallards and geese, but certainly offered no place to camp.

We followed the compass north, sometimes poling against the mucky bottom with our paddles, probing narrow passages, turning back at dead ends, restlessly moving forward like an ant that has lost the communal trail. I kept standing up in the bow, hoping to see an opening in the horizon, an end to the swamp and the beginning of open lake.

The first hint of lake arrived in the wind, a cool freshness. We followed the last few shallow passages, marsh grass thinning out, open water expanding. Blue lake stretched away to the east, blending seamlessly with the pale afternoon horizon, an oceanic vista. Directly across the lake, a range of rounded bedrock hills and a sprinkling of forested islands contrasted with the low wet landscape of the delta. Still a half-dozen miles away, we could clearly make out the town of Fort Chipewyan on the bedrock shore. A radio tower speared the sky on a hilltop, and the town wrinkled over the rock like a village on the Maine coast.

We paddled along the border of marsh grass, searching the southern shore for any point of elevation, any potential camp. The delta spread for miles, nowhere hospitable. Gulls and terns played the winds, searching the shallow water for food, raucously piercing the air with their cries. The contrast of fresh air and moving winds, the distant skyline, made me imagine arriving at the Atlantic from the depths of a South American river, the sudden joy inhibited by an awareness of threatening space.

Along the fringe of delta, the grasses and weeds tamed the waves. We pushed through green matted vegetation thick as braided rope, the lake bottom half a paddle length beneath us. Anchored in silt, huge weathered tree trunks, whitened by wind and sun, dotted the shallows. The southern shore stretched ahead interminably, more of the same. Anywhere we got out, we'd sink to our hips.

We came up to a grounded tree four times the length of our canoe, a foundered Moby Dick besmirched with bird whitewash. I tied up to an arthritic-looking branch and stepped out on the broad back of wood, pacing its length to work out my legs and let my aching shoulders loosen up. Marypat crawled crabwise over the load and joined me. Overhead, the gulls and terns we'd displaced scolded and dove toward us.

"I wish we could cross the lake. Those islands look so damn inviting." I was studying the map to fix our position. "They're almost five miles away, but they look like a fifteen-minute paddle."

The wind blew out of the southwest, directly broadside to a crossing. The shallow water near us heaved with large swells, held down by the thick ropey vegetation, but farther out we could see the choppy waves, the flecks of white-capped water. We'd already come thirty-five miles, never once getting out of the canoe.

"We could sleep in the boat if we had to." Marypat looked at the town through binoculars and then swept the horizon behind us in search of a dry spot. "Maybe we should wait a while and see if the wind dies." Clambering back over the load to the stern, she stretched out to snooze, her feet propped on the gunwales, blue visor pulled down over her eyes, life vest bunched up for a pillow. I stayed on the tree, walking the length of trunk as if it were a ship deck, feeling for a change in the wind.

We waited at the log for hours, alternately resting in the canoe or standing up to check conditions. To paddle ahead seemed pointless, to cross, dangerous, so we stayed. By the time we decided to leave, the sun lay near the horizon just off our bearing, the wind had dropped, and our restlessness had come to a peak.

"Let's go, Marypat. I think we can make it."

As if preparing for a whitewater run, we snapped up the deck and girded ourselves for waves, unhitched the bowline from the huge, natural anchor, and pointed across the lake—the first major crossing of the summer. For almost a mile the boat was held back by weeds, leaving a path through the wavy green strands behind us. When we broke into deeper water, the canoe rocked more heavily, fighting a slight choppiness. The islands seemed tangibly close, minutes away, even as the time stretched on and my arms labored under the weariness of a forty-mile day. I counted strokes in sets of a hundred, forcing my eyes away from the islands until I finished a set. In the center of the crossing, miles from either shore, the wind freshened. We kneeled and turned so that we quartered the waves, lengthened the distance as a result.

Waves sometimes broke over the edge of the deck. I felt the boat tip and wobble in troughs, the wind steadily building. The island shores slowly became visible, spray breaking on the large rocks. Still over a mile to go, we turned more downwind and made for the nearest rocky outcrop, waves by now an alarming size. Closer yet, I could hear the crash of surf, see the orange lichen on boulders. I started to look for a landing spot. The lake water was much colder than the lower river. I remembered rescuing my brother out of a frigid northern lake after a nearly fatal capsize on an earlier expedition, numb and stiff with hypothermia, and wondered if anyone from Fort Chipewyan would do the same for us if we went over.

Landing proved difficult. The bow crashed and bumped in the rocky crevice we entered, and water slopped over the stern. I jumped off the bow plate, hauled the canoe up the granite slope, and grabbed Marypat as she leapt for the slippery shore.

"No good. No good." I stumbled among the rocks in a state of nervous agitation. "We were lucky. Dammit, I didn't want the first crossing to be that borderline."

Marypat heaved the canoe farther onto the island, her hair wind-blown and scraggly. "Hey, I was pretty nervous, too, but I didn't want to spend the night on that log, either!" We looked back across the lake, the delta a thin green line, a very distant horizon.

PART III

THE MAGIC OF LAKE ATHABASCA

The change in environment hardly
could have been more dramatic. For weeks we had dealt with mud and
silt and a closed-in horizon, a world in which we became oppressed by
our anxiety. We had become used to landing barefoot in order to cope
with ever-present mud, to finding piles of sand in the tent, grit in our
sleeping bags, grains of rock in our dinner. Even the water in sidestreams
had become silty and discolored on the lower river, coating the water
jugs with a permanent gray layer of sediment.

The bedrock island felt like a doormat at the entranceway to the
north. Solid rock adorned with colorful reindeer lichen, beds of sphagnum moss, granitic boulders, cold clean water for the taking. I hopped
up and down the shore from boulder to boulder, fatigue and fear
forgotten, hardly able to restrain my relief and excitement.

"What's that?" Marypat was listening for something behind the
wind.

There was another background sound, a kind of moaning wail. It
came from over the top of the island. We climbed up the rock, the noise
intensifying, and found the other tenants—a pack of five or six sled dogs,
all howling into the wind. At least they were chained to trees, each with
a water bucket nearby. We retreated to the other side of the knoll, not
about to abandon our safe haven because of a few mangy canines.

Instead of calming in the evening, winds kept building out of the southwest, sending four-foot waves smashing against the shore. We had to move the canoe to the top of a ledge and weight the tent down with our packs to keep it from blowing away. Our crossing had occurred in a narrow, fortuitous lull. Two hours later and we would have been paddling for our lives.

Natives had spotted us from town. While dinner cooked on a fire sheltered from gusts in a rocky crevice, several boats cruised by, circling the island for a better look at the visitors. No words were exchanged, hardly anyone waved. The powerful boats slammed past in the surf, brown impassive faces aimed inquisitively at our camp.

Once in the tent, I couldn't sleep, in spite of the pleasant ache of fatigue. Winds buffeted the fabric like giant paws. Our sleeping bags lay on a mattress of moss in a rocky depression. My mind worked back over the day, the astonishing contrast between morning and evening. "You awake, Marypat?" I rolled over to face my partner. "Can you imagine how agonizing today would have been if we'd been part of a larger group? Every one of those little route decisions in the delta would have turned into long discussions, everybody reading the map differently. God, we'd still be tied to that tree!"

Marypat groaned and laughed. "Finding the lake would have been the easy part, too. Picture three canoes tied up there, all of us trying to figure out where to camp, whether to cross, how long to wait for the wind to die!"

"With the bears and everything, there have been times when I wished we had company," I continued, "but I sure like not having to negotiate every pissant little detail. I like our quiet style."

"Me too, Al. I'm really glad we're alone." Marypat's voice was muffled. She squirmed deeper into her bag.

"Let's make tomorrow a rest day. What do you think? We've earned a break."

Marypat's eyes were closed, her breathing slow. "Sure," she managed. "I don't care."

I lay awake, listening to the wind, the rollers breaking against shuddering rock. We're in good shape, I thought. On the lake by August first. Even with wind delays we should have plenty of time to make it before fall weather starts in.

* *

Wind wouldn't have allowed our departure in the morning, in any event. Waves pounded the island from across the lake, and the time off felt like a snow day in seventh grade, a gift. I kept looking over the blue spread of horizon, standing where the spray-laden wind hit me in the face, feeling the rock through my boots, tracing lichen patterns with my fingers. I harnessed my enthusiasm to tackle chores—laundry, a bath, catching up in my journal, writing letters.

Except for the peak moments of bear fear, when I wished desperately for company, I had shed the longing for society. Even so, letters became a substantial link to the people we'd left behind. Writing down experiences, the things that occupied my mind, gave me a strong sense of connecting, even if I couldn't get letters in return.

During quiet paddling stretches I sometimes communed with a friend, reworking memories, hearing snatches of old conversation, verbalizing my new thoughts. When we passed a community and dropped off a bundle of insect-smeared, travel-worn envelopes, I continued on in a glow of satisfaction, having made contact.

By evening the wind calmed, and in the morning the lake was as smooth as a park pond. We visited Fort Chip only long enough to mail our letters at the post office, located in the front hallway of someone's home, and then we headed down the rockbound shore of Lake Athabasca. Crossing the first few inlets and bays, winding among islands, a rustic version of northern suburbia dotted the shores. White canvas wall tents marked summer fishing camps, with drying racks for fish set up like skeletal tepees. Every island seemed to have its complement of dogs. Ramshackle cabins loomed through the sparse spruce forest.

An enthusiastically gesturing man hailed us to the shore of one island, and then held the bow off the rocks while we talked. Two bulky women dressed in loose ankle-length skirts sat shyly behind him in the rocks, not once looking up at us. Pete White Deer rattled off an impressive list of friends and relatives for us to greet in Fond-du-Lac and Stony Rapids, towns still so many lake miles away that I hadn't begun anticipating our arrival there.

For the first time we paddled without the aid of current, the boat propelled by our arms and backs alone. Used to the jockeying motions of moving water, we felt held back by the quiet lake. Our paddle blades entered the water on a changed note. Granite cliffs fell sheer into the deep lake. Peregrine falcons flew out from rocky perches on swordlike wings, their flight a fast arrowing, alarm calls sharp and piercing. On a windy day the cliff faces would offer no safe landings, but we broke through smooth water in their shadow, landed at narrow ledges to take pictures, our tiny wake lapping minutely against ancient rock.

It was our forty-eighth day out. We stopped early to sew in a new tent zipper from the repair kit, and camped on a high point overlooking the calm lake. Zipper failure in bug country is more than a nuisance. A tent is the only safe zone when insect onslaughts become intolerable; without a tight door, there is no sanctuary. While Marypat stitched in the replacement, I searched for driftwood, finding the tracks of our nemesis on a nearby beach. A new environment, but still infused with threat.

By dawn the personality of the lake had transformed. Even from inside my bag I could hear breakers on the rocky point. An east wind pressed against the tent, its raw momentum gathered along two hundred miles of lake surface. Damn! We should have gotten more miles in last night.

With the canoe in the restless water behind a nose of granite, the packs loaded into their accustomed spots, deck snapped down, Marypat eyed the rough surface from the bow. "It doesn't look good to me," she said, her heavily clothed body twisted around toward the spacious horizon.

"Well, if we can't do it, we'll stop. We can at least try right along shore and see how bad it is."

Each wave presented an individual challenge. One steep and sharp-fronted; the next cresting with snarling foam while we rode to the top; still another broad-backed and benign. While the canoe twisted and slammed through the gray water, I watched and estimated the procession of obstacles, adjusting to quarter into the larger waves more directly. If I missed the angle by a fraction, or underestimated a wave, water slurped across the deck or washed over the diving bow. Within two hundred yards, we'd had enough. Once around the end of Shelter Point, a fluid topography punctuated with whitecaps promised an even more frightening prospect.

A crescent beach curved whitely at the back of the bay we headed into. A native camp sprawled at the edge of the woods along one side. Outside a canvas wall tent, two girls sat by a fire the size of a steer-roast pit. When we approached, they became agitated, standing up and nervously mincing away from the fire. I thought of half-wild horses who have been out to pasture too long and have to be lured in. As it became clear that we intended to visit, they actually ran off into the forest, woodland nymphs slipping away from foreigners.

Our bow grated into the sand. The water in the small bay was calm and still. After thirty seconds or more the older girl materialized out of the woods, acting as if she had been on some errand. Bare feet, tight blue-jeans, dark hair halfway down her back, her slim face in the shy averted pose we'd noticed in the women who accompanied Pete White Deer.

"It's too windy on the lake. Is it all right if we camp here?" I sensed my intrusive status, wishing we'd just gone to the other side of the bay and waited. The girl said nothing.

"Do you speak English?" A nod, but still no look, even her thin body half turned away.

"We'll just wait for the wind to die." I pointed down the beach with my paddle. Another nod. She turned back to the fire where her companion had sneaked back out of the trees, dragging her naked feet through the cool sand.

The beach was littered with trash. Old cowboy boots, diapers, plastic bags, tin cans, bottles, bits of yellow line. Obviously a well-used native camp. The canoe unloaded, but left halfway in the water as a symbol of our readiness, I watched the tumultuous lake. Marypat curled up out of the wind to snooze. The girls played at kicking a blue rubber ball in the sand a hundred yards away.

I had become capable of long periods of quiet contemplation, a kind of mental estivation, not concentrating on any specific train of thought but drifting, feeling the wind, watching the moving water—with images of our journey, thoughts of family, whimsical pictures of the near future performing an uninhibited slow-motion dance through my mind. Time consciousness in the sense of looking at a watch never occurred to me anymore. I checked the sun, tracked a cloud across the sky, caught sight of a particularly large wave colliding on the rocky point, sat still while the day moved past.

I rarely considered the issue of expedition purpose anymore. It seemed a fretful digression, a stale attic. With the summer memories a fluid current, the prospect of country and thrill and quiet contemplation ahead, the why question never came up. We lived a wilderness existence simplistic in the extreme, but harboring profound and fully occupying depths as well, depths impossible to quantify.

I could feel my body firming up, sloughing off the layers of fat, my arms and shoulders powerful again, my pants loose at the waist and my belly flat. At the beginning of the journey I had been in the worst physical shape of my life. I had felt undeserving of the challenge, unworthy. But with the demanding effort below Fort McMurray, I began to take pride in my half of the machine that pushed us across the north, to wear aches and soreness as badges.

A boy emerged from the wall tent, seventeen perhaps, wearing sweat pants and a T-shirt that advertised Miller beer. He and the older girl poled a skiff into deeper water and chugged into the waves just off the point to pull in a net. Hair streaming in wind gusts, the slender girl hung over the bow, completely slipping from view in the wave troughs, hauling in a net weighted with huge glistening fish that flapped from the strings every few feet.

After the boat returned and the group sat at the fire filleting fish, I couldn't resist imposing myself, couldn't resist hunting up the camera and slinging it behind my back. I trudged toward the gathering.

A tape player crooned Tammy Wynette. The older girl held a baby on her lap while the boy/man pinned one of the monstrous flapping pike on a board and hacked away at the live fish with little of the native dexterity I would have expected.

"Desmond," he said, after I'd said hello. "My wife, Darlene." He pointed the bloody knife at the shy girl. "My daughter, Daphne. And Darlene's sister, Linda." He hardly paused in his efforts. I had taken his wife for a twelve-year-old. A fawn of a girl, but she played with her daughter naturally, at ease with motherhood.

The girls stayed in the background, deferential and silent, but Desmond turned almost loquacious, telling me they were out camping for the weekend, trying to smoke fish, although they didn't really know how. He sawed through several pike, saying he didn't mind if I took pictures, the girls giggling at my interest. I stayed until conversation lapsed and then said goodbye, slogging through the sand to report my anthropological findings to Marypat.

"If there was ever an attractive spot for a bear, this is it! They have food all over the place. It's as if they're baiting a live trap. And all that fish hanging there. Any bear in the province could home in on this place!" The blatant lack of concern displayed by residents made me cringe at the thought of my own timid behavior in bear country. Cringe, but not abandon the attitude.

At twilight the winds hadn't abated and we set up camp reluctantly, admitting to the ignominious forward progress of roughly two hundred yards for the day. "If you get up first, even if it's really early, make sure you wake me." My cocky confidence about our time cushion had been significantly diminished by wind and wave.

2

Wind. Without form, invisible, odorless, unpredictable as lightning strikes, yet capable of stopping us as effectively as a wall. Everything else might be perfect—a sky untainted by cloud, the sun a warm breath, ourselves rested and prepared—yet the wind could spoil the party as abruptly as a police raid. It troubled our days, harassing our attempts at forward progress.

For a week we spent as much time windbound as we did paddling. At dawn we emerged to study the lake, watch the clouds, feel the air. On some mornings it was a waste of time to get up, the wind and roiled water an unappealing sentence, obvious from the inside of the tent. At no time were we were confident of lasting calm. A twenty-five-mile day could be followed by two days of siege. Calm mornings deteriorated and turned nasty within a mile-and-a-half of camp.

At least the shoreline offered a panoply of choice locations in which to wait out delays. Rock points as graceful as whalebacks, sand beaches untrammeled by human footprints, spruce-fragrant woodlands unsullied by trash and carpeted with crowberry. We pitched the tent on mattresses of moss so absorbent that even torrential downpours left no standing water. Sunsets performed lingering shows that we watched from front-row seats on the patient bedrock.

Dawn was often blessed by stillness, our voices hushed, the canoe wake a scratch across a mirror. A mile from camp the first breezes blew the bugs away, cooled our faces. But often the early relief of air would strengthen and reach for us across ruffled water, awakening the lake. More than once the wind rose so quickly we were unable to compensate for it, to make plans. Plunging through rough water, buttoning down the cover as we went, shouting to each other, we were forced to land at the first feasible spot, whether on a forbidding outcrop or a dingy island. Landings like that had the feel of amphibious beach assaults under mortarfire, waves a repeated cymbal-crash against coastline, our canoe a piece of flotsam. The bow person leapt to shore as the bow struck, abandoning the stern person in the floundering craft to weather the battering lake until the boat could be stabilized.

With winds blowing off the land, paddling became an exhausting ordeal. Progress was possible as long as we clung to the protective lee along the shoreline, but the miles were paid for with aching wrists and shoulders, our arms complaining at the joint sockets from the strain of lopsided paddling. Trip notes logged our stuttering movement: fifteen miles, two hundred yards, twenty-five miles, three miles, no progress, sixteen miles, every day an anomaly.

Marypat accepted delays with a measure of resigned equanimity I found both admirable and maddening. Her usual response was to drag out her sleeping bag, build a windbreak out of packs, and go to sleep. Meantime, I would pace the shore just out of reach of the tumult, listening for a change in pitch, measuring the height of the waves, refiguring our mileage average in light of the new postponement.

My manic frustration fueled attacks on chores. I'd bathe, wash a few socks in a pond of water, spread out equipment to dry, build a fire to make coffee and then methodically drink the whole pot, write a letter, and return to prowling the shoreline. Would we be trapped for an hour or a week? I unfolded the map to study ahead so often that the creases frayed and split apart.

Some days we packed and unpacked the boat three times, repeatedly encouraged and then repulsed by fickle wind shifts. Rolling up the tent, nesting pots, storing plastic bags of food in the right stuffsacks, covering our traces, lashing the load had become so routinized that we could have set up and broken camp blindfolded in a hurricane.

Fiddler Point, Graywillow Point, Thousand Island Bay, Cracking-stone Peninsula, Saint Mary's Channel, Lobstick Island. Home for an hour, two days, overnight, the landmarks a litany of progress along the lengthy convoluted shore.

The lake offered a positively schizophrenic range of experience. For a day and a half we were trapped on a barren rocky island the size of a modest living room, perhaps two feet above lake level, vegetated by only a few desertlike shrubs. Marypat saw the best in the situation and named the rocky dot Nest Island; I stuck to a less charming label pressed upon me by the ubiquitous evidence of the nestees. Forced by wind to make an emergency landing in four-foot waves, we were imprisoned there by a continuing barrage that never slackened.

By the second day, when waves diminished a bit in size by afternoon, I lobbied for departure—more out of desperation to escape than from any true conviction that we could make much headway. But the lake altered character with the speed of a quick-change artist adopting a new disguise. The wind died. The waves lost their angry, white-capped chop and swung under the boat in a lazy waltz. It was wonderful to paddle the calming swells, our blades biting through water free of airy resistance, our ready shoulders working under the long cool rays of the low circling sun.

The sky shaded from a pale washed-out blue to the beginning peach of sunset, and far east across the open water the first bruise of night inked the sky. Fifteen miles we made, bite by bite, past points, across bays, along islands, through narrow shortcut shallows where big pike swirled the muck like northern gators.

By sunset the lake turned utterly calm, the air cool as a whisper of fall, and an island camp presented itself in magnificent contrast to the forlorn bit of real estate we'd been forcibly marooned on. We headed toward a rocky knoll of granite, scaled with crisp curls of lichen, carpeted on top in deep sphagnum shag, and equipped with a watery crevice perfect for a canoe berth. In the dusky light, we sat on the top of the ancient loaf of bedrock and watched a group of thirty-one loons. Quietly gabbling, popping their heads down to survey the other dimension of their lives with sharp glittery eyes, they swam purposefully by in front of our camp. The neighborhood review committee.

3

Lake Athabasca captivated us with beguiling beauty and then terrified us with implacable power. At dawn we paddled a surface smoking with mist, smooth as a satin sheet. Far-off islands looked to be suspended just above the water, their spruce hair wavy in the liquid distance. We stole across the mouths of bays quiet as looters in the giant's lair. Even loons seemed reluctant to break the dawn world with their wailing bird howls, and rode sedately on the smooth surface.

For days at a stretch we avoided the mainland, feeling secure on small islands, like sleeping in moat-encircled castles. Fear of bears lost its edge. Only rare sightings intruded on our days. Along one steep shore-line, a sow sent her two black cubs scrabbling up a jack pine and lumbered aggressively to the edge of the rock cliff, vigilant, her hot gaze truculent and unequivocal. Six-foot willow shrubs smashed under her paws like blades of grass. Would she leap in after us? "It's okay, Mama, we're just goin' along our way."

The lake was thirty, thirty-five, forty miles wide. As the southern shore faded out of view, we felt unbalanced by the loss of horizon. Out toward the big open water, the space looked oceanic. We traveled along the edge of a liquid Sahara. Although we stuck close to the northern shoreline, crossings in front of cliff faces could be severely unnerving experiences. Dark rock scarps dropped sheer into black water, swells gulping into mossy crevices. Sometimes there were miles between landing sites. Places like Crackingstone Peninsula: half a dozen miles of straight bedrock dropping into deep cold lake. We battled the last of that massive jut of rock in four-foot whitecaps, wordlessly paddling for survival. The bow pitched and dove and shed water like a powerless submarine adrift in the North Sea. We kept close to the cliffs, not because they offered security but because we were terrified to leave land. Rebounding waves slapped back from the rock, torquing the canoe with wicked twists, glimpses of mossy crevices deep underwater visible through the smooth wave valleys. When we made Saint Mary's Channel and ducked in behind the first islands, it felt like coming into a fire-warmed living room from a howling winter blizzard. Palpable safety.

Later on, calm weather stretched for days, and we took the lake in greedy swallows, paddling from quiet dawn to hot breathless afternoon, when we stopped out of fatigue and arm weariness. Twenty-five miles at a whack. In the evening camp, we sat side by side with the map on our knees, remembering the points and islands and bays as the pencil dotted in the satisfying day's trail.

While paddling I watched the lake bottom pass: boulders, ledges, the shadow of spooked fish. Canada flipped by under our keel. Rock by rock, a continent fell away behind the stern. For hours at a time we talked only when tracking our position, mesmerized by heat and stillness and the rhythms of work, our strokes a mantra that led us inward, the concert of our locomotion so ingrained as to require no thought.

We were a competent team. The boat felt as natural beneath us as our feet on the ends of our legs. We knew just how to hit waves, the most efficient way to lash in our load, just how much of a stroke was needed to correct our direction. The nicks and dings and loom of the canoe had become as familiar as a family member. We camped efficiently as well—the tent going up without need of conversation, firewood collected, meals prepared, chores attended to—self-contained and complementary as factory workers who have toiled side by side for decades.

Afternoon conversations had been turned into a regular ritual, a device to help the miles pass, a mental sedative for our aching shoulders. On alternating days we each were responsible for a discussion topic. Who were the five most influential people in your life? What would you occupy yourself with if you never had to worry about making money? Describe in detail your ideal home. If we were to get married, what sort of ceremony would you want? What the hell kind of question is that?

Lake Athabasca had thoroughly bewitched us: islands weighted down with blueberries, beaches that stretched for miles, the stirring call of loons at twilight, campsites that couldn't be bettered until the next one came along, the sparse spruce-lichen woods and bedrock ridges smoothed and combed by the heavy landscaping influence of ice sheets. In the warm afternoons after a strong day of paddling, we stripped off our clothes and lay on the smooth warm bedrock, polished as statuary, our bodies cooled by breezes. Bugs, never as severe as we had feared, were almost nonexistent by mid-August. We reveled in our health, in our self-contained competence.

Loons were gathering into flocks in preparation for their southerly flight. Small groups swam with restless energy off shore, beating their wings on the water and calling out as if hoping for an echo. We had a cheap tape recorder along and recorded a trio of active loons from a campsite. When we played the tape back, the birds went into a display of comic consternation, looking at each other as if suspicious of trickery, checking underwater, sending out answering yodels, baffled by our unwitting practical joke.

Lodge Bay, Easter Head, Strike Point, Fish Hook Bay, Narrow Bay, out of Alberta and into Saskatchewan. Gradually we put the lake behind us. August nights were really dark, no longer the tentative dusk while the sun cat-napped just out of view. We saw the first northern lights of the summer, green frost in the fling of sharp stars, and woke each other up to share the spectacle from the tent. Some mornings had the feel of fall, nippy enough that I procrastinated leaving my warm bag, the chore of starting a fire a cold business and the wait for the first cup of coffee a minor torture.

In time, like earlier challenges, the lake became a known quantity, and our thoughts leapt ahead to the next hurdle. Afternoon discussions turned more and more directed, focused on the shadowy winter season that we had made no arrangement for. Describe your image of the town of Stony Rapids. What do you think Cliff Blackmur's fishing camp will be like? Will he remember us from our letter? Our talks degenerated into strategizing sessions, philosophical debates. I presented the few options as I pinpointed an island landmark on the map. "First, we should stop in at the fishing camp and see what it looks like. Then, we can go into Stony Rapids and start looking for places to hole up for the winter."

Marypat added her fantasies. "Maybe we could find an old trapper's cabin and fix it up. We'll have probably a month before the weather turns wintry. It would be great if we could trade work for a place to stay. What do you think the benefits of staying in town are versus living in the bush?"

The truth was, all we had were the name of a fishing camp we'd written to, asking about caretaking for the winter; the name of a couple Alan Woods had told us to look up in Stony Rapids; and our faith in the tendency for things to work out. But, taken together, that wasn't much security to go on.

Big lakes had always bored me before. I disliked being able to see so far ahead, the day's goal visible from the lunch spot. But Lake Athabasca's beauty and freshness and dynamic shoreline and ability to terrify seduced me completely. I lost hold of my impatience to get across it.

We were getting across it, though. The southern shore hove back into view like an old reassuring friend, the lake narrowing toward the funnel that at some indistinct point becomes the Fond-du-Lac River. We made notes to ourselves, fine-tuning logistics for the next summer, preserving tidbits of fresh knowledge: fewer crackers at lunch, add powdered milk to the cocoa, subtract one pair of socks, one less T-shirt, more nuts for baking. In a way, the first summer provided a test run for the more rigorous second leg of travel. Every ounce of weight and bulge of bulk would be critical. The first thousand miles had been forgiving in ways that the second would be harsh.

Within twenty-five miles of Fond-du-Lac, Saskatchewan, human litter sprinkled the landscape in distasteful splotches. Native camps were trash dumps: Pepsi cans, black garbage bags, bones and feathers, saplings crudely axed down for spruce-bough bedding. I suppose that in the old days it mattered little that camp refuse got left behind. Eventually everything decayed, but the habit has remained unchanged despite the indestructibility of modern products. Graffiti was spray-painted on the Precambrian rock in neon greens and pinks, the universal self-aggrandizement of teenage infatuations: Billy loves Tina.

The dominant white church was our first glimpse of Fond-du-Lac, eight miles away, the building stolidly facing toward the big lake, the rest of the settlement scattered like a wrinkled robe around it. We stroked up to and past the Chipewyan reserve town in the self-locomoted style that had been abandoned by the natives for decades. Not a canoe in sight. Fiberglass powerboats with shiny big horsepower motors, the police launch, a bright float plane oddly anchored among the watercraft like a moose in a dairy herd.

More garish graffiti: Hollywood, Billy Adams. Shabby houses with weathered clapboard partially painted, doors agape, spilling children onto the pebbly shoreline. A woman leaned indolently on a doorjamb, her house like a cave behind her. Wooden boat skeletons rotted on the beach, transected by a high-water mark full of styrofoam chunks, plastic bottles, pop cans. Whiffs of oily smoke from a burn barrel lent a grimy aftertaste. A few people watched us pass, openly curious but not inclined to wave at two Anglo faces shining from a canoe.

Conscious of the threat of sudden winds and enamored of the winding alleys between islands, we chose a route through a covey of stunning bedrock knobs along the north shore. We took the two-mile open water stretch across Grease Bay in a beeline, the twinge of adrenaline that pumped up my paddling speed on open water as strong as ever, and camped on another well-used island.

The fishing camp we were headed for lay five or six miles distant, located, as best we knew, somewhere in Otherside Bay. Large islands would facilitate our crossing to the southern shore that we'd lost contact with since our vigil on the weathered log across from Fort Chipewyan, more than two hundred paddling miles to the west. In the calm translucent twilight, a string of boats aimed toward Fond-du-Lac sent an insect-like buzz through the still air. "I wonder if those boats are from the camp?"

We could have paddled on into the fishing operation, the mileage only a matter of an hour or two, but we resisted reaching the end of our simple life. Sixty-three days out from Jasper, Alberta, and the wrenching dislocation from society, we found ourselves reticent. Arriving at camp would signal the beginning of the next intimidating phase of our journey. Thinking back, days and experiences ran together like the filaments of converging rivers. Day Fifty-Six or Thirty-Nine? Fourth week or seventh? How many full moons had we seen? Day of the week? Long gone. I remembered experiences with a clarity that shocked me when I realized they had taken place a month before. My memory swam with bear faces, ledge drops, the taste of blueberries, the exquisite curve of sand in a bay, the smell of burning driftwood, the ripple of river felt in my knees, none of it etched on a linear calendar, as if the interlocking gears of structured existence had slowly come unmeshed.

Unexpectedly, the final crossing turned out to be the most dangerous of the entire lake. Even with the most judicious use of islands, we couldn't escape several open stretches. Across the first one we beat head on into a growing east wind and then ran with the waves to tack to land, hissing down the front slopes of the dark liquid mountains. Once in the lee of an island, the lake was so completely motionless that the memory of turbulence half a mile away seemed hardly credible. The winds increased so that the second crossing became a pitched battle, water repeatedly breaking over the bow, the canoe a wild thing beneath us. We had no choice but to run with the waves, going away from our destination in order to cross without capsizing.

Once near land, the shallow water allowed us to inch forward, but minuscule progress came at such an expenditure of energy and frayed nerves that we gave up the attempt and shot into a sandy cove, the wind hurling us forward onto shore. So close to our destination and yet unable to eke out the last two miles.

The beach-fronted cove provided one of the prettier windbound prisons in the string that stretched back across the lake, but I wanted none of it. While Marypat curled up on the warm sand, I pulled out the grill to make coffee. An aluminum boat appeared off the point, wallowing heavily on the rough lake, trolling slowly back and forth in front of us, as if taunting our inability to move. Surely a boat from the nearby camp. Now that I had reconciled myself to the end of our lonely travel, I was eager for the next stage, curious about the camp, jazzed up for the change.

After Marypat woke from her nap, we played gin rummy using a stuffsack for our card table, taking up time, watching the lake. "It looks like the waves are smaller, MP." I stood up to get a better view of the white-capped vista. "Still not calm enough to leave, but better."

Another two rounds of cards. "It has definitely gone down. Should we try?"

"It still looks pretty rough to me. Let's give it a little longer."

The lake smoothed out. Back to the boat, out around the point. "We don't even know where the camp is for sure," Marypat called back from the bow. "It could be way down the far side."

I looked over at the retreating shoreline across the bay, miles off. "I don't think so. I'll bet it's at the foot of the bay."

Around the point, gusts smacked us in the face. What had appeared to be a calming trend had, instead, been a shift. Broad, three-foot swells generated by the east wind still heaved the canoe up and down from the side. New waves, an angry lathering, came at us head on, kicked up by the fresh south blasts. The boat rocked and wallowed and bucked along every axis. No camp in sight.

"We shouldn't be out here, Al!" I looked to shore, an uninviting thicket of willow and alder, the landing an angular bed of boulders. "The water's shallow here. Even if we went over, we could stand up. It has to get better as we go farther into the bay." If Marypat had been in the stern, she would have turned us in to shore over my objections. But I kept on course, determined to arrive now that we were on the final approach.

The wind screamed at us, our paddling speed an exhausting crawl, the shore going by in increments of inches. "Hey, is that a windsock?" Something white fluttered like a flag on the end of a willowy point ahead. A hundred yards further along, we could see the ridge line of a building. "There it is, MP. Finally!"

Right up to the last stroke the wind fought our arrival. The camp sat at the very bottom of a bay, screened behind a low rocky peninsula, the Otherside River tumbling into the lake along one side. A red-stained lodge and log cabins hunkered on the top of a low rise, the camp girded by a long dock with a string of aluminum boats tied like horses outside a crowded saloon. As we paddled up, an energetic figure emerged from the lodge and strode down to meet us—worn bluejeans and checkered shirt, sharp blue eyes, an encouraging smile.

"You must be Cliff Blackmur," I said.

"I wondered if you'd make it. We've been watching you." Cliff pointed to a wooden boat ramp. "Pull over there and we'll get the canoe out of the water." I felt like a military scout just returned to headquarters after a harrowing mission to the front lines, juxtaposition of desperate struggle and calm serenity within minutes of each other.

Nosing the canoe around the dock, I was proud of our ease with the craft. Cliff grabbed the bow line and hauled us up the smooth ramp. I stepped out with cramped legs and stood beside the red canoe heeled over on the peeled log surface, suddenly out of its element. I had no way of knowing it then, but we wouldn't paddle our loaded vehicle again for ten months.

PART IV

INTERLUDE

INTERLUDE

Our decision to spend the winter in Athabasca Camps came with disorienting swiftness. Three days after nudging the travel-scarred canoe bow onto the boat ramp, we impulsively committed ourselves to caretake the camp over the lonely season. Doing so, the taut bubble of concern about winter arrangements suddenly collapsed, leaving us at loose ends—elated at the fortune of things falling into place so soon, but left clutching the still-warm memories of summer with no new challenge to occupy us.

Cliff broached the subject within an hour of our arrival. "We'd sure like to have you stay here over the winter." Just like that, in our laps. "You should go into Stony Rapids and look around before you decide, mind you," he added. "I'll take you in when I fly over to do errands and you can see what you think."

I could only laugh. My forehead still stung from the blasting wind we'd paddled against; my shoulders felt slightly separated, ligaments stretched from the strain. Through the bank of windows at the front of the lodge, the blue lake we'd inched across tossed and heaved under the lash of wind. Marypat and I ate ham sandwiches on white bread.

Two days in camp. Patterns of summer had imprinted themselves on our senses. Access to laundered clothes, hot showers, stupendous meals, and fishing tourists couldn't disrupt the rhythm stamped on our psyches by sixty-three days of repetition. We lived by new rules but felt like im-

posters. We slept in our tent pitched behind the lodge like an incongruous space module. I woke at dawn ready to hunt for wood and study the
map, but the red canoe stayed in dry dock and the days passed in dis-
jointed progression.

The flight to town made me realize how parochial our perspective
had been all summer. It took twenty minutes to cover forty miles, a distance we would have crossed in two or three days under bicep power, bar-
ring wind delays. Underneath the plane spread the northern bush:
spruce bogs, stands of poplar, lakes as dense as stars in a dark sky, frothy
streams descending to the huge lake. Bays and inlets and islands, depths
and shallows that painted the lake different hues, beaches and cliffs and
rock-strewn shore, shoulders of granite trending south and west under
the ancient grooming influence of ice. Contours of landscape unfolded
that we had only imagined from map study and hints seen from the
canoe.

Cliff flew the Cessna 185 with an abstracted, dashboard-fiddling
manner that reminded me of making a daily car commute. Marypat
clicked pictures out of the back window until it made her airsick. Pine
Channel, the Fond-du-Lac River, and then Stony Rapids, buildings and
fuel silos clustered at the base of fast water where the river widens out in
swirling eddies. I thought of an osprey plummeting toward the water
after a fish, talons outstretched, as Cliff set the plane down into the
strong solid flow.

I suspect that Cliff knew only too well that a trip to town would tip
the scales in his favor. For someone who cherished a sentimental vision
of wintering in a remote northern village and capturing some sense of
nineteenth-century settlement life, Stony Rapids was a severe letdown.
Chipewyan teenagers toted boom boxes down the dirt streets. Vehicles
raised dust tornadoes on the roads. Snowmobiles rested in every yard.
The hint of burning trash wafted in the breeze. Flea-bitten canines ran
in scrofulous packs. A huge generator plant dieseled away behind town,
providing power for videos, televisions, toaster ovens, microwaves,
Christmas-tree lights.

The vacant home or abandoned trapper's cabin we had fantasized
about inheriting for the winter turned out to be just that: fantasy.
Housing was tight and cost far more than our budget allowed. Prices in

The Bay store were astounding: eggs at three dollars a dozen, cheese for six dollars a pound, onions at a dollar each, a gallon of white gas cost ten dollars. Cliff picked up a small bag of miscellaneous groceries for camp and spent eighty bucks.

While he hammered out logistical details at the local aviation company in preparation for the next group of fishing guests, we climbed the hill to the only cafe in town for a cup of coffee. The White Water Inn originally had been run by natives, but had never turned into a successful enterprise. Following a period of mismanagement, the hotel/cafe was bought and restored by a non-native couple, the people Alan Woods had told us to look up.

Ed White recognized us as soon as we opened the door. "You must be the canoeists," he held out his hand in greeting. "Nobody ever looks so calm and healthy around here!" His wife and partner, Margy Michel, poked her head out a serving window from the kitchen and called a greeting. "Alan told us to expect you. Welcome to Stony!"

The cup of coffee expanded to cheeseburgers, French fries, and homemade pie under Ed and Margy's encouragement. Ed bantered with customers. A young, compactly vigorous, quick-humored man, he exuded an appetite for projects even in the way he cleared tables. Margy, trapped in back under the tyranny of fast-food orders, took part in the conversation by hurling exclamatory remarks through the window.

They reinforced our impression of Stony Rapids as a poor place to winter on a tight budget. "There's really nothing available in town. As long as you have a snowmobile, I'd stay at the camp," Ed said as he wiped up a freshly vacated table and tossed the towel in a bin eight feet away.

"We'll come to visit you!" Margy added with a quick smile.

At one of the several coffee breaks the next morning—clients already out on the lake with guides, and the camp momentarily somnolent in their absence—we confirmed our decision with Cliff. Confirmed it, but quickly added our list of concerns—housing, transportation, communication, access to supplies. Cliff responded with ready solutions.

He proposed constructing a winterized log cabin that would be our home, promised to buy a snowmobile, had design theories on the best sort of wood stove to weld together, and ticked off remedies to any number of minor problems we came up with. All of this to be accomplished within the next four or five weeks, at the same time that the camp handled various groups of clients.

"Hell, we can build that cabin in two weeks!" Cliff's exuberant confidence left me more doubtful than reassured.

"Really?" I felt as if I'd signed up for an exotic tour about which I understood few particulars and during which I had no choice but to depend heavily on the expertise and trustworthiness of a cocky guide.

"Just relax for a few days," Cliff said, on his way out the door. "There'll be plenty to do soon enough."

In the afternoons we'd take the empty boat for a lap on the bay. I'd think back and remember the wide stage of sky, the cooled winds, the heft of paddle in my calloused hands. I realized how much I missed talking with Marypat and sharing our simple days.

I understood for the first time what relief must have come to pioneers when they opened the bush and beat back the wilderness; the security to be found in a clearing. Athabasca Camps is an opening in a vast wild ocean. Bears regularly tipped over burn barrels in the nearby dump, and a pale wolf patrolled the shore of the bay in the evenings.

Within a week we inherited our own temporary cabin, ridiculous luxury—hot shower, wood stove to take the chill off, bunk beds with flannel sheets, a small desk for writing. A shy curious weasel visited us through a crack in the wall, quicksilver shadow of wariness tempered by an almost suicidally inquiring nature. A squirrel wreaked havoc on our leftover food supplies until we secured them in glass jars and plastic tubs.

Camp life was hectic, and absorbed all our energies. Washing dishes every evening, running unending loads of laundry through a heroic overworked washer, preparing meals for as many as fifty people, packing shore lunch boxes for fishing parties, cutting and delivering firewood, cleaning cabins, filleting fish, loading or unloading planes and boats. Add to that a perpetual state of crisis management—running out of propane, rescuing a boat that sheared a prop on a rock, chasing bears out of camp, running out of food.

Always in the background there were major construction projects— docks, boat ramps, outhouses, wall tent platforms, bunk beds, tool sheds, a pump house, a barbecue pit. We became part of the camp staff, along with Bob, a shareholder in the business and our evening cribbage instructor; Stella, Cliff's partner and essential cog in camp operation; the native guides who ran the boats on the lake and slowly became our friends; and the camp dog, Bandit, who raised the alarm over new arrivals and staked out treed squirrels with limitless patience.

Two weeks went by without our making a start on the cabin. Suddenly it was dark before 10 p.m., northern lights wreathed the black cold sky, hard frosts firmed the ground and turned the dawn air brittle and sharp, the poplar turned a pale tint of yellow.

On September 2, along with several guides, I cleared the brush off the proposed cabin site, set in against the woods and protected from the northern winds. Cold sleet drove at us out of low clouds. After selecting the five long logs that would lie parallel to form the cabin base, and setting them roughly in place, we were forced to stop.

Work stuttered along. Bad weather, lack of materials, daily crises— the construction rarely went uninterrupted. Absurd problems consumed entire days. Because we ran out of two by twos, we had to rip long lengths from two by sixes with an inadequate power saw. Doing so, I succeeded in burning out the saw bearings and brought work to an abrupt halt. In order to get under way again, we had to fly to Stony Rapids, drive the camp bus to Black Lake, spend a hundred bucks on an even less adequate saw, and return to camp. Another day lost. A chainsaw clutch burned out one afternoon. Cliff developed an inflamed tooth that debilitated him with pain. Then, on days when everything seemed ready to proceed full bore, horrendous weather set in to make outside work impossible.

In Cliff's scheme, the one insulated cabin would be used by winter caretakers and then double as an additional tourist space during the busy season. We would be the trial tenants. Between bouts of building, design theories flew thick as equations at a scientific conference.

"It should just be left as one big room," Cliff said. "That way the heat circulates efficiently and all your space is usable." Eli, the most charming of the older native guides, described a stove made out of a sawed-off fifty-five-gallon drum. "Oh yes, very nice stove. Stay warm." Should the bed be high off the floor or low down? Which wall would the cook stove go against? How high should the side windows be? Did we need a porch?

Bit by bit the cabin rose from the ground—floor insulated, door frame braced, logs peeled and hewed to lay relatively flat then pegged together with ten-inch spikes. Materials at hand and problem-solving limitations relegated us to Neanderthal solutions. Floor not quite level? Jack up a corner and find a flat rock to put under the base log. On September 17, three walls of the cabin were up, but we had to stop work in a snowstorm.

To her chagrin, Marypat had little to do with the building. Camp life demanded a crew to keep food coming, cabins clean, laundry done. All summer we had shared cooking, switched paddling positions, carried his or her fair weight across portages, yet she was left out of much of the cabin raising. Instead, she and Stella ran the camp. Whenever she found time to pitch in on the cabin, she received unnecessary "help" from a work crew who didn't fully appreciate her physical capability. In frustration, she gave up trying except on minor, out-of-the-way tasks.

Eli's wife, Angela, came from town to live in the camp after the last clients left. Marypat spent much of her time at the guides' wall tents with the older Chipewyan woman. At night she'd teach me new Chipewyan words learned over cups of black tea in the afternoon—bear, *sus*; black fly, *hooney-tonney*; northern pike, *uldai*; that's good, *lazoon*. In the lull between work and supper, we both received language tutorials, invariably providing comic relief with our infallible ability to mangle Chipewyan pronunciation.

Twice, Marypat went out with a boatload of natives to pick cranberries. On the first trip they shot a duck along the way and stopped for an impromptu picnic. The plucked bird went into a pot of boiling water with a dash of salt, simmered for a few minutes, then was served—head, feet, entrails, and all. Marypat, a rather fastidious eater, maintained falsely but adamantly that she had just finished lunch, much to the disappointment of her hosts.

We cultivated the natives' acceptance. Once left alone at the camp, the friends we made, both Chipewyan and white, would very literally be our safety network and only social outlet. We quizzed them on details for winter. When would bears start hibernating? When would the lake freeze? Where did they run their trap lines? What did they do at Christmas? Would they come visit us?

September 21. We nailed the final sheets of plywood to the cabin roof and were spiking a rough porch railing in place, when a sudden commotion near the lodge drew our attention. A moose had been sighted crossing the lake narrows in front of camp. Eli and another guide were already shoving off in a boat, pulling the starter rope, loading a rifle. The big bull stood at the halfway point in the crossing, knee-deep on a shoal of rocks. He was black against the bright blue lake, big rack like grotesque petrified ears.

The moose was too late in recognizing his peril. Like a spectator, he watched the boat approach. By the time he realized the violence the two men intended, he had time for only a short floundering surge. The single faraway crack sounded like the noise from a toy gun, but the animal seemed to deflate and then sink in the water. In another minute, the boat appeared off the near point, laboring, towing the moose by a rope looped around an antler.

Butchering began immediately. The huge animal lay on the black rocks, soft underbelly wide and round as a barrel. The impossibly long tongue hung stupidly out one side of its mouth. A Chipewyan child asked in a high worried voice about papa moose. All the Indians laughed and chorused, "Poor papa moose!" An air of grim festivity charged us all, a primitive killing adrenaline made everyone a little tipsy, a little fierce.

Knives and hands, sticky red with blood, tore at the animal, stripped away hide, separated muscle quivering with the memory of life. The hind quarters were so heavy that it took two people to lift them, the bone head at the hip clean and round and cream-colored, never before insulted by sunlight. Soon the moose that had been going about the business of crossing a lake was reduced to a slippery, chaotic mound of red meat.

Hide, lower legs, stomach, and head went to the Chipewyan; tongue, heart, and liver to the whites. Meat was split evenly between the two. Only the pink, spongy lungs and intestines were left on the rocks. Air bubbles frothed listlessly out of the lungs, bright crimson pools of blood turned dull and lichen-colored. Stained knives and bloody hands were rinsed in the numbing lake water. As the sun disappeared, it grew cold quickly. We filed across the rocks back into camp, quietly giving up the scene of death, our winter meat cache suddenly overflowing.

Like the quickening water at the head of a rapid, we moved at an accelerated pace toward our time of isolation. Marypat and I made two trips to Fond-du-Lac by motorboat to arrange winter supplies and get mail, hoping also to establish contacts who wouldn't forget we were out in the bush when winter descended.

Our home made lurching final steps toward completion. September 26, roof gable ends insulated and covered; September 27, interior walls paneled; September 29, center partition built and bed installed. One of the guides' sons sold us a used wood stove for the cabin. Cliff hadn't yet mentioned a departure date, but I sensed that his thoughts were disengaging from the camp, slipping to the south like the flocks of geese and ducks streaming away from the northern land.

Rather than purchase a snowmobile, Cliff arranged with one of the younger guides, Don McDonald, to be our contact, responsible if an emergency came up or if we needed a ride to town when cabin fever set in. During a final brief visit to Stony Rapids, Ed White expressed concern over the situation. "Boy, I don't know. I wouldn't like to be that far out with no transportation." Margy soothed my worries with promises of visits, but Ed shook his head. "You just don't know. Too many things can happen."

We borrowed old snowshoes from a Fond-du-Lac man. The circumference of land open to us steadily puckered in, becoming a kind of noose, hardly larger than the camp clearing. Until freeze-up, we could drive a boat to town, but that option would be lost soon.

October. At night the sky looked sharp and deep as black ice, and we hurried down to our cabin to start a fire. Bears visited the natives' wall tents two nights running to try to abscond with the moose hide. Eli shot after them in the darkness but missed. Once, on the way back to our cabin, we were stopped mid-step by the indescribable sound of bears caterwauling on the far side of the river, mournful lusting emanations from the shadowed woods.

The guides were hunting for "chicken," or spruce grouse, in the evenings and would eat birds at their tents rather than come to the lodge for dinner. Angela cut strips of moose meat to hang from a loose log framework above a smokey fire, the meat shriveling and turning brown. Ravens and gulls and eagles squawked contentiously over the few scraps left at the butchering site.

At breakfast on October 3, Cliff made the surprise announcement that they planned to leave that afternoon. "Looks like a system moving in. We should get out ahead of it."

"Today?" I stammered, incredulous. "For good?!"

All the odds and ends we'd been stringing along were crammed into one morning. Installing the cook stove, moving the radio telephone aerial, hooking up the wood stove, fitting the windows. We scurried around like chipmunks hoarding winter food. What about all the things that weren't done? An ice chisel for getting water, a start on winter wood, the chainsaw that hadn't been fixed . . . ? The last guides rolled up tents and left for town, promising to see us soon. A misting rain drove us to an even faster pace.

The floats on the overloaded Cessna barely held the plane out of water. Goodbyes were hurried, distracted, preoccupied. We shook hands and embraced in a kind of numb haze, the suddenness of transition making emotional reconciliation impossible.

For the final time I held the wing strut as Cliff squeezed into the packed cockpit and checked the instruments. "See you next spring," he said cheerfully, turning the key. Stella and Bob waved and made leave-taking noises, and the plane plowed off away from the dock.

They roared into the rain for an eternity, the sound of straining full-out engine diminishing until I felt certain they'd have to return and unload more weight, but finally we heard the freed pitch as the plane lifted from the water. Marypat and I stood on the wet dock with our winter pet, Bandit, listening to the faint engine in the gray sky. Slowly the plane curved back toward us, dropping out of the low clouds, waggling wings. Overhead our friends' faces strained for a last look at camp.

My throat clenched with the same awful loneliness that I'd felt when we'd swept away downstream from Jasper. The camp was a ghost town. Memories of human vitality endured, but lacked the reassurance of movement, the security of voices. Our own noises echoed off buildings cloaked in a wintry mist of funereal gloom.

The summer solitude had lasted nine weeks. At best, winter isolation stretched ahead for thirty, probably more. Thirty harsh winter weeks. Alone.

PART V

FALL

Illness and disease in the wilderness rarely concerned me. Outdoor life kept us healthy and vigorous, strong and lean, immune from common sickness. Infrequent contact with germ-laden humanity lulled me into believing that we traveled along an aseptic trail, hermetically sealed from danger. The prospect of accident occupied center stage instead. A capsized boat, a chainsaw mishap, breaking through ice, a tree falling wrong—the possibilities were so numerous that to dwell on them could paralyze you altogether. Prevention was a necessary corollary to our existence, not a buzzword. But it was insidious infection, a repellent illness, that threatened our winter endeavor almost before it began.

For a week or more before the camp closed, I had played host to a mysterious local skin infection on my belly. At first I assumed it was an inflamed black fly bite, but it didn't act normally. A small area grew red and swollen, without itching, then finally ruptured into an open sore, oozing out a plug of pus that left behind an impressive cavity. Treating the site with liquid antibiotic and a bandage, I figured the wound would heal and that would be the end of it.

Not so. On the drizzly day the plane left, I discovered a similar swelling on my face. According to the chapter on infections in our medical text, my problem was abscesses, localized staphylococci infections that usually disappear on their own after opening up and draining.

The text cautioned that if infections grew, spread, or broke out in new spots, they could quickly become cause for concern. Facial outbreaks were particularly dangerous, since infection could directly threaten the brain. The book recommended immediate evacuation for stubborn or spreading cases.

Terrific. Not even twenty-four hours alone, the lake heading toward freeze-up, few real contacts to depend on, and we faced a threat from an entirely unexpected quarter. The only reassuring element was that we did have one of the appropriate antibiotics along in our first aid kit. But I resisted jumping into a program of medication.

Over a period of several days, I applied warm compresses to the affected area, drawing pus to the surface, where I hoped it would then drain. The infection continued to grow, swelling my face. The dire warnings in the first aid book soon convinced me to start medication.

There was plenty to keep us busy during the day. Each morning we searched the woods for a stand of dead trees, preferably jack pine, and set to work bringing them down, trimming branches, cutting long lengths, and hauling them out of the forest to a stack by our cabin. The noise of the camp's decrepit chainsaw, the oily cloud of exhaust, struck me as intrusive and obnoxious, and after one bout with it we decided to cut our wood by hand, using axes to fell trees and a bucksaw to split logs into stove lengths.

I worked with a gauze pad on my face, ugly poison seeping out of my swollen cheek. In the evening I drew more pus out with warm compresses, the stream of infection seemingly endless. In the late-night darkness, waking to pop another pill, I'd lie in the silence wondering if I had diagnosed the problem accurately, if the medicine was correct, if we were being foolish not to seek outside attention.

Meanwhile, Marypat and I floundered awkwardly trying to regain a balance with each other, to accustom ourselves to the sixteen-by-twenty-foot den, to stop expecting company, to accept the shimmering desert of space and quiet hours before us. Bandit actively played out her own symptoms of transition distress. Every morning she'd whine to be let out, and then race up to the lodge, as if expecting to find breakfast in full swing. At night we had to call her away from Cliff and Stella's cabin, where she waited like a forlorn child for the old routine to resume.

Winter posed a new and unnerving batch of worries. We blundered along, jumpy with the knowledge that any number of entirely conceivable mishaps might prove disastrous. How much firewood would be required? If we didn't cut enough initially, would we be able to harvest more in the deep snow and cold of mid-winter? How much propane would we use? Would five or six bottles last eight months? Would the radio telephone, our only link to the outside, go on the blink as it had several times in the last month?

With over a hundred long lengths of wood piled up, we began sawing and stacking the winter supply. Using a crude homemade sawhorse, we switched right and left arms with each cut, and trundled the wheelbarrow loads of wood to a protected side of the cabin, beginning a pitifully tiny stack under the eaves.

Slowly, the cabin molded into our home—insulation stuffed into air leaks, shelves for food, a calendar nailed to the wall, books on a shelf, hooks to hang the lantern from, favorite reading spots, a system for washing dishes.

We made rounds through the camp, reluctantly stored our canoe for the winter, checked our clothes for mending jobs, shifted the center of life to the new cabin, the lone focus of movement and warmth—the only chimney puffing smoke, the only windows glowing with lantern light. The neighboring structures were skeletal and dormant, unnecessary appendages.

My face slowly healed, the wound finally drying up and scabbing over. I stopped taking medication after the suggested period, only to discover another swelling on my leg. Shaken, I started popping pills again, deciding to take them until they ran out.

"What if the infection comes back even after that?" Marypat voiced the question that loomed unavoidably in my own mind.

"I guess," I answered, "we'd have to go get help."

We talked no more on the subject, but I checked my body for signs of change, good or bad, like a ship captain suspicious of mutinous leanings in the crew.

At dawn I found myself most vulnerable. Doubts and fears skated on the thin ice of my self-assurance. Out the front window lay gray light and a soft stillness, the spruce across the bay like a ragged paper cutout against a silver sky. I warmed my skin against Marypat's, belly to back, mammals seeking succor, and fought the creeping urge to avoid the day, to stay in bed. Winter ran ahead in my mind like a misty road, empty and unvarying and endless.

Have to have a routine, I'd think, get outside every day, stay busy. But I comprehended the stories of winter malaise, the undermining cabin-bound lethargy that could eventually leave one listless and stupid with inaction, unable to rise to a challenge, drawn inward, the central fires down to a candle flicker.

Already the nights were cold. Zero, ten below, frost like confectionery sugar on the willows below the windsock. The shallow bay froze with transparent ice that would take most of the day to melt again. Snow sifted out of the sky and only reluctantly dissolved on the ground. We learned the quirks of the stove, the best draft settings, how to encourage but not overdo the fire. Tramping the forest for fuel, the earth felt hard as a sidewalk and the deep beds of moss broke and fractured underfoot, our steps wreaking devastation.

In mid-October, the bay didn't melt one afternoon and the skim ice thickened again that night. Was this it? We counted on one final trip to Fond-du-Lac—a small list of purchases, mail collection, firming arrangements with Don. When the ice lingered in spite of a warm afternoon, we decided to make the run.

Even at that, we had to smash a path out of the bay, rocking the camp boat in its frozen berth, ramming up on the elastic ice, and then jumping against the aluminum boat bottom to break through, leaving a trail of small fractured floes behind. Once out in the river current, a path of moving water provided a kind of marked channel to the big lake, where deep wide water held off the oncoming season.

Throttle full out, the boat spanked on a straight course to the native settlement, more than a dozen miles of exposed water from point to point. Wind, engine, and wave overwhelmed all but the most energetic bellowing communication. An hour later, skirting a herd of barely submerged whaleback rocks, I cut the motor and drifted up to the town dock.

A float plane rubbed against the pilings, and a harried pilot supervised the loading of an incredible mass of supplies. A Chipewyan man on the way to his trap line kept bringing more: canned goods, wall tent, toboggan, malevolent-looking traps, rifles, fuel, lanterns, axes, and, stretching down the dock, a double line of mange-ridden, crusty-eyed sled dogs. We picked our way through the debris, nodding to the distracted pilot, and walked the gauntlet of canines, calves tingling in expectation of snapping jaws.

Don McDonald lived on a high shoulder of bedrock overlooking the lake narrows. On an earlier visit, he had told me that the two-bedroom house cost two-hundred-fifty dollars, an average price on the subsidized reserve. The house looked quiet and lifeless even from a distance. Close up, we confronted a padlocked door, boarded windows, an abandoned home.

"What the hell? I wonder if he moved."

His parents lived next door. His father, Muglar, sat at the kitchen table drinking tea, and warmly invited us in to join him.

"You just missed Donald," Muglar said, filling our mugs with the strong black drink. "He went north to trap with his family about an hour ago."

"He did?!" our level of anxiety rising. "For how long?"

"Oh, just for the fall. He'll be back around Christmas, I guess." Muglar's cheerful prediction was a stunning contrast to our consternation.

The remainder of our town visit did nothing to improve our outlook. The Bay store, stuffed with geegaws we had no use for, had almost none of the basics we needed. Timex watches, gaudy yarn, ball caps, snowmobile parts, sweat shirts, and frozen food packed the shelves, but spare lantern parts, sawblades, ice chisels, fresh onions, and candles were absent.

At the post office, a piece of shirt cardboard nailed into the peeling paint next to the door assured us that we had arrived during business hours, but the way in was undeniably locked. Across the alley, we were told, lived the woman who ran the operation. Next to her door, on another rectangle of thin cardboard, a sign read, IF THE POST OFFICE IS CLOSED, DON'T COME HERE!!! Marypat and I looked at each other. I knocked.

With a minimum of explanation, we convinced the postal matron to retrieve our mail. A chubby child attired in Pampers yanked on my back pocket while we watched the woman rummage through an alarmingly disheveled pile of envelopes and packages, eventually emerging with a thin sheaf of letters.

"That's it?" I questioned, not at all confident that a complete search had been conducted through the warren of drawers, shelves, bags, and stacks in the dimly lit back room.

"All of it," she replied, a finality in her tone that brooked no opening for appeal.

Eli was out cutting wood. The schoolteachers we hoped to meet were busy with classes. The Catholic priest, a Frenchman who'd lived in the north for fifty years, couldn't be found. We fled from Fond-du-Lac on a losing streak, no less foreign as a result of the visit, the few needs we'd come to fill still wanting. A cold wind numbed my jaw and stiffened my gripping hand on the return ride. We kept silent, bundled in thought, and stayed near shore, the boat pounding through swells.

On October 17 we admitted to being frozen in. For days the weather alternated between freezing rain and wet snow. At night the temperature dropped near zero, sometimes below, and the entire bay grew a skin of ice. Only the river channel was free of the wintry grip. A prolonged thaw might still reopen a way to the big lake, but we had to get the camp boat out of the water before it froze in inextricably. The job consumed most of an afternoon.

While not thick enough to safely stand on, the ice fought our progress all the way around the dock. At first it looked as if we might be able to slide the boat on top, but the frozen surface bent and broke through. For hours we pounded a pathway with our feet, a pickax, or the boat hull, a foot at a time, until we passed the end of the dock and reached the ramp, finally keel-hauling the heavy craft out of reach of the lake. I hung up the engine and drained the oil, cutting off the last form of transportation that could realistically get us to town.

2

Crisp fall weather overwhelmed our bleak thoughts with exuberant beauty. Frosty nights, flames on the clouds at sunrise, days warm enough to work in shirtsleeves. The new season came as an awakening, an invigoration—as well as a warning of the dark and cold to come. It seemed ironic that the turning season signaled an oncoming torpor, a kind of death, because an undeniable joy suffused those days. We should all die as leaves do, brilliantly.

The clean air made me notice new things in places I'd walked past for weeks: symmetrical drill holes made by sapsuckers in a fat birch; the rusty carpeting of blueberry bushes on a rounded knoll; trees propped against each other framing a fragment of sky.

Tall grasses along the edge of the river turned tawny, giving off the color of lion mane at sunset. From a high bank upriver we could see the final burst of yellow and gold in the birch and poplar stands, a profligacy of color. The larch turned rusty and then golden, the short needles like a coat of fur on the branches.

Cold nights gathered together late flocks of agitated birds. Loons, mergansers, geese, snow buntings, massing together as if requiring a consensus before moving south. The buntings blew across the ground like flurries of confetti, feeding up and moving on in a nervous frenzy. Only the geese made noise as they passed by, the other birds intent on conserving energy, focused on their single-minded purpose.

I imagined the bears excavating dens in sandy bluffs or finding small rocky caves, their fur rolling on top of fat layers they'd built up gorging on fish, berries, insects, seeds. We still came across their tracks after snowfalls and found claw incisions in the poplar bark. Squirrels built up tremendous piles of shredded pine cone and forest litter, then tunneled into them, creating shelter and food source at the same time. We found little domed muskrat houses in river backwaters. On the freezing bay, rodents sitting on thin ice shelves studiously gnawed on willow branches with an air of worried concern, as if wondering whether this year they began preparing too late.

Our own activity differed little from the animals'—sniffing out leaks in the cabin chinking, hoarding and organizing food, mending clothes, measuring the swelling stack of wood against the hunger of the stove. Cutting wood by hand seemed unobtrusive, commensurate with the quiet around us, our arms staying firm with the work. We grew intimate with the qualities of trees, knowing the smell of pine or spruce, the tendency of poplar to get waterlogged; soon we could assess the burning time of a log by how difficult it was to cut.

Almost daily I tipped and hefted the propane bottle to see how quickly we were using it up, fueling my anxiety over a thing we could do nothing about. "You just checked that yesterday," Marypat would chastise me.

"I know, but it feels pretty light already!"

At night we heated a pan of water on the stove and swiped at the daily dirt and sweat with a washcloth. I ran out of antibiotics and surveyed my body for signs of betrayal. I thought myself cured, but the discovery of a tiny pimple would send me into a cold sweat, wondering if I was still poisoned.

Afternoon walks began to establish a territorial circumference of ground, the paths like capillaries or tentacles, extensions of our domain. Straight into the woods behind the cabin, a trail led off parallel to the lake shore, eventually cresting a bouldered rise on a point overlooking the open lake.

We could either tramp along the lake's edge or wind through the woods back from shore. On the exposed margin, we took note of the incremental growth of ice, each day firming against land, thickening and losing its transparency, closing off the channel of moving water like a predator moving in on weakening prey. At the point, where the gray jostling waves resisted winter, a margin of candle ice marked the battle zone between seasons. Loose ice tinkled like a crystal chandelier as waves undulated through the pack; the traveling rhythmic humps finally flattened out completely under the stiff, unforgiving sheets.

"God, the lake looks cold," I'd say, shoving my hands into my pockets. "Let's walk back through the woods."

In the forest, back from the water, wind couldn't reach us and our feet shuffled through a bed of leaves and brittle crackling lichen. Traditional native camp clearings looked out on the bay—old fishing spots, marked with fire scars and inevitable bits of ancient trash, making me imagine firelit circles and the sounds of guttural Chipewyan conversation.

Our path led through stands of huge poplar and birch trees, increasingly skeletal and denuded, a black-and-white photograph. Inexplicably, I never got over the feeling of being observed in those spacious overarching groves, and kept glancing about as I moved, catching shadows at the corners of my vision.

Our favorite paths led up the Otherside River, a world of motion and sound and dynamic change. Even out of sight of the water, the flowing rhythms came to our ears like wind. The river expressed our combative wish to hang on to fall, to prolong our freedom, to stave off the silent white suffocation.

We called the main path Wolf Trail after finding the large doglike tracks in a wet snow, leading us off in chase for miles. The tracks were twice the size of Bandit's, wide padded saucers of canine stealth, and couldn't have been two hours old in the just-fallen snow. Bandit clung to us, growling softly in her chest, hackles in a perpetual ridge, and we kept watching for the svelte slip of wolf ahead. Later, more wet snow falling on us, we followed the tracks off the trail and walked up on three abandoned wolf beds under a spruce, three thawed circles in the snow, new flakes still melting inside.

The river's battle against the oppression of ice provided us with a spectator sport. A fresh dam of ice would force the current into backwaters and side channels, flooding low spots. Then on a warm afternoon, the flow might flush out a blockage or regain the use of an old channel. But the ice insidiously spread and thickened, creating fresh rapids and eddies and whirlpools, sending creamy submarine sheets along the rocky bottom, building in layers along the banks, growing in wide pieces from island nuclei.

We watched from lonely grandstands—a sandy bluff on an island, or an opening beneath a stunted jack pine full at the top with an old eagle nest; an esker ridge far up the river over a fast narrows, or the midst of a thicket of gigantic poplar trunks.

In a matter of one day, it seemed, the bright colorful burst of season was gone, the sacrifice to winter made. All the leaves were shaken to the ground, the larch needles blown from their branches, a dead browning layer covered the earth. The paths froze solidly, no spring left underfoot, and snow that fell, stayed. The last hurrying birds flew south, the final windblown flocks of buntings skittered across the yard, and a gray light sifted onto the country, a muffling inexorable settling.

On our walk that day the river looked black as ebony, slow as oil with the cold. The ice had won. Even the fast open spots seemed submissive, sheepish, admitting defeat. One late merganser swam along the ice edge, looking bedraggled and abandoned, paddling in the confined cold space. I urged the bird to fly on, to escape before it was too late.

And we moved toward camp in the gloaming, suddenly in a hurry. The small cabin sent a smoke plume into the gauzy sky, a comforting sight. Our home. Evening movements already fell into a pattern— armload of night wood, a tin of starter sawdust for the morning fire, check the temperature, close the door against the season.

3

There are two schools of thought on the matter of overnight fire maintenance. One holds that keeping temperatures in a reasonably steady comfort zone is worth getting up in the night to stoke the stove. The other school maintains that uninterrupted sleep is worth the rigor of arising in below freezing temperatures to restart a dead fire. We held with the latter philosophy. We preferred sleeping in cold air to overstuffing the stove and suffering sweltering heat waves until after midnight. If we woke up shivering, there were more blankets close at hand. Besides, developing a kind of thermostatic vigilance through the night meant that we usually slept poorly.

But every morning, quick-footing around the frigid cabin, our allegiance to the practice came into serious question. Sliding tentatively out from the languid warmth of bed, our movements immediately sped up, bodies firing on all pistons to produce internal heat, breath visible spurts. As we dressed, small exhaling shouts escaped us, like surfacing after a dive into a mountain lake. "Whoo! Whoo!" Fumbling with socks, underwear, slippers.

What we lacked in real warmth, we made up with vehemence of action. Clanging the stove door open and shut, tossing in heavy logs, firing up a flame under the coffee pot, dancing a soft-shoe shuffle around the floor, rubbing our hands together—until the first blush of warmth filled the cabin and we cozied up against the stove like purring cats, cup of coffee gripped with both hands.

On several nights we brought the thermometer inside, curious to know where the mercury bottomed out, but our scientific inquiry lost its charm when we discovered dawn readings in the 5°F range. Cold enough that we didn't need to know the details.

Every person we'd talked to, every account we'd read, stressed the importance of developing a disciplined daily routine to ward off cabin fever. The practice requires an act of will, and like an exercise program, the regimen is easy to shirk. Why get up in the morning? It's dark and cold. Why do even the most basic chores, for that matter? No one admonishes you to get going. No paycheck rewards your efforts every two weeks. Why bother?

Before winter, when I heard of people who'd slipped under the spell of cabin-bound lethargy, hardly moving, almost descending to a state of physical and mental hibernation, I wondered how anyone could allow themselves to slide so, why they couldn't see what was happening. But it's as easy as going to sleep. Maintaining a minimum vitality is far more difficult. Without a job to go to, a round of daily busyness, a routine becomes the framework onto which you nail your sanity. No matter that the discipline is entirely arbitrary, the activity and structure are critical.

Once the stack of wood reached the eaves along an entire twenty-foot wall of the cabin, we felt insured against the cruelty of cold, a treasure more comforting and tangible than money in the bank. After the first burst of organizing and stockpiling, chores dwindled to the point where an hour or two a day covered the necessities. Life support became simple in the extreme. We had no car to start up, no snowmobile to tinker with, no pipes to freeze, no electricity. Our needs centered on hauling water from the lake, keeping the fire lit, feeding ourselves, and caring for small appliances like lanterns or sawhorses.

Each morning, at least theoretically, was devoted to personal projects. I'd settle at the kitchen table, in front of the south-facing window, and work on the writing outlines I'd sketched over the summer. On the far side of the partition that divided the back half of the cabin down the middle, Marypat roosted at a small desk where she practiced her drawing or created beading jobs. Within ten feet of each other, we might as well have been in separate office buildings, achieving the same quality of mental distancing from each other that we had in the canoe. The only interruptions came when one of us went for another cup of coffee or the cooling cabin prompted us to hand a stick of wood through the stove door. Even Bandit recognized the quiet time and entertained herself outdoors or lay in the corner, occasionally letting loose loud sighs, like an exasperated child waiting for things to get interesting.

The ice forced us to pound a hole for water every day, an errand often postponed until after lunch, our "work" behind us and whatever zenith of warmth the day bequeathed at its height. Using a long pry bar as our blunt ice chisel, we kept free of ice a square hole large enough to accept a five-gallon bucket. On particularly cold nights, the ice froze several inches thick, sometimes necessitating the use of a pickax to widen the well. Even if we didn't use up our water reserves, we reopened the hole each day; if we waited forty-eight hours, chopping through the thick frozen layer required a major effort.

Laundry became the most loathed duty, put off until the last pair of socks or underwear signaled unnegotiable necessity. Hand scrubbing the clothes in soapy water warmed on the stove proved tedious, but was a positive treat compared to the pain of the rinse cycle and the messiness of drying. We would cart a bucket of washed clothing to the water hole and swirl each article in the icy well. Then, hands painfully numb, we wrung out shirts and socks and underwear that would freeze as they emerged from the hole.

Drying was a two-stage process. The first took place on the clothesline outside as pants and shirts stiffened into comical mannequin poses in the cold; during the second, soggy clothes adorned every hook and beam in the cabin, dripping into buckets and onto the floor and slapping our faces soddenly as we moved about during the day.

The cleanliness of our bodies also demanded redress. For the first month, we made do with wholly inadequate sponge baths, taken in the minimal privacy behind the partial wall that divided the cabin. Sloppy, only marginally effective, almost embarrassing in the graphic and blunt attack on crucial areas, sponge baths were indulged in only because there was no alternative.

One night after a singularly unproductive bout with the washcloth, I lay in bed scheming plans for an ad-lib shower system. The major pitfall was that the process would have to take place outside. But I was determined anyway.

We had a five-gallon black plastic container complete with flexible hose, nozzle, and turn-on valve. Inside, no rafter or beam could raise the contraption high enough to do the job, and in any case, no workable containment device could keep the water from making a mess. Outside, however, we could use a tree limb or a roof beam to pulley up the bag, and ignore the runoff. Still, the formidable problem of physical exposure remained.

The first experiment took place at a calm 4°F. We heated three gallons of water on the stove and filled the container. At the back of the cabin, a rope pulley that looped over the roof beam raised the contraption to a convenient height, and then anchored to a full propane bottle. With a square of plywood on the ground as a foot platform, soap and shampoo resting on a chest-high log, the shower was primed for its victim.

Under the warm spray I barely noticed the cold. Except in a wind or in really frosty weather, when my leg hairs froze as I washed my head, the experience was remarkably enjoyable. Once cleaned, I'd languish under the last of the hot flow, procrastinating until the shower suddenly snapped off. Then came a cursory toweling off and a rubber-booted sprint to the front door. Any breeze made that brief naked run an icy torture. But the rigors of personal hygiene were nothing compared to the joy of total cleanliness and invigorating corporeal renewal. Sponge baths immediately became history.

Afternoon walks were perhaps the most important anodyne against emotional demise. The daily excursions acted on our souls the way the weekly shower flushed off the buildup of dirt. It didn't much matter how far we walked, whether the day brought beauty or gray monotonous skies, or whether we made new discoveries. The very act of bundling up, strapping on snowshoes, and scrunching off through the snow made our isolation less weighty, our perspective less likely to turn inward. When we missed a day, an indefinable dissatisfaction settled over me, an unease. A tendency toward irritability crept into my interaction with Marypat, my patience with Bandit grew short.

All summer we'd taken in surroundings with a large-scale view, the perspective of those traveling on through, measuring a vista in miles, taking country in batches. Now, on our walks, we began appreciating the smaller scale, laying temporary claim to a territory limited by our restricted ability to travel.

Gradually my eyes adjusted to take in the close things—erratic weasel tracks, the way new snow piled on pedestals of flat fungi on birch trunks, hollows left in snow by sleeping grouse, evocative river backwaters, the thicket in which we sometimes saw a black-backed three-toed woodpecker. After a walk, the cabin felt more like a secure den at the center of known country than an imprisoning cell of isolation.

Before dinner, before beginning the evening ration of lantern light, we regularly played a round of cribbage or Scrabble, the games another plank in the edifice of routine we built around us. They represented our social interlude, the equivalent of tea time or cocktail hour. Often we played by candlelight; sometimes the cabin was so dark we had to hold our cards inches from our faces.

There is no overestimating the profound importance of light. Candlelight, firelight, lantern light—flickerings against darkness—we became experts in their subtleties. With white gas at ten dollars a can, we rationed ourselves stringently to avoid overconsumption, lighting the lantern only when we couldn't find our way around and turning it off again when we went to bed, where we read by candlelight. Within the radius of a lantern we could write, read, do dishes, perform all but very close work, although eye strain eventually became a matter of concern.

Of course, nothing compares in power and brilliance to electricity, a product we grew up taking for granted, ours at the flip of a switch. In the cabin we had a small generator, chiefly for charging radio-phone batteries, and a very short supply of gasoline. Once a week we set up the little plant and treated ourselves to "generator night"—one bare bulb hanging from the rafters in a sixteen-by-twenty-foot space. For four hours, until the gas ran out, we could sew, write letters, read small type, relax the squints we perpetually wore at night, and luxuriate in the glow as though we had captured our own private sun. Then the generator sputtered and missed, running out of gasoline, and we scurried for matches and candles before darkness and quiet engulfed the cabin again like a silent tidal wave.

Other than the telephone, our only contact with the outside came from a small transistor radio, which brought in one CBC station. We listened to the news of a world from which we felt profoundly severed—earthquake and flood, space disaster, nuclear tragedy, military adventurism, the stock market. We might as well have been another species, except that the information affected us emotionally. Yet the news had no connection to our immediate lives; it could have been soap opera. However, that didn't stop us from listening: late-night talk shows, morning news, musical specials, call-in discussion programs. As weeks passed, we developed a round of favorite radio spots and incorporated them into our schedule.

Once accustomed to the pattern and demands of our life, growing comfortable with our ability to manage it, we adjusted our pace to those requirements. Missing a daily walk or shirking a day's writing caused a round of self-imposed recriminations, sometimes even a bout with depression. I worried that the slip in discipline might be the first sign of deterioration, that the day's weakness might become a trend, and warned myself that another breach would be unpardonable.

Small, unexpected problems confounded us, seeming to clutter the day as if we were already scheduled right up. After weeks of steady use, the sawhorse broke under the onslaught of dozens of heavy logs, but we put off its repair for days, making do awkwardly with the crippled device, the job of reconstruction growing into a major hurdle. When I finally forced myself to get outside and build a new one, using the original for a model, the project took only an hour or two and turned out to be an enjoyable morning's work. Why didn't I do that sooner? Unexpectedly, the same routine that protected us from emotional slippage also served as a crutch that enabled us to shirk spontaneity and flexibility.

4

On November 1, my thirty-third birthday, Eli came from Fond-du-Lac. The big lake was freezing. His was the last boat still in the water, but he planned to make a final run to his trapping cabin, down the lake shore from us, and would bring our mail if we could meet him at the point.

We were ready to leave within minutes, actually having to restrain ourselves from going too early, reminding each other that rendezvous arrangements in the north are so susceptible to change that meeting times simply can't be counted on. Punctuality is almost an impossibility.

But we were lucky. Half an hour after we reached the point, poised at the edge of the bay ice, we heard the sound of an approaching boat. Bundled up heavily, Eli and three of his sons idled up to the icepack, waving a cheerful hello, our first visitors.

As they pulled the heavy boat onto the ice shelf, Eli announced that they'd have lunch with us before going on. A large pile of mail heaped onto our sled. While we tramped over the now thick ice toward camp, Eli pointed out spots in the bay to be wary of. He carried a small hatchet with which he periodically chopped a quick hole to gauge ice thickness. "Be careful here," Eli gestured to an area just away from shore. "Lots of times, thin ice." He pounded the spot to demonstrate; with two blows the hatchet broke through, black water bubbling up as if pressurized.

I never did get all of Eli's offspring figured out. He and Angela gave birth to twenty-one children, an enormous family even by native standards, and the relationships were confusing in the extreme. Some of his grandchildren were older than his youngest kids, for instance. Sometimes it seemed that half of Fond-du-Lac had Adams for a last name. We met only a small sampling of the family, but still managed to be hopelessly confused by the web of lineage.

His boys were quiet and reticent, but possessed a quality of self-contained poise that seemed to mark all the Chipewyan we'd met: quick to respond, ready to see and appreciate humor, observant, comfortable with silence. The Chipewyan had none of our difficulty with conversational lapses. If there was nothing to say, they didn't lather up the atmosphere with inconsequential nattering. Their conversation was devoid of the extra niceties we are taught as part of our socialization, the pleases and thank-yous. "Do you want some tea?" "Yup." "A cookie?" "Yup." "Some more food?" "Nope. All done."

Finished eating, smoking a cigarette and drinking coffee, Eli looked around the room. "Good cabin," he said, approving. Then he noted that our woodpile was impressive. "Lots of wood. Should last till Christmas."

Christmas! Hell, I figured we had nearly enough for the whole winter! Marypat and I glanced at each other with raised eyebrows.

But Eli went on. "One of my girls almost drowned yesterday." As if he were telling us that a new shipment of snowmobiles had come in. She'd gone out night snowmobile-riding with a friend on the new ice and broken through. The machine immediately sank to the bottom, and the two riders spent twenty minutes floundering in the water, yelling for help, unable to crawl out, until someone heard the shouts and sent a boat out after them. "Lucky," he said, finishing his coffee.

Death by accident was common. People drowned, froze to death, or perished in plane wrecks so frequently, the possibility of terminal mishap never wholly retreated from their minds. As a result, the Chipewyan retained a disquieting equanimity about their chances of survival. Death was as tangible and sudden as a crack in the ice.

Eli and his boys left the cabin with an abruptness we could have interpreted as rude, but understood as simply an extension of their direct social habits. "See you," Eli said as he pulled on his cap and mitts. Out they went, heading for their trapping cabin, leaving us to savor our mail. The memory of the crowded room was cut off so suddenly, only the cloud of cigarette smoke confirmed their presence.

For a month that the Chipewyan refer to as fall, November proceeded to get colder than we thought strictly necessary. On fourteen nights the temperature plummeted to between -30°F to -50°F. Average maximum daily temperature for the entire month was 2°F. On many mornings the propane turned sluggish or refused to flow altogether, forcing us out to wrestle with the metal bottles, holding a torch to the valve stem or pouring boiling water over the top. Touching the metal with bare hands induced a searing, firelike sensation and turned the tips of our fingers white with frost-nip within seconds.

At night, in the brittle blackness outside, trees popped and cracked like musket fire, tortuous sounds loud enough to hear inside, where we huddled together under a mound of blankets. The cold attacked with a palpable hungering force, sucking out heat from the cabin like marrow from a bone.

And light steadily fled from the land. The sun receded southward in a march almost measurable in daily increments. We were lighting the lantern earlier each evening and then, grudgingly, for a time each morning. The sun arced briefly over the forest, a pallid medallion more symbolic than real, its rays at a long ineffective angle. I fought my tendency to retreat with the sun, to dwell on an image of our descent through a long, darkening tunnel to the low ebb of the year. In the somber light, my optimism represented a conscious repression of the temptation to give in.

In the evenings, the contrast between inside and outside temperatures could come as a physical blow. When I had to venture out on a trip to the crisp outhouse seat, the cold air seared my lungs as if I were breathing brandy. Eager to warm things up, we often stoked the stove too enthusiastically and turned the cabin into a sauna—75°F, 80°F, 90°F—so hot that we did dishes without any shirts on while through the cabin wall the temperature sank to -40°F. Heat forced us to open the cabin door for relief, and refrigerated air swooped into the room with a vaporous pounce.

If it hadn't been so brutally cold we would have spent hours in front of the cabin with our heads tipped back, for the northern lights were alive and pulsing. Nearly every clear night the sky flowed and rippled with displays. Most often a kind of watery green, but sometimes a wraith-like white or pale red, the lights shimmered and moved, intense in one part of the sky and then shifting to another quadrant. Sometimes a solid arc, like a spotlight, at other times like delicately waving curtains, the northern lights roamed the star-cluttered dome free of restriction. Snow squeaking underfoot, we would walk beyond our porch, the forest utterly still around us, and watch the show until the chilling cold drove us in.

Even the big lake finally succumbed to the ice, but not without complaint. As the armor grew and hardened, the lake groaned and shrieked with eerie, titanic moans. We walked out as far as we dared and listened to the noise of the struggle, the movements so massive and profound that I thought of them as plates of the earth grinding together. At times, shock waves of sound migrated right under our feet, like seismic tremors, a lonely organ chord. Pressure bumps like tiny Mid-Atlantic Ridges heaved up along cracks.

In the ponderous quiet, any sudden noise sounded like a shout in an ink-black cave. The popping trees, groaning ice, owl hoots—outbursts in a land otherwise so still that the silence felt like wind in the ears. On calm nights I could stand on the porch and hear the last ribbon of open water flowing in the river almost a half-mile away.

Clear bright days woke us up, invigorated our spirits, prodded us out of the cabin for the few light hours. We celebrated the good days by pushing at the edges of our territory, exploring new land, finding companionship in the creatures that have chosen that stringent and demanding landscape for their homes.

One morning we woke to a yard full of willow ptarmigan. Like albino chickens, they clucked and waddled about, plucking buds off willow and gleaning seeds from grasses, plowing wobbly furrows through the powdery snow. They seemed like a bevy of portly aunts and uncles from out of town—purposeful, comfortable bourgeois, with simple aspirations and a cheery countenance. Later on, during our walk, we found dozens of them along the lake shore, roosting like round ornaments in the willows, tracking up the lake with their feathery print, leaving burrows in the snow where they wiggled in for the night.

Marypat put out a simple bird feeder in front of our window, a plywood platform onto which we placed leftovers or small piles of nuts. Gray jays, their piratical behavior essentially unchanged from summer, arrived within minutes of a new food deposit. Then boreal chickadees, living examples of plucky indomitability. Minuscule bits of energy, they are the avian equivalent of voles, animals with no earthly business being alive and prosperous in the exiguous north. While I bundled up in layers of wool, polypropylene, and down, I would watch those cinnamon-tinged dynamos attack pine cones and flit energetically among branches in -30°F air. At times of deepest cold, even the uncompromising ravens holed up until warmer air brought them out again, their glittery opportunistic eyes gleaming with a lust for survival.

Most glimpses of wildlife came secondhand, our observational abilities no match for their vigilance and stealth. Well-beaten snow-shoe-hare runs cobwebbed around our cabin like a metropolitan street plan, but months went by between sightings of the perfectly camou-flaged rabbits. They took the liberty of gnawing on the plywood of the outhouse, attracted to glue or paint, and even taunted us by rasping away loudly on the base logs of the cabin in the middle of the night.

Up the river, among the jumbled blocks of ice, the tracks and slides of otter documented the playful habits of an animal truly undaunted by cold—first, sliding along the ice on their bellies, and then plopping fearlessly into river water so cold as to be almost liquid ice.

The snow sprouted tracks: lynx, marten, mouse, squirrel, weasel, moose, and the straight dainty line of fox at a trot across the lake. In the gray afternoons, a great horned owl sent its call into the cold vastness, an arresting sound, a mesmerizing threat to small lives. On one of our trails we found the scattered remains of a ptarmigan—explosion of white feathers, spot of crimson, grain-filled guts—and the wide wing imprint of swooping owl.

Wolves were everywhere around us, but kept out of sight. Their tracks encircled the cabin, dotted the bay, our trails, the woods behind camp, as if they indulged a timid curiosity but knew better than to barge in. Bandit would rush to the cabin window, ears up, hackles raised, faint rumbling growl in her chest. I thought she recognized distant kin, but felt so estranged that she didn't know whether to fear or welcome them.

One black night I woke to see Bandit at the window, head cocked, a trembling tension in her form. Something had wakened me as well, perhaps a dream. Then it came again, more a vibration in the air than a sound—the haunting exultation of wolves, that primal, throbbing song, and then harmony as others joined in. Their penetrating howls raised the hair on my neck, exhilarating and terrifying all at once. Involuntarily I held my breath and pulled tighter on the bed covers—but I also longed to join the pack, scent the shifting air and prowl the night.

Two days later, Marypat was pounding open the water hole while I finished a writing project. I looked out the window to watch her at work and saw a pale gray wolf trot onto the bay just across the river from her. She saw it too, and stopped to watch, when another appeared, head lowered to the scent of the first animal's path. And another, until there were four of them, confident as warders of a preserve that was unquestionably theirs. By that time I had left the cabin and hurried toward the water hole. The wolves noticed us, but we might have been two ravens standing on the ice for all the attention we warranted. They trotted slowly and steadily across the bay, seventy-five yards away.

We were suddenly desperate for their company. Could they pass by with no recognition of our existence, as nonchalantly as we would walk past someone's labrador on the way home from work? We sent out a little chorus of yips and barks, coyote howls. That did it.

They stopped and studied us. Who are you? Now we had their attention, but didn't know what to say. They waited, and we were mute. Two of them sat on the ice. The lead wolf paced fluidly toward us and stopped, attentive. The low red sun shone warmly on the thick tawny fur. Small whiffs of visible breath curled up past the wolf's muzzle. Two of the animals crossed the bay to sit at the edge of the spruce forest. They were quiet as rocks.

When I first heard one of the wolves howl, I didn't credit my senses. I thought perhaps it was wind in the trees. The sound surrounded us, seeming to simply rise out of the air, impossible to place, coming out of the depths of the animal's chest, a wolf that I faced across the white bay. The howling embodied an ineffable blend of wild emotion—threat and acquiescence, hunger and playfulness, all of life.

After that we saw the wolves almost daily for a time, trotting across the bay or along the edge of the forest with a complacent air, their acceptance of us further reassurance that we had settled in and nailed down a territory.

5

The arrival of mail set off spasms of excitement between us. "Listen to this," one of us would chortle, and read out some surprising anecdote. Any mawkish sentiment lurking beneath the surface flowered into bloom with the news from the social network we had so conclusively left behind. Postcards, pictures, advent calendars, crayon colorings from our nephews, all went onto the cabin walls. At difficult times, we caught each other standing in front of the pictures in a sentimental swoon.

My brother Craig wrote a long letter and, almost as an aside, mentioned that he and his wife, Beth, might be interested in joining us for the second summer of paddling, if we were open to it. He could have had no idea what a paroxysm of mental and conversational dialogue that would set off.

Initially, we both reacted negatively. "We set out to do the trip alone and we should finish that way." End of subject. Except that we kept turning it over in our minds, weighing the rewards of companionship, shared adventure, other outlets for conversation, the greater security of a larger group. At the same time, even as we longed for social stimulation, we understood that accepting another canoe into our endeavor would necessitate an adjustment of profound proportions.

On walks, over dinner, even late at night in bed, we roller-coastered through the arguments for and against having partners. Our original rigidity softened. "Whose expedition image are we living up to anyway? This is our trip. A year of solo wilderness living is lengthy by any standards. Why not enjoy company for the final two months?"

When one of us felt right about inviting them, the other expressed doubts. Even in agreement, we questioned our objectivity. In the end, weeks later, we decided to ask them along, agreeing that once the decision had been made, we needed to be realistic about adjustments and not fall into the trap of comparing the qualities of experience.

Early the next morning, we made radio telephone contact with Craig and Beth. To them the invitation came as a startling development, a possibility they had thrown out on an off chance more than a month earlier and since let fade. They had, in fact, begun tentative travel plans with other friends. By the end of our conversation, they had caught a measure of our enthusiasm and seemed prone to join us, but unable to commit.

With all the back and forth of our discussions, I had no idea how set on companionship I had become once our tendencies had crystallized. The realization that we might not even have the option of company, that they might turn us down, made us desolate.

"Look, we have to reconcile ourselves to the possibility that they'll say no," I blurted out as much to myself as to Marypat. "If they can't go with us, we're just back where we were all along. If it doesn't work out, no big deal."

But it was a big deal. The fantasies had already flourished. That night the radio horn blared and I heard my brother's voice on the line. Right off I could tell that the answer would be no. We talked of unrelated things, the main subject skirted like bad ice on a river crossing. "Well, Al, I have some bad news. We'd love to go with you, but can't renege on the plans that other people have already started to count on."

After I hung up the phone, the cabin felt still and stale, the emptiness outside a force pressing against the walls. We went to bed in the dark silence, our minds struggling to right our capsized expectations.

Almost as soon as I'd connected the phone in the morning, the horn startled me. Craig again. "We'd like to join you next summer. In fact," he continued, "we're counting on joining you!" Craig's voice had the jazzed vigor mine had had a few days earlier. My cabin-echoing dawn whoop levitated Marypat out of bed and brought her trotting around the partition with a "What's going on?" expression.

Maps on the table, new calculations for equipment needs and increased food supplies, a logistics checklist to send south with the next mail delivery—our energy for the next summer blazed to life, the prospect of variety and company a tremendous boost to our spirits.

Marypat shook me awake one night, the cabin black as tar. "I think we should get married."

"Huh?" I rose from the depths of grogginess like an air bubble in oil.

"I want to marry you. I've been thinking about it and wanted to tell you."

"Is this a proposal?" I had hold of the topic, but still came up well short with my response.

Marypat had always been adamant in her belief that marriage was out of the question. She rejected the conventional trappings, the societal expectations that come with the package, the potential for stagnation and complacency that lurked on the far side of the threshold.

For years we had known we were committed for the long term, but the legal nicety offered no relevance, seemed beside the point, actually posed the possibility of a threat to our relationship's balance. Whether or not we possessed a legal document proclaiming our conjugal state mattered not at all.

But on the expedition we began to appreciate the other function of a wedding ceremony, the acknowledgment of our commitment within a human fraternity. The more we thought about it and discussed it, the more we came to see the occasion in equal measure a statement of commitment and a celebration of social bonds. In that light, the legal formality remained a side issue, while the process of sharing a significant moment with the people we loved became the focal point. What had changed as a result of our solitary trek had little to do with the deepening of our involvement, and almost totally to do with a heightened appreciation for our human circle.

The topic had first come up during the summer as one of the daily discussion questions. As fall progressed, we approached the issue from time to time, the acute awareness of our societal needs motivating our thoughts. The idea of a wedding soon after the end of the expedition had an almost irresistible appeal. We decided to announce the plan at Christmas, either by mail or radio telephone, and thus created another future prospect to plan for and anticipate.

6

Nearly a month passed without a visitor after Eli's final boat trip. The big lake froze solid and snow lay more than a foot deep in the forest. After Eli's assessment of our wood supply, Marypat and I had foraged vigorously for more fuel, building up what we hoped would be an inexhaustible stack of amputated wood around the cabin. The deep cold hung on, and the stove gorged on jack pine with an astonishing appetite.

On the day before Thanksgiving, the temperature up near zero, snow trickling out of a thick matting of cloud, Bandit deafened us with her thundering warning, barking at the window as if hordes were sweeping out of the spruce forest. Once out on the porch, we could hear snowmobiles long before they sped through the willows and crossed the small bay to the cabin.

The sound of a snowmobile motor has to be one of the least attractive mechanical utterances man has given birth to. Only chainsaws and dirt bikes rival it for sheer obnoxiousness. But from inside the cabin at the back of Otherside Bay, the distant crescendoing whine meant one overriding thing: company. Company and, maybe, mail. Besides, snow-mobiles in the north are the equivalent of automobiles. They are the only reasonable surface transportation available. As a vehicle of utility rather than recreation, they are a good deal more palatable.

Two strangers arrived, huge bulking men on new machines, each hauling a toboggan. "Hello!" we shouted through the shattered air. "Come in for coffee."

Stan, a Resource Department officer out of Stony Rapids, and his assistant, Bill, swept snow off their pants and boots before coming inside, then proceeded to unlayer, becoming progressively less imposing as the clothing came off. Traveling to Fond-du-Lac on their monthly round, they had heard word of us and decided to swing in to see who we were. I had forgotten how long it had been since we had talked to anyone new, especially someone who spoke fluent English.

With Eli and most of the Chipewyan, conversation sputtered along monosyllabically. English is their second language, used only in conver-sation with fishing tourists, the police, and The Bay manager. Even though children are taught in English, they switch to Chip in the school hallways and at home.

Stan, although native, had spent some years farther south and spoke English easily. We battered him with conversation, Marypat serving cookies, cranberry bread, tea, and coffee, gastronomic bribes with which to prolong their stay. Small puddles of meltwater collected under their dripping clothing and cigarette smoke hung like smog in the cabin.

When the short afternoon light began to fade, the men reversed the cumbersome process of undressing, re-armoring to combat the wind and cold. "It's good riding weather," Stan asserted. "Cold enough, but not bitter."

"Are you coming back this way tomorrow?" I asked. "It's American Thanksgiving. Could you stop for dinner?"

"Sure," Stan said willingly. "We should be back about noon. And we'll bring your mail."

They straddled their squat machines, fired up the engines, and roared toward the settlement, loaded with a batch of our letters, leaving us so thoroughly stimulated that we had to tramp off on a long walk to plan the Thanksgiving meal and savor our new acquaintances.

With an event to prepare for, we were out of bed in the early darkness, elaborate menu in the works. Moose roast, instant potatoes, gravy, cranberry sauce, fresh-baked bread, a pie, dehydrated vegetables, a repast that strained the limits of our scanty capacities.

I should have known better than to expect them on time. Noon passed, and one o'clock, the food cooling along with our enthusiasm. By three o'clock I figured they had gone on by or had been held over another day, but half an hour later, twilight settling over the lake, Bandit went into her welcoming cacophony and the two men motored up.

They made no excuse for being late, assuming that we understood the six-hour fudge factor that comes with northern travel arrangements. No mail. They had been unable to find the postal matron before leaving town, but they promised to bring it another time.

Stan and Bill seemed unfazed by the prospect of driving forty-five miles back to Stony in the cold night as they pitched into our wilderness version of Thanksgiving dinner.

A lantern hissing overhead, the room bulged with an air of festivity. The noises we made serving and eating the meal brought forth upwellings of nostalgia, images of family holidays triggered by the click of utensils or the polite conversation and long chewing pauses. Only when I glanced out the window and saw the barely distinguishable lines where the white bay ran up against the black forest, did I come abruptly back to reality.

Stan's job put him in an unenviable no-man's land of confrontation and isolation. Essentially a game warden, he had to administer restrictions to a native population used to harvesting fish and game when and how they liked. They literally assumed it to be their native right. That freedom remained largely unchanged, but Stan enforced such things as the legal size of gill nets allowed for fishing, and faced the nightmarish task of ferreting out the varying applications of policy for treaty and non-treaty natives, thereby enmeshing himself in a legal cat's cradle of daunting proportions.

Natives resented his intrusion and more often than not ignored his edicts or flagrantly rebelled against them. Worse yet, the bureaucracy that theoretically stood behind him proved susceptible to fickle political pressures. Already precariously extended in enforcing an unpopular law, he often found his support backing off, his supervisors succumbing to native complaints by telling Stan to lay off.

Observing the guides in camp, we had witnessed examples of their game-harvesting capacity. Eli netted fish by the thousands for winter dog food. Don talked about shooting forty or fifty grouse in an afternoon. The men went hunting for moose or bear as if they could never have enough. They did utilize the animals, and we saw few instances of wanton killing or wasteful butchering, but the sheer gusto for game was substantial. Stan only enhanced that impression. "An unofficial survey of these northern communities found that an average family kills forty caribou each year," he told us.

No wonder that it had been ten years since the caribou herds came this far south in the winter. Fond-du-Lac and Stony Rapids were located at traditional caribou crossing points, narrows in the waterways where seasonal harvest could be depended on. Now the natives have to fly or snowmobile north to find caribou herds. The last time caribou wandered south onto nearby Wollaston Lake, it lit a savage fuse in the native and white populations, and set off a spree of indiscriminate slaughter so shocking that even people who weren't there talk about it with disgust.

"I'd like to go even farther north." Stan pushed his empty plate away and tapped the inevitable cigarette into his hand. "The farther away from cities and big government, the happier I am, eh? It's good here, but farther up would be better."

By the time the two men left, the night sky had pulled a black tarp across the lake. The stars were dense and close, and the temperature slid below -20°F. "It's usually easier to stay with the snowmobile trail by headlight than it is in daylight," Stan reassured us before firing up his machine.

Like a suburban couple tidying up after a dinner party, we cleared dishes, heated wash water, put away leftovers, fed the dog. The cabin reverberated with the warmth and presence of guests. Satiated by the meal, our spiritual reservoirs brimmed as well. "Friends, Marypat," as we finished up the dishes. "What wealth it is to have friends. Tonight was like an original Thanksgiving."

Social eruptions discombobulated the pace of our routine, leaving a turbulence of excitement in their wake. It took days to regain the quiet, long-term perspective. Pumped up by social interaction, our invigorated outlook would have crippled us with restlessness if we had let it reign. Like athletes submitting to the lonely isolation of training after an exhilarating contest, we wrestled down our excitement.

In mid-December, Don McDonald returned to Fond-du-Lac with his family. We knew because his wife called on the telephone to ask for money—a woman I had met once, with whom I had exchanged half a dozen words, calling to request a loan of one hundred dollars.

"Where's Don?" I asked her, completely taken off guard by the call.

"At his sister's house," she answered.

"You ask Don to call me," I told her, and hung up.

"Christ, you won't believe this!" I exploded. "They go away for over two months without letting us know, and then want to borrow money as soon as they come back. They even had the gall to call collect! Why can't they borrow money from somebody they know, for crying out loud?" I paced the cabin.

By the time Don called back, I had worked myself up to an indignant pitch, but he entirely defused my bluster by blandly asking, "What did you decide?"

"Well," I sputtered, "what's the money for?"

"Roseann is pregnant and needs to go south for a checkup. She could use some spending money."

"Didn't you make any money trapping?"

"Not yet. I have to send the pelts in first."

"But what about your family?" I asked. "We only have enough money for our trip."

"The government checks aren't in yet," Don blocked off another avenue.

"When could you pay us back?" I started to cave in.

"Oh, by January."

Silence. Despite what seemed like an outrageous request by a man who had abandoned us almost immediately after agreeing to provide us with transportation, I still recognized Don's potential importance as a contact. We had a long winter ahead and well might require his help. If we antagonized him, would we pay a price later when we needed a friend?

"Will you sign an agreement saying you'll pay us back?" I felt stupid making the demand, but stubborn at the same time, recognizing a need to put Don on the spot.

"Sure," he answered, in a flip way that indicated what he thought of a piece of paper as a binding contract.

"When will you come to pick it up?" I completed the commitment.

"Tomorrow."

"Okay," I hesitated. "We'll cook up some moose if you can come at lunch time." My tendency was to placate any sense of confrontation, to bury the uncomfortable tensions and get onto more friendly ground.

At noon the next day, another moose roast simmered on the stove, but no sign of Don. No phone call, no approaching snowmobile. The gray afternoon crept by and we ate the moose for dinner without company.

"It can't help but piss me off," I vented my anger. "I don't care if the Chipewyans have different ways of looking at arrangements. It's just a matter of common courtesy!"

Don arrived twenty-four hours late, with no excuse for the delay. He pulled off his moosehide mitts and I shook his hand on the porch.

"Where have you been?" I couldn't resist the question.

"Too foggy yesterday," Don said.

The weather seemed identical both days to me, but I let the subject drop. "We have leftover moose if you want some."

I served Don a plate and watched him eat. "The meat's dry," he said after several bites. "Cooked too long."

"Yesterday at noon it tasted pretty good," sarcastic edge to my retort.

I pulled a hundred dollars out of my pocket, eager to make the distasteful transaction and be done with it. "Thanks," Don said.

I fetched the scrawled I.O.U. I'd prepared and asked Don to sign it. The scrap of paper seemed ludicrous, the formality an insult, but I felt imposed upon, recalcitrant. Don chuckled and signed, the paper obviously meaningless. What could I do? Take him to small claims court?

Past the odious exchange, I asked Don about his time trapping.

Don's rounded smooth face displayed little emotion, his voice was soft, his sentences direct and unadorned. He had the sort of undefined physical build that easily passed as chubby and toneless, but I knew it disguised great strength and a quality of enduring toughness. I'd seen Don heft a twenty-five-foot beam onto his back and carry it seventy-five yards.

He had taken his entire family north with him—the government subsidizes the transportation of native trappers as an incentive to work. Roseann was six months pregnant at the time. They had an infant and two young children along. The cabin they'd lived in for two and a half months measured nine by twelve feet, had a dirt floor and two small windows covered in plastic. I thought of the deep cold we'd experienced and imagined living in an uninsulated tiny cabin stuffed with a family of five.

"How did your trapping go?" we asked.

"One marten, two fisher," Don said, briefly.

"That's all?" I couldn't believe that in nearly three months, after an expensive journey into the Northwest Territories, he'd returned with three measly pelts.

"I didn't trap that much," Don lit another cigarette. "I shot lots of caribou, though. There's about twenty that I left up there and have to go back to get later on. I have to go now." Don pulled his parka on and opened the door.

When he'd left, I couldn't shed the feeling that I'd been taken advantage of. "I wonder if we'll see that hundred dollars again," I said to Marypat.

7

Just days later Don's father contacted us. "Eli and I have been talking," he said. "We want you to come to town for midnight mass on Christmas Eve."

"Really? We'd love to!"

"You can stay at my house. I'll send Donald to pick you up the day before Christmas."

My mixed feelings about Don and the loan paled in the glow of the invitation, became, in fact, tinged with a strong dose of guilt. What was a hundred dollars? Here were people who thoughtfully extended their hospitality to us, essentially foreigners, without any prompting or obligation.

The qualitative contrast between our interactions with Don and his father focused a generational pattern I had noticed before. Generally speaking, our contact with the older natives had been marked by politeness, an open hospitality, and dependability. Dealings with Don's generation, our contemporaries and younger, were laced with a tension and discomfort that never really faded away. Spontaneous interactions, social bantering, cruised along with superficial ease, but the potential for conflict gave dealings a tart edge. Once on less safe ground—work, money, arrangements that involved commitments—I felt the way I do when portaging a canoe across muskeg, always aware that the next step might take me up to my hips in mire.

Beyond the cultural divergences that posed substantial obstacles to understanding, the contrast in generations starkly illuminated the conflict of a society leaping from a traditional, largely pre-industrial lifestyle to the twentieth century, complete with punk rock, video, and drugs. Donald's peers stand at the crux of that leap.

The older Chipewyan grew up paddling canoes, driving dog teams, living in seasonal camps dependent on the movements and habits of wildlife. Their skills focused on hunting, trapping, fishing, knowing the ways of wild things, and their conversations dwelt on the issues attendant to those pursuits. For them, the technological leap occurred after maturity. Airplanes, powerboats, snowmobiles, electricity are as much an amazing curiosity as a reality. While they accept the change and utilize the advanced technology to make their lives easier, their outlook is annealed by the old ways.

Don's generation bears the brunt of the abrupt transition. Brought up by parents who followed caribou herds, still restricted by many of the ancient limitations, they watch "Three's Company" on television, listen to The Police and John Cougar Mellencamp on the radio, and eat Eggo frozen waffles for breakfast. For our part, we shared the representative guilt of a society responsible for overwhelming the native lifestyle, imposing values and expectations of a radically disorienting nature. The resulting interplay made for an awkward dance on an uncertain surface, a wary circling encumbered with baggage so all-encompassing that the participants only rarely achieved any perspective that enabled them to escape its effects.

Muglar's invitation would provide the first opportunity to leave our tiny territory in more than two months. Reminded of the season, we brought in a small spruce tree and anchored it in a tin bucket by a front window. Short on ornaments, we made do with cut-out stars from foil coffee packets, strung popcorn and cranberries, and an odd assortment of shiny balls sent north by family. Marypat nailed a spruce-bough wreath to the front door.

I worked on a poem for Marypat's Christmas present, and encouraged her to go for walks alone so I could secretly fashion a pair of chopsticks out of straight-grained poplar.

My weather notes indicate our increased tolerance for bitter cold. On a day when the lower temperature reached -38°F and the high peaked at -13°F, I remarked that conditions were moderating. For a ten-day stretch, low temperatures ranged between -30°F and -60°F, while highs never exceeded -15°F. Average maximum temperature for the month of December was -5°F, but it left an impression not nearly as harsh as November had.

Winter solstice loomed as the most significant moment of the season. No wonder primitive people made such a fuss over celestial movements, the coming and going of light. Our occupations took place in a state of twilight, sometimes a week at a time passing between pools of good light. Even the brightest sun came from such a long angle as to hurl startling shadows the length of skyscrapers in front of us.

Since October we'd been sinking into a well of darkness. Our emotions often reflected that descent, a black mood seeping into our thoughts, usurping optimism as darkness conquered the sun. I steeled myself against the encroachment by developing a kind of bovine patience, a tunnel vision restricted to the simplest life maintenance.

We slept long hours, our tolerance for darkness growing short, the escape an attitudinal addiction. The sun in mid-December didn't show itself above the forest until almost eleven, and slipped below the earth rim around three. At its height, the pale yolk-colored globe stood only a hand's width above the horizon, catching us at the very edge of its circle. I imagined it hoarding light in the southern latitudes, irre-sponsibly forgetting those toward the far pole.

On December 21 we set the camera tripod on the bay and snapped hourly pictures of the sun, recording the lowest transit of light. Five pictures, from first glimmer to final flame. That night we awarded ourselves double cocktails and generator light, an optimism infusing us in marked contrast to our position at the deepest recesses of the well. January, winter's fortress, lay ahead of us, and long months before any appreciable lightening of winter would occur, but that night, it mattered little. The sun would remember us and begin its tortuously slow return to warm and light our lives. Who could despair? Our spirits began climb-ing the next morning with the sun.

PART VI

WINTER

Considering it was a momentous occasion, leaving camp at Christmas required so little preparation as to make the departure unceremonious. Dump out the water, unhook the radio phone, let the fire die, close the door. Finished in a matter of minutes.

Don arrived only two hours late, fastidiously punctual by northern standards, pulling a toboggan behind his snowmobile. Marypat and Bandit squeezed into the canvas-sided modern travois, jammed in with our holiday contributions—pie, cranberry sauce, cookies, a case of pop left over in camp—and wrapped up in quilts and sleeping bags for the bumpy ride. Face into the wind, I rode shotgun, standing on the back of the toboggan, slinging around corners or over bumps on crack-the-whip rides.

The impact of departure hit home as we left behind the tiny circumference of our domain and drove onto the wide frozen expanse. The same stretch of lake that we first paddled across, using islands for windblocks and beating against waves, now felt like northern pavement.

The lake was a borderless white room—ridged sculpted floor marked by jutting heaves of ice, grooved by the invisible currying of unimpeded winds. A ceiling of hazy low-hanging clouds blended seamlessly with the suggestion of a horizon. White walls of swirling snow completed the disorienting surrealistic scene. Myopically we followed the tracks of other machines, trusting to a common destination and sense of direction.

Thumped and slammed by the rigid surface, Marypat took the brunt of punishment, protecting the pie on her lap, tucking her feet under Bandit's belly for warmth. Don and I switched off driving, going until our accelerator thumb turned numb, then relinquishing control and taking another stint on the toboggan. The white/gray world remained so unrelieved, the faint path we followed so indistinct, that my eyes went out of focus from the strain. The lake shimmered like an arctic version of a desert mirage.

An hour later we bobsledded through the willows, scattering ptarmigan like feathered snow flurries, rocking into Fond-du-Lac by the back entrance—across yards, past abandoned pickup trucks and staked-out dog teams—to arrive at the back porch of the McDonalds in a pale cloud of exhaust. A group of sulking canines howled at us forlornly.

A human tempest raged in the small two-bedroom house. Children and adults trooped in and out rummaging through the boot pile, hovering in the background, watching television in the living room, bursting in with questions or requests, a revolving door of Chipewyans. Our reticence evaporated as we caught hold of the pace and confusion, drank tea and coffee at the kitchen table, and made ineffectual attempts at conversation like shouts in a gale.

The house glittered with holiday ornaments: tinsel, strings of styrofoam bells, a two-foot-tall fake Christmas tree, lights and candles hanging and glowing from every imaginable anchoring point. Whenever I walked out of the kitchen, I whacked my forehead softly against a golden bell dangling from the door frame.

Not about to squander our rare visit to town, we set out before supper to pick up a few supplies at The Bay store and collect mail at the post office. Outside, the windswept streets were already gloomy with twilight. Cowering skeletal dogs skulked in shadowy corners, and the incessant whine of snowmobiles hung in the air like the drone of a giant insect hive.

It seemed to us that all eight hundred residents of Fond-du-Lac were out on last-minute errands. A dozen snowmobiles sat haphazardly outside the store, while inside a confused mob scene inhibited our ability to find what we needed. The two of us were the only white faces in the store. Few of the items we wanted were in stock, but fortified by our ability to make do, we just shrugged and joined the hour-long line to the cash register.

All the native transactions took place on paper, no cash changing hands. Charge slips for tremendous purchases were routinely written and filed away, settled when the government checks arrived: $920, $850, $545. Fantastic sums for purchases so few that they made it out the door in a single load. It took the clerk a minute to adjust to our cash payment and remember the steps for making change.

A group of older men, Eli among them, loitered at the back of the store, smoking cigarettes and chatting, oblivious to the confusion. When we waved to Eli, he acknowledged us with a reserved nod that gave the impression he didn't wish to appear overly chummy when among his peers.

At the post office we again overcame the discouraging sign on the door and prevailed upon the postmistress to open up for us. "Lots of mail," she said, unlocking the door and flipping on a light. A large shipment of food we'd been waiting on for over a month finally had arrived, and along with it an almost embarrassing pile of Christmas boxes and letters, a load so large that we had to get Don to pull it behind the snowmobile.

The scene back at the McDonald house did nothing to allay the giddy amusement-park sensation that the town visit had provoked. If anything, traffic and commotion increased as we sat down to a meal of caribou steaks, instant mashed potatoes, and canned vegetables. Everywhere around us lay evidence of the cultural fault line between primitive and modern. A television, complete with video recorder, animated the living room with a flickering glow. Powered by a huge diesel generator, a toaster oven, stereo, and other electronic gadgetry cluttered the house. Yet the temperature was maintained by stoking a wood stove, and the water supply had been hauled by hand from a hole chopped through the lake ice. To use the bathroom, one sallied out through the canine gauntlet to the outhouse.

Our hosts recalled the round of existence they'd known in their childhood. At that time, families stayed in bush camps for entire seasons, fishing in the summer, hunting caribou and trapping in the winter. Settlements had functioned as little more than supply and gathering points. Everyone had traveled by canoe or dog sled and English had been a foreign and little-heard language. Muglar remembered an elder who had foretold the coming of the featherless silver bird.

While most of the children had moved out of the house, several of the youngest still lived at home, and Muglar and his wife cared for a granddaughter as well. "Her mother is too young to take care of her," they explained. I wondered how young that might be in a culture that accepted fifteen-year-old motherhood as unexceptional.

The little girl had complete tyrannical latitude in the house, and was treated with a benign lack of discipline that we would consider a prescription for disaster. Muglar would pick her up with an exasperated chuckle and cuddle her on his lap, a look of resigned bemusement on his face. In a settlement that few people left, a tendency toward ingrown, even inbred patterns had developed, but the maintenance of extended families was a fact of life. Neither the elderly nor the young were abandoned in the native society.

Midnight mass at the Catholic church provided the focus of the holiday in town. The population was 100 percent Catholic, and all but a few settlement drunks attended the service. While Muglar's family prepared themselves, we went over to Eli and Angela's for a visit.

The two homes presented a shocking contrast. While the McDonalds' resembled a carnival, the Adamses' was as quiet as a convent during morning prayers. We wondered at first if the house was deserted, but found Angela on a couch, beading moccasins. Eli, she said, had gone to make a contribution to the church, but would be right back.

While we waited, a drunken neighbor staggered in for a visit, but Angela beat the surprised man back out the door with a vehement stream of angry Chipewyan. I fully expected her to grab a broom and give him a sharp spank to encourage him on his way, but her fierce demeanor relaxed into a chuckle when she came back to us.

Eli returned, the earlier aloofness I had noticed evaporated. "Hello!" he boomed, his spry figure and thick black hair making him look closer to forty than sixty. "Good man," he greeted us, as we regrouped around a formica table in the kitchen.

A Mr. Coffee machine rumbled on the counter while a copper tea kettle stayed warm on the wood stove. In the corner of the kitchen a large moose leg stood anchored in a pail, furry hoof sticking up like an incongruous fencepost in the clean kitchen. Vaguely out-of-focus religious prints and Scripture quotations hung on the wall, but no Christmas tree or decorations marked the holiday.

Angela poured tea, moving her bulky shapeless body with an unhurried grace and economy. The exercise of bearing twenty-one children no doubt gave her figure reason for fatigue, but she carried herself with authority. Her brown arthritic hands had the gnarled look that hinted of hide tanning, meat pounding, and tough beading projects; fingers blunted and knobbed and abused, but they moved with a dexterous competence mesmerizing to watch.

A trickle of visitors ebbed in and out—family members, older couples, no one bothering to knock. People appeared at the door, slipped off shoes, and joined us in the kitchen. The initial impression of taciturnity lasted only until the first smile crinkled their faces and lit their eyes.

With the older people, language difficulty relegated discussion to the most basic level; we spent most of our time searching for words or straightening out misunderstandings. "What is the Chip word for musk ox?" "Huh?" "You know, like a buffalo, but with big horns." We made horn gestures with our hands. "Lots of shaggy hair. They live up north. Maybe we'll see them next summer." The Chipewyan looked at each other, shrugging, trying to figure what we were getting at, finally shaking their heads. Then, fifteen minutes later, Eli would understand our question and go into a spate of Chipewyan, the other company nodding with comprehension and going, "Ah!" and the word would be produced. Conversation went on like a quiz show, everyone clutching at clues and making improbable intuitive leaps.

Later, when we returned to the McDonalds', we found the house relatively calm, only five or six people inside, all dressed for the service. Walking to the church, our small group joined the general flow—quiet talk and the sounds of brittle snow underfoot, a wide black sky overhead, the big lake a sensation of openness to the west.

We climbed upstairs to take balcony seats and watched the pews fill below us, the air warming with body heat. Women sat on one side of the aisle, men on the other. Most people genuflected and crossed themselves before sitting. Many older people held rosary strings, toying with them absently like worry beads. A mosaic of fur coats, beaded moose-hide, and leather jackets formed below us. Nearly everyone wore a pair of the moosehide mitts dangling from their necks on bright yarn strings, decorated with beadwork designs characteristic of the Fond-du-Lac band.

Suddenly, without any signal, an eerie Chipewyan chanting began. Led by a woman toward the front, the undulating singsong occasionally broke out with lines from Christian hymns, the familiar phrases an evocative pulse. Men and women sang alternating parts; at times the chanting died away, only to build and crest again like summer waves on a granite shore.

The priest appeared in vestment, carrying a crudely carved, wooden baby Jesus, which he laid in the manger. The chanting tailed off and the service, weighty with ritual, began. The priest gave mass entirely in Chipewyan, a language he spoke with practiced ease. Two teenagers acted as altar boys, and the congregation responded to the litany with memorized phrases. Communion made up by far the lengthiest section of the mass, the entire town filing down gender-segregated aisles toward the elderly white priest, a shuffling line of dark hair, fringed hide shirts, beaded mitts. After, the congregation moved quietly back out into the deep black night, each family walking home in the early hours of Christmas day. The town appeared dwarfed and dingy under the sharp pure darkness.

Fully expecting to find our way to bed, we were startled when another three-course meal got under way. At one in the morning, we tucked into the table in front of a ham dinner, white man's food contrasting with the caribou steaks of the afternoon. Even a small ham constituted no small gesture, probably having cost forty or fifty dollars at The Bay.

Around three o'clock, bloated with food, exhausted by the abnormally long day, we were shown to our bed, generously awarded one of two bedrooms in the tiny house. I slipped off to sleep, serenaded by the endlessly cruising snowmobiles whining outside and wondering if Chipewyan children believed that Santa made his rounds by snow machine.

*   *

My Christmas morning memories are replete with dawn risings, large trees overshadowing a formidable stack of gifts, and the childhood anticipation of a gluttonous binge of present opening. But in the McDonald household nobody stirred before ten-thirty, when I heard the stove door hinges creak and the first logs of the day thump into the box. Gift-giving assumed a minor place. We received a box of chocolates. Only the youngest children got more than one present, and most gifts were modest and utilitarian—a pair of socks, a watch, beaded moccasins.

By early afternoon a rising wind shrieked through the exposed streets, nearly obliterating our view of the lake. Despite the social excitement of the visit, and the generosity we'd been bathed in, I was subverted by a readiness to return to our log home. If we got trapped in town by bad weather, we might be there a week.

I went to Don's to visit and drink coffee. He agreed that we should hurry if we wanted to get back that day, and we soon had the toboggan bulging with our Christmas loot from home. Once Marypat and Bandit were precariously astride the boxes and mail, we departed, saluted by the unavoidable pack of roving dogs.

Back on the armored lake surface, jarring toward home, I turned for a final wave and found the town already swallowed up in a white bank of wind-driven snow, gone as if the visit had been a vivid production of fantasy. The return trail had drifted over, sculpted clean of tracks, our route an intuitive reckoning. Blowing snow stung our faces like tiny shrapnel and forced our eyes into slits. Wind sliced through our clothes. We clung to the lake shore as a blind person to a guide, the border of trees the only hope of keeping our bearings.

Once we turned into Otherside Bay the forest protected us from the strongest wind, a welcoming calm in our known territory, the familiar landmarks as comforting as a home-town street. Don stayed only long enough for a cup of hot tea, leaving again even before the cabin thawed out, the bitter taste of our previous transaction a faint memory.

A second stage of Christmas began once we'd restocked with water and stoked the heat again. The supply boxes spilled their contents across the floor replenishing food we'd run out of weeks earlier, a fresh store of books, writing pads, spare lantern parts, candles, the simple materials that made the difference between comfort and hardship.

And gifts. Letters, books, a bottle of bourbon, warm clothes, packages of canned fruit, evaporated milk, gourmet soup mixes, T-shirts, cocoa, canned lobster spread, two cans of beer that miraculously escaped the clutches of customs officials and managed to arrive unfrozen.

The phone horn rang with calls from home, poor connections and the stilted conversation of radio contact no match for the warmth of feeling. We announced our plans for a post-expedition wedding, setting off distant tremors of enthusiasm.

Hours later, silence wrapped around the cabin, we stood in the middle of the warm room and held each other. Marypat said, "I feel so unbelievably wealthy."

By morning our holiday euphoria was markedly diminished. We sent the old year out and welcomed the new under the curse of racking sickness. Our defensive systems had been caught napping, turned slothful by inaction. Gargantuan colds. Throats as sore as if we'd swallowed knives, heads the size of basketballs, bodies arthritic with achy stiffness.

It gave us small comfort to hear that most of Fond-du-Lac suffered with us. I called Muglar to thank him for his hospitality and found that he'd been laid low as well. "I've been dead for three days!" he said, which was a pretty fair assessment of our own condition. Maintaining our fire, hauling water, rising from bed demanded all of our energies. In Fond-du-Lac they called off the New Year's dance because of the epidemic.

2

When northern people want to make a case for the difficulty of winter, it is January that they talk about, the dark heart of the season. Cold clamps down like an unrelenting vise, the sun appears reluctant to return, the days are gray and unrelieved, wildlife holes up in dens and burrows, and people avoid traveling as much as possible. January, in my mind, was hump month. Once past it, we could coast toward spring.

On afternoon walks my bearded face turned into a white mask of hoarfrost, even my eyelids frosting up. When I blinked, the lids stuck together momentarily. Ax handles snapped in half with the slightest mis-hit, rubber hoses broke apart at a touch, wood didn't so much split as shatter at a blow from the ax. The ice at the water hole thickened measurably each night, already four feet from the surface we stood on to the bottom lip. We chopped steps into the ice well in order to reach the water and battled back the relentless crystalline growth on a daily basis, just to keep the hole wide enough for our buckets. A skim frosted over the surface within seconds of lifting out the last load of water.

Temperatures within fifteen degrees of zero struck us as balmy. At -10°F, I journeyed to the outhouse without a coat and chopped at the ice clad only in a long-sleeved shirt, wearing a pair of light gloves. My weather notes summarize a day when the temperature ranged between -12°F and -2°F as "overcast, breezy, warm."

Our own reaction to the daunting conditions was to retreat inward, physically and mentally. Writing, drawing, reading, transported by a line of poetry or a piquant interview on the radio. We read voraciously, the padded silence of our environment encouraging complete absorption into plots and characters unimaginably foreign by comparison. During the summer, days had flowed together, a seamless cyclic rhythm, hours and minutes meaningless, place names and river mileage and wildlife encounters the benchmarks. But in January my frame of reference had taken another leap. The flow of the year passed in ever larger chunks, a varied but uncompartmentalized passage. Whole weeks and months slid by in a fluid current with us bobbing along in midstream.

"Shower day again?" I'd remark. "It's generator night already?" Or, "Look at that full moon. Has it really been a month?"

January crept by. No visitors lifted the mantle of our focused inward existence. When the cold didn't have us clutched in a grip as sharp as an owl's talons, more snow fell to deepen the layers of silence. Our sled trail to the water hole cut through corniced drifts, and if we stepped off our beaten track, we went to our waists in the powdery depths. After a new snowfall, we set out purposefully to rebreak our system of trails, tramping down webbed walkways with the same dutiful sense of ownership as city residents shoveling their walks. On our tours we periodically checked each other for white patches of frost-nip, sometimes cutting a walk short to return and thaw our feet in warm water.

Standing on the porch at night, I couldn't hear a sound. Quiet to the horizon. The pack of wolves had gone, probably traveling north to scavenge at the edges of caribou herds. The live things still in evidence went about quietly, subdued and humbled by the dark and cold time. No waves lapped the shore, no current tickled the banks, only the riverine lights in the sky hissed across the blackness. Balanced at the crux of the season, each of us hunkered protectively around our own warm heart, selfishly banking the coals of our personal fires.

3

February 1. As if to signify the passing of winter's core, Ed and Margy called to announce plans for a visit. Plus, the temperature peaked out near zero, a perfect traveling day. Inspecting our cabin, we realized that the room had begun to reflect our introverted musty state. The prospect of company fired a purgative round of sweeping, scouring, shoveling, and feast preparation. Around mid-day the sound of two snowmobiles augered the first human contact since Christmas—Ed and Margy on one and Ivan, a pilot and engineer, on another. Ivan's machine, a clattering hulk, certainly seemed worthy of an engineer's attention.

The clean cabin turned into an instant disaster area—coats, boots, and hats scattered on the floor and furniture. Margy unloaded a boxful of gifts: beads for Marypat, candy, fresh fruit, homemade pie, a boxed liter of wine. Bandit timidly skirted the confused scene, consternation over her hunger for attention—and then her inability to cope when it came—a perfect pantomime of our own conflicted response.

Circled around the usual company fare of moose roast and trimmings, we loosed a deluge of pent-up conversation on our guests. I watched Marypat blathering on about some political belief or local observation, while the rest of us tolerated her exuberant excess. Comparing notes later, she told me I had been guilty of exactly the same infraction. After dinner we conducted an upriver tour along our favorite trail, taking show-and-tell pride in pointing out spots of particular interest—the place we'd seen a spruce grouse, the last part of river to freeze, a good fishing hole.

Our native visitors had relieved the solitude, brought us supplies, and broadened our understanding of the traditional way of life. But Ed, Margy, and Ivan were peers. Conversation clipped along unimpeded by language barriers. Similar values and experiences gave our visit the easy comfortable quality possible only among members of our own tribe. The talk never stopped. When it came time for the trio to gird up for the three-hour return trip, we felt we had only begun to tap the available topics.

"Oh, you'll start seeing people more now," Ed assured us as he snugged the lashing on a spare gas can and checked his load. "In February and March people get out."

For days after they left, the charge of the encounter kept buzzing like extra voltage through our nervous systems. "God, I hope I didn't scare them off with all my talking," Marypat worried. "I just couldn't help it!"

The visit constituted such a minute island in the ocean of isolation—one afternoon out of a five-week period—yet the human contact dominated our memories.

A week later it happened again. Late in the day we heard a small plane overhead and ran out to see if someone was giving us a friendly buzz. The white plane zoomed in low over the trees, right over the cabin, banked around over the bay, and returned while we waved from the porch. On the next pass the plane angled alarmingly low toward the lake, on what looked like a crash course.

"I think they're landing, Marypat!" I leapt from the porch and waded around the point to look, but couldn't see the plane. "Let's get dressed and go out there."

We found them half a mile out on the bay, the furrows of the plane's skis like giant snow-worm paths. Ivan and his girlfriend, Diane, were protectively tucking in the tiny fabric-winged plane. When we reached them, Ivan was hunched over an army surplus, wick-style heater, getting ready to light it and put it inside the engine to keep things from freezing solid.

"I haven't ever tried this before," he told us, "but it should work, if I'm lucky."

Pampering the plane, even for a short stay, entailed installing the heater, wrapping the nose in engine covers and quilted sleeping bags, and hauling the battery back to the cabin with us.

"Can you stay the night?" we asked.

"Well," Ivan looked one last time toward his plane. "I've never left her away from a hangar all night before. We thought we'd visit for a while and see what we wanted to do."

Within an hour it was clear they would stay over. After a thrown-together dinner, Diane and Marypat launched into spirited conversation on one side of the cabin while Ivan and I competed for air space on the other.

"I really don't like flying in the winter," he told me. "Almost all our business is taking natives north to hunt caribou. It seems like all I do is land Indians on the ice, watch them pick off helpless animals, load up the meat, and fly them back."

I expected most northerners, living where hunting and trapping are cultural mainstays, to be pretty hardened about killing game, but Ivan seemed sincerely upset by the status quo.

"There's no skill or effort put into a hunt," he continued. "I fly around until we spot a herd, and then put her down on a lake. The Indians get out and stand next to the plane, shooting a dozen animals sometimes. Some of the caribou limp off wounded, but the Indians say it's too cold to go after them. After I get back to the hangar, it takes me hours to clean the blood and hair out of the plane."

Ivan thumped the table with his fist. "I just don't like killing the caribou that way!"

He told me about a recent local plane crash. A new pilot had taken natives up to hunt caribou and been surprised by a whiteout on the return trip. "He wasn't trained in instrument flying." Ivan shook his head. "Lost his bearings. Just flew into the ice on Black Lake at a hundred-fifty miles an hour. All they found were body parts and bits of plane."

The night turned clear and bitter cold. Ivan wanted to go check the plane and refill his heater with camp gas, in hopes that it would keep burning all night. He and I trudged back out on the bay, northern lights like arcing spotlights in the star-stuffed sky. Frustrated by our mittened clumsiness, we stripped to bare hands to unwrap the engine and refill the heater. Contact with metal seared our fingers, a bone-numbing burn. Even without seeing, I knew my fingertips were icy white. Between small tasks like unscrewing a gas cap, we blew into our hands and smacked them together painfully.

"I have no idea if this heater will last all night," Ivan spoke over his shoulder as I followed his small muscular figure back to the cabin. "If it's frozen in the morning, we'll deal with it then, eh!"

In the clear cold morning, bellies warmed with coffee and a stack of pancakes, Ivan and I returned to the plane, carrying the battery, dreading what seemed certain to be a lengthy session with an engine frozen solid, lubricated with oil the consistency of soft asphalt.

Ivan unhooked a corner of the quilts and opened the engine cover enough to stick his hand in. A beatific grin creased his face. "Stick your hand in there," he said, stepping aside. It felt as warm inside the engine as the inside of our cabin. "Wow!"

Ivan almost chortled with relief and satisfaction. "An eight-hour heater!" he crowed.

Battery bolted down, covers stowed away, Ivan squeezed his heavily padded body into the cockpit and cranked her over. As near to immediate ignition as anyone has a right to expect after a -40°F night. The grin became a permanent fixture on Ivan's face, but he covered his elation by checking the dash, tinkering with instruments, and working the rudder, as if to imply that he expected nothing less from his plane.

We began to wonder if our weekly shower ritual had a causative relationship with our social life. The next weekend, shortly after we completed the cleansing process, the sound of a visiting snowmobile again caused an initial reaction of surprised confirming glances at each other, followed by a rush to the door. It was Ed and Margy, their identities hidden to the last by the neutralizing anonymity produced by seven or eight clothing layers.

Taught by their first visit to avoid the round-trip marathon in a single day, they came prepared to spend the night. Their heavy insulated boots clumped into the cabin, shaking the floor with weight. Layer after layer of jackets, face masks, sweaters, mitts, overpants amassed into a whopping pile of wool and synthetic and fur, puddles of melt-water spread onto the floor.

To bestow a special distinction on the evening, we got out a bottle of rye and declared generator night, turning the cabin electric for four hours, alternately opening the door to cool things off and adding logs to the stove to heat the room back up. Our home lost its usual vulnerable quality and became cocky and assertive. The card games lapsed into long interludes of conversation. Even after the generator sputtered out and we replaced the hard electric bulb with the ruddy ghostlight of candles, we kept dealing cards, pouring each other fresh drinks, making batches of popcorn, like old friends at the weekly poker party.

The next morning at breakfast, Ed mentioned that Stony Rapids had a Valentine's Day social dance scheduled that night. "Too bad you can't come to it," he added. But I could tell by his fidgety preoccupied silence that Ed was scamming something. "You know," he started, tapping the edge of the table for emphasis, "that snowmobile is brand new. I'll bet it will take all of us in."

Momentary silence. At first I dragged my heels, reluctant to leave the known warmth and serenity of our comfortable cabin, while drawn impulsively toward the adventure. "What about getting back?" I asked, throwing out niggling obstacles.

"Someone's always coming this way." Ed neatly steamrolled my objection. "One of the pilots can probably drop you off on a flight. Look, if the snowmobile can't handle the load, we'll just turn around and bring you back in!"

Inside of an hour we closed the cabin, swaddled ourselves cumbrously in winter clothes, and roared out of camp, four people and a dog behind a straining snowmobile.

The forty-five-mile run took nearly three hours. Temperatures stayed in the -30°F range with a cutting crosswind adding to the already severe artificial windchill created by our forward motion.

Ed and Margy rode up front, hunchbacked behind the windscreen, Margy's nose inches from Ed's rounded back. Marypat and Bandit squeezed uncomfortably into the wooden-sided toboggan. I rode in back on a small extension of corrugated roofing tin that made up the toboggan bottom and acted as an efficient heat conductor, remorselessly sucking warmth through the soles of my mukluks.

Periodically, we'd stop to limber up and pull out the coffee thermos. The frozen lid came off with difficulty and the cup trembled as it passed from hand to hand, the hot liquid searing our supercooled lips. We peered at each other's faces in search of frostbite.

"Looks like you got nipped on your cheekbone there," Ed pointed out a spot of white on my face. "How do I look?"

Two or three times the engine died, each time conjuring up images of trudging twenty miles to town or bivouacking overnight under the popping trees. The spark-plug wire kept loosening and falling off, until we finally effected a repair with some thin wire and a strap of duct tape, the repair kit staples. By the time the fuel silos in town appeared in front of us, we all moved like wards of an arthritis clinic, our jaws frozen stiff as if the cold had rusted them in place.

At the White Water Inn, remarkable luxuries blunted the effects of the cold ride most satisfactorily. Hot baths, a television movie channel, hamburgers, and a heated room—a weekend trip to Europe couldn't have promised more.

The dance took place in a corrugated Quonset hut with a concrete floor, a building euphemistically referred to as the Community Center. When we walked over at nine-thirty, the temperature already stood at -40°F outside, but inside, body heat warmed the cavernous room uncomfortably, and a choking pall of cigarette smoke would have given pause to the most hardened Los Angeles commuter.

Over two hundred Chipewyan were bent on getting their share of the finite booze supply. Rather than buy beer by the glass, people got it by the tray, and systematically worked their way through the forest of cups. At the front of the room a disc jockey played country-and-western music on a vintage phonograph, the tinny songs swallowed up in the metal building.

Marypat and I finally pioneered the dance floor, along with a few younger couples, and eventually the drinking pace settled down. The concrete floor filled with dancers, older couples jigging in a kind of Appalachian clogging style, the women dressed in long skirts and thick hose, plain black shoes on their feet. Younger couples stuck to the standard cling-and-sway style, more inhibited than their elders.

The effects of alcohol were evident. People pretty regularly missed their chairs when they sat down, and every table had representatives who cradled their heads in their arms, oblivious to the racket. Somebody puked in a corner. And fights began to break out, quickly nipped by a cadre of efficient bouncers who operated on orders to be ruthless. The simple solution to fist fights was to toss the combatants out the door into the -40°F night, where, presumably, animosities would be overwhelmed by the confrontation with death by freezing.

I had never been around a group of people who viewed fighting as the natural and inevitable result of normal conversation. But at one point I found myself cornered by a man whose tone grew more and more belligerent as time went on, and who began cracking his knuckles and making hostile gestures as he said things like, "This is my land!" or "I don't want to see you traveling in my land!" Before we came to what seemed the unavoidable conclusion of the encounter, Marypat rescued me with a request to dance, and my new acquaintance wandered off in search of fresh diversion.

By midnight most pugilists had been tossed out or worn out, the liquor supply was largely exhausted, and more serious dancing got under way. Marypat had become a popular partner, especially for the older men, and rarely had a break from the exertion. One old but energetic partner kept jigging faster and faster, Marypat enthusiastically keeping pace, until he suddenly stopped in mid-step, breathing heavily.

"You tire me out," he said, gripping Marypat by the elbows for support. "I'm seventy-six years old. You dance too fast."

A Chipewyan grandmother held the floor to the last, alcoholic euphoria or a sinewy constitution powering her along until, petticoats flying, she tipped over backward on the concrete in the middle of a particularly emphatic move.

"Oh no, she's broken her hip for sure!" I started to stand up. But she rolled up like a slightly out-of-condition gymnast, hardly skipping a beat of music.

Leaving the Quonset hut in the early bitter-cold morning, we maneuvered through clots of natives standing about in the night, apparently immune to the temperature, wearing short jackets and tight jeans, continuing whatever socializing they hadn't finished inside.

"Some of those older people still have to walk home," Ed told us as we headed back toward the inn. "The lady who fell down at the end? She has a three-mile walk to make, wearing that skirt and a light coat. I don't know how they do it! Most of these people would never normally act like that, but liquor is trouble every time."

I remembered Earl Kay saying that 90 percent of the problems in the north could be directly attributed to liquor. I thought of our distasteful summer encounters in the town of Athabasca, and contrasted them with the warmth and generosity we had enjoyed in Fond-du-Lac at Christmas, or the easy friendship of the natives who visited us at our cabin and had taken Marypat cranberry-picking with them.

Because of widespread alcohol abuse in the north, most native settlements have outlawed liquor altogether. Even so, a brisk bootleg business manages to supply people willing to pay outrageous sums for a bottle. Many older Chipewyan, people like Muglar and Eli, had experienced the debilitating effects of overindulgence and, unable to control the habit, had given up drinking completely.

Our trip back to Otherside Bay took several days to materialize. Ivan's plane developed mechanical problems after landing in lake slush, and nobody else seemed to be traveling west with room for passengers. Time to enjoy town comforts and visit with friends.

While Stony Rapids had only a few hundred residents, small by comparison to several nearby reserve communities, it functioned as the transportation center for the far northern tier of Saskatchewan. It was the only viable northern community that offered air service and a hotel and cafe.

Amenities came only with effort, however. Overnight comfort and convenience, taken for granted in less isolated places, were the product of rigorous labor at the White Water Inn. Ed and Margy cooked meals, waited tables, cut wood to heat the building, hauled water from a town well so guests could enjoy showers, pumped and hauled the hotel sewage, met guests at the plane when requested, arranged impromptu fishing trips in the summer and rented snowmobiles in the winter—and coped with an endless string of daily crises with matter-of-fact competence and cheerful humor. It was the first hotel I'd ever been able to say was worth every cent of the asking price.

Ed and I spent an afternoon hunting firewood by snowmobile. The trip involved fifteen or twenty miles of driving, several hours of floundering through hip-deep snow in a burn area, fighting with a reluctant powersaw in -30°F temperatures, and hauling back a toboggan-load of logs that repeatedly frustrated our attempts to lash them effectively in place.

The exciting moment of our foray came on the return trip, crossing the expanse of Stony Lake. Ivan, out test flying a 185 he'd been working on, spotted us and zoomed in for a low greeting. Northern pilots garner a sadistic glee from startling the wits out of unsuspecting travelers. The plane's skis came over us at a level that made me duck, and the blat of the engine roar hit us like a shock wave. I turned to see the plane wings waggle a farewell.

Enjoyable as the town visit was, we began despairing of ever getting back to the cabin. I had an image of the closed-up water hole thickening to a point that would require a chainsaw to cut through it. The spell of deep cold hung on.

But our way back surfaced as suddenly as had Ed's initial suggestion to come to town. A pilot Ivan knew had an empty flight going over to Uranium City. He called to offer a drop-off in Otherside Bay, if we could leave in fifteen minutes. We were there in ten. Less than an hour later, he landed us over a mile out in the bay, understandably sensitive to the danger of slush closer to the mouth of the river. As soon as we stood clear, he was off again, blasting us with the blizzard of his slipstream as the plane labored out of snow drifts and into the pale sky.

4

Our little cabin felt as if it had been abandoned for weeks. Inside, the still air bit our faces with cold. Everything had a brittle, fragile quality, ready to shatter at a touch. Marypat built a fire and, as smoke streamed from the chimney, I spent the rest of the morning bludgeoning the ice at the water hole with the blunt end of a pry bar, so we could dip up the life-sustaining liquid with our buckets.

It startled me to find how much I had missed our home, how content I felt at returning. With winter half gone, with friends in town, the cabin that had felt in October like a lonely unknown burrow in a vacuum of wilderness had become our chosen haven, the place I missed within a day or two of leaving it. In a curious way, given the short time I'd lived there, it felt as strongly like a home as anyplace I'd ever settled.

Sixteen feet wide and twenty feet long. Six paces by eight. Much of the inside cabin space was given over to our bed, the stove, and other furniture. The living area consisted of two narrow aisles, one on either side of the room partition, and a wider front section congested with the stove and a table. Because of the inescapable mass of time spent indoors, I had never come to know a small space more closely. Every knot in the floor, the corner where no amount of chinking stopped air from coming through to send fingers of frost along the wall on cold nights, the square views out the front windows, the unevenly joined pieces of plywood, the sound of the opening door, squeaks in the floor, the minute topography of our house.

The freezing, inexorably heaving ground under the cabin made the front door so tight one month that we had to rasp off wood to get it closed. The next month, the shifting earth made the fit so loose that the latch hardly caught, and cold air sucked through the crack as if filling a void. Every view, every household idiosyncrasy, every sound and texture became familiar, as if the cabin were a set of loose clothes we broke in and wore over the winter.

Marypat and I lived in excruciating intimacy, unable to avoid or escape each other in the compressed space. The ability to wander away literally entailed an act of imagination, an exercise in concentration. Physically, we remained within ten feet of each other for essentially all of eight months. No aspect of living, other than trips to the outhouse or walks taken alone, unfolded in privacy. On the cold nights, in order to avoid venturing outside, we peed into a slop bucket eight feet from where our partner slept.

Dressing, showering, eating, working, relaxing, sleeping, all of it accomplished as if we were hobbled together. Loosely bonded Siamese twins. Even outside, we walked together, took up opposite ends of the same saw, helped each other carry heavy logs, teamed up to jockey the water sled from the water hole to the cabin, and navigated the thin ice crossing to the garbage dump in wary tandem, each carrying a long pole in case we broke through. We had worked out the dynamics of a rescue beforehand.

If a thought played on my mind, I had only two ways to go with it, inward or to Marypat. Compromise and negotiation underlay every move. How long a work session lasted, when to turn on the radio, when to eat, whose turn to get up and start the fire, whether to play cribbage or Scrabble, what book to read, where to sit. Every small movement and disruption affected the equilibrium of the other person, as if each of us carried a magnetic field that attracted or repelled the other's.

Emotional eruptions broke through the surface of our tight lives like frightful volcanic storms. We'd catch ourselves arguing about absurd meaningless points as if our future lay in the balance.

"Let's go out and get some wood, Marypat."

"Why? It seems like we've got plenty."

"I've been watching the stack. This cold spell has shrunk our supply down incredibly. I'd just feel better if we had more wood. Besides, today's a good day for being outside. What if we get a bunch of new snow and couldn't get around?"

"But I'm working on a drawing." Marypat sat at her desk, colored pencils littered around her, the disruption of her work an obvious annoyance.

"Can't you take a break?"

"Can't we cut wood another time?"

Neither of us was willing to let go, digging into argumentative trenches, our patterns at odds. The argument had an evil will of its own.

Defeated, angry at myself and at my irascible cabin mate, I'd stump around getting dressed to go outside, flinging clothes in corners, making an ass of myself.

"Where are you going?" Marypat's working rhythm had evaporated. Irritability brooded between us.

"Outside." And I'd be out the door, Bandit at my heels, leaving Marypat to try to reassemble her shattered mood.

Cabin fever. A malady born of confinement, of boredom, of bumping into each other. The mind turned restless and conniving by inactivity and limited stimulation. Sometimes we could deflect it. Catching ourselves in the middle of a pointless debate, we'd shrug it off like an annoying article of clothing, brand the argument a cabin-fever outbreak, and go for a walk or cut wood to defuse the tension, teaming up to face the threat.

But also there were poisonous times, when we lacked the perspective to identify the tension or the will to avoid it, and we fought like animals held too long in a cage, the unnatural proximity breaking out in meaningless disturbing conflict. Later, recovered from an outburst, we would be sheepish as alcoholics after a binge, frightened by the destructive emotional storm, reawakened to the fact of our dependence on each other.

Even the small disagreements frightened us with their potential. The prospect of an atmosphere of acrimony—a bilious cloud of discontent hovering within the tiny living space, invading our bed, between us like thunder—terrified us. When the prospect of irreconcilable conflict peeped over the horizon like a black planet, the realization of our need for each other beat it back into darkness. We balanced along a line between necessary support and the need for space and privacy, like high-wire artists who know that no net waits below to catch them.

While saddled by the closeness of our living quarters, we were graced with a luxury of time and serenity of setting. Without the pressure of an externally imposed schedule, we could indulge in discussions for hours, and often did, spending whole chunks of a day reminiscing about past adventures, continuing a debate about our spiritual beliefs, sharing the plot of a book.

The same expanse of free time that could threaten our stability also bestowed an immense wealth upon us. The horizon of time exposed my insignificance, dwarfed my productive efforts, and yet, the lack of tension, the freedom to ponder thoughts, the power to indulge my whims, infused me with a sanguine outlook.

Isolated together, marooned and secure, Marypat and I couldn't help but understand each other more deeply. Physically we yoked up for the heavy labor around the cabin. Emotionally we gauged the need for support and challenge, almost barometrically sensitive to shifts in mood and attitude. In the mornings we discussed our dreams. At night we shared a reading candle. Breaking trail through the woods, we stepped in each other's tracks like foxes.

5

Against my better judgment, but unable to keep myself from it, I had begun counting toward spring on December 22, the day after solstice. Though the cold deepened for months and winter held the north in an unrelenting grip week after week, I took great heart in the return of light. We delayed firing the lantern some nights until we were reduced to finding our way around with arms outstretched like blind people, as if by this ploy we actually made the day longer.

When the first brief thaws arrived, they were, in a way, cruel jokes. We knew they could not last, but the surge of restless excitement rose regardless, like the wakened sap in trees. Disappointment was inevitable, the return to winter a foregone certainty, the short fragrant warmth a tease. They were cruel, but I wouldn't have liked to do without them. The brief warm spells were a promise, a pledge of more to come.

Even as early as February, the weather warmed up on a few days, sending tendrils of balmy air into the north. At least it felt balmy to us. The temperature stayed above zero overnight only three times all month. But during the last week, the thermometer soared to near freezing, an unbelievable heat wave when we hadn't seen 20°F since November.

Squirrels, invisible since before Christmas, suddenly appeared above ground, busily shredding pine cones on platforms of snow, sending Bandit into a joyous but ineffectual frenzy of hunting. Ravens wheeled in the sky, their complaints like the sound of nails being pulled from wood.

On walks through the forest we wore only light jackets and no hats. Small pockets of warm air, tinged with the scent of spruce sap, caressed our bare faces, stopping us short to inhale and taste. Animal tracks laced and looped through the snow, and I read exuberance in the hops and strides, playfulness in the long wiggly otter slides. Our ears were assailed by the small scrabbling sounds of life.

The earliest whiffs of spring, exploratory, diffident, quick to retreat, still managed to coax a few birds along—birds that must have been wintering just over the southern skyline, and who, I imagined, were imbued with the same restless urgings that we were.

Small flocks of white-winged crossbills or common redpolls arrived like advance scouts probing the hostile frontier, bravely boisterous to keep up group morale, reconnoitering the still-daunting hinterland— but then vanished, as though they were issued only a three-day pass. The twittering of flocks in the upper branches of forest sounded like school-children at recess.

So what if, after a day, winter reasserted its dominance with savage vengeance, sending all creatures back into their burrows, snipping off the buds of enthusiasm. Spring was assured!

Visitors became a fairly regular occurrence, as though the restless-ness caused by longer days and mitigating temperatures had become epidemic. Planes buzzed low over the cabin almost daily, the loud greeting unfailingly successful in getting us out on the porch to wave. Eli pulled up one late afternoon, driving a dog team, his approach signaled only at the very last by the jingling bells on the dog harnesses, a sound that created absurd Santa Claus images in my mind.

Chopping up whitefish with a hatchet, he threw each dog a third of a frozen fish to keep them busy while he visited. "Like wolves," he said, watching them gulp their portions with a single flash of teeth. "Eat everything. Bones, heads, all of it."

He wanted to set a trap or two nearby and asked us to check them if he wasn't able to come back for a few days. "What if we find something in them?" I questioned, knowing but dreading the answer.

"Wear gloves," Eli said. "Put your hand around the neck, or twist the head." He demonstrated with his gloved hands, a quick, methodical twist so practiced that I almost heard the snap of a spinal cord. Eli pulled a small frozen marten out of a coat pocket, stiff as a log. That day's catch.

We avoided Eli's traps for days, afraid to find something struggling there, but when we finally checked, found nothing. I walked all around the sets nearest our cabin, leaving my man scent, notifying the small creatures, and fervently hoping they took heed.

Eli's son Albert roared up a week later, fresh from his trapline, and showed us the lynx he'd just killed, limp and warm in his arms, large padded feet hanging down as Albert held him up by the neck for us to admire. "Worth four hundred dollars," he said, grinning.

Visitors in February kept mentioning the possibility of an ice road. In the same way that northern residents speculate about the arrival of barges when the water is open, the brief clearing of an ice road, linking northern settlements to roads in the south and making it possible to bring up a load of supplies by semi truck, provided fodder for weeks of heated conversation.

In the first week of March, the ice road was punched through across the lake to Fond-du-Lac, and from there to Stony Rapids and Black Lake. A convoy of semi trucks followed a heavy plow across the ice, hauling precious gasoline, food, snowmobiles, crates of Pampers, and hardware. Scouts in front took ice cores to check thickness and probed the way like desert travelers fearful of quicksand.

Ed and Margy called, a giddy edge to their voices. "The ice road is here," they told me. "We're going on a road trip! Want to meet us?"

"Wait a minute! Meet you where? To do what?"

"We'll call you just before we leave," Ed had clearly been strategizing for this one. "You walk out to the road, and we'll pick you up."

As usual, plans for our return were vague and glossed over.

"You'll get back. Ivan can fly you. Maybe you can pick up a ride with the trucks. No problem."

Marypat and I exchanged glances, a quick conference, a shrug of shoulders. "What the hell," I said. "Sure! We'll be there."

A few hours later we embarked on our third trip away from camp since October. The cabin closed behind us, Marypat, Bandit, and I headed out on the lake, primed to rendezvous in an hour on the road. Recent winds and deep drifts made walking arduous, the packs on our backs adding to the difficulty. All along, I had assumed that the ice road would follow the same path as the snowmobile trail, which crossed the mouth of Otherside Bay. At the most, a forty-five minute walk. I kept looking for signs of a road scar or a passing vehicle that would give us the precise location.

Finally, I saw what looked like a snowmobile traveling past, and took out binoculars to be sure. "Damn," I muttered, when I focused in.

"What's the matter?" Marypat asked from my side.

"Well, first off, that's not a snowmobile, it's a pickup truck. It only looks like a snowmobile because it's so far away. The road is all the way across the lake!"

To begin with, our plans to join Ed and Margy were inexact. Neither party knew the actual route of the road. One group traveled by snowshoe, the other by truck. One started from forty-five miles away, the other from three or four. The potential margin for error covered an area roughly five miles by four. We had started off by underestimating the distance to the road by roughly 300 percent.

"We better get moving," I put the binoculars away.

Trudging across the vast white lake—snowshoes alternately sinking into drifts and scraping across a hard wind-grooved surface—had the feel of marching across a Siberian wasteland. The likelihood of missing our meeting overwhelmed me. Once the light failed, sighting the far shore would be impossible.

We straggled on across the ice. Distances on the unvaried surface proved deceiving. The far shoreline looked no closer even after long stints of fast walking. I worked up a sweat, despite the cold air. The road almost appeared to move away as we approached, like a mirage that tantalized but never materialized. As we drew nearer, I made out a truck driving up from the east. Could it be them? It seemed unbelievable that, given all the variables, our two parties might intersect with such choreographed perfection. The truck moved closer, but I couldn't see faces. I hurried ahead. No honk, no flash of lights, no waving hands. The truck drew up and went on by, as if we weren't there.

Marypat caught up. "That had to be them!"

I turned to her. "I wonder if those jerks were playing a joke."

As if in reply, we saw the truck returning, now could make out familiar smiling faces. We all crammed into the cab of a three-quarter-ton truck. Three dogs scrambled about in back, occasionally leaping out and causing us unplanned stops to recover them. Boxed wine and quantities of dubious homemade beer fueled a level of celebration that sucked us into its vortex like the winds of a tornado.

The truck continued on its boisterous way, winding along the north shore of the lake to Fond-du-Lac. The road followed almost exactly the same route we had taken by canoe, skirting the wide bays, curving through flocks of islands, creating a bizarre case of déjà vu as we saw the same landscape we had watched go by in our canoe wake. I shook my head and laughed out loud.

"There's our last campsite, Marypat," I pointed to a frozen knoll off to the north.

A convoy of semi trucks idled at the brink of lake ice in Fond-du-Lac. Drawn up like Conestoga wagons on the Oregon Trail, the trucks and their drivers had a good deal in common with early pioneers. To the west, the lake stretched off under gauzy low clouds, the road discernible only for a few hundred yards before it blended into the general whiteness. Half a dozen trucks, emptied of their wares, would follow the single plow back across mile after mile of black ice and pressure ridges, the spread of lake wide as any prairie, over treacherous and undetectable thin spots in the ice. We heard stories of the weight of trucks actually setting up waves in the ice if they went too fast or if the trucks bunched too closely together.

By comparison, we were on a joy ride. The journey into town had no purpose beyond its own small absurd adventure, and we played it to the hilt. Natives shook their heads at the conglomeration of tipsy whites, as baffled as I had been by the Chipewyan behavior at the social dance. For hours we busily did nothing, cruising the two or three streets, chasing down canines enticed out of the truck by strings of howling sled dogs, and puttering aimlessly about with nothing to do, thoroughly entertained nonetheless.

Our return to Stony Rapids, following the beam of a single truck headlight, seemed to take half the night. At least we didn't have to worry about making a wrong turn in the dark. The road held us in a deep rut, almost a tunnel. Inside the truck, we sang bawdy songs, rambled off into spontaneous fits of horribly rhyming group poetry, and then lapsed into breath-catching silences, the murky, white, featureless world going by the windows, truck wheels treading with impunity on top of water dozens of feet deep.

The ice road lasted only a week, just long enough for the trucks to come and go, and then collapsed with disuse, the northern settlements abandoned again, the road drifting over so that travelers went back to using the old snowmobile track.

Marypat and I spent two days at the White Water Inn before Ivan offered to fly us back. He flew at his preferred altitude, something well under a hundred feet. "I like to window shop," he explained. He flew low and acrobatically enough to identify and follow moose tracks, the broad ridges along the lake a good deal higher than the small plane. "I see so much pretty country," Ivan pointed to some fast, open water in a river, "but I never get to touch it."

He took us on a tight loop above the land near camp, the wings canted over so that I looked straight down at the forest below. We could see our trail network, our claimed land, and recognized the landmarks we'd become familiar with over the winter. At the most turbulent rapids on the river, the water had already begun eroding the ice. Ivan skimmed in over the willows, ptarmigan flushing out from under the plane skis, and landed us on our home bay.

Alone again at the cabin, relieved at the silence, I suddenly saw how far we had come from the timid and nervous state of mind with which we had begun the winter, when we set out across the expanse of season like paddling the first tentative miles through unmapped country. Looking back over the last months gave me a sense of satisfaction, like glancing over my shoulder at my broken snowshoe trail across an untracked meadow.

More important than the physical accomplishments, the stacks of firewood, and successfully overcome obstacles, I treasured the knowledge of friendships, an emotional warmth like the weight of an extra blanket on a cold night. The difference between March and October had as much to do with the wealth of companionship as with the matured confidence in our ability to survive.

PART VII

SPRING

Except for the Christmas visit to Fond-du-Lac, we had lived lonely, self-absorbed lives from October to February, weeks and even months going by between human contacts. After February it seemed we achieved minor celebrity status. Our Stony Rapids friends had come to view Otherside Bay as a vacation destination, their rustic getaway, and came as often as they could. A Saskatchewan radio station somehow got wind of us and called on the mobile phone for an interview. We became an informally established way station for travelers. Guests dropped by frequently enough that we grew shy about the timing of our showers, for fear visitors might arrive during our naked sprint around the cabin.

One exceptional afternoon in late March, fifteen people crammed into the confined quarters of our home. They arrived unexpectedly, the whine of snowmobiles obliterated by howling March winds, the crush of humanity suddenly materializing out of a swirl of thick snow in front of our porch.

Several miles down the lake shore from us, the Fond-du-Lac school had a winter camp, an organized attempt to teach traditional skills. A few settlement elders had been coerced into the project, camping out for the weekend with several teachers and any students who could be enticed along. Apparently the blizzardlike conditions had curtailed planned camp activities, and when two teachers announced they were going to visit our cabin, an entourage of thirteen teenagers clamored to come along for the ride.

For an hour or two I questioned the cabin's structural ability to withstand the onslaught, half expecting the walls to collapse on top of us. While mittens and hats flew through the air and a Chipewyan whirlwind gusted around us, we tried to visit with the teachers. Conversation had as much chance as a black-fly hatch in January. Before any major damage occurred, the teachers rounded up their charges for the return trip, the two snowmobiles almost invisible under the load. They left us with an invitation to visit their camp.

The native camp had been pitched in the woods at the back of a small bay, screened from view by spruce and jack pine, the smell of burning wood our first sensory clue to its location. When we snowshoed up, Eli and another man, August, were harnessing their dog teams. The older men operated two of the few remaining dog teams in Fond-du-Lac. Snowmobiles had so completely supplanted the older form of locomotion that the youngsters, who were there for instruction, had no experience with dogs. Dog harness, sled, and men were tied into a contorted, writhing mess in the snow. The men alternately called out, "Ha!" and "Whoa!" to which their dogs responded with sudden starts and stops while the drivers worked snarls out of the traces. The dogs frequently let their enthusiasm overwhelm their obedience and had to be stopped bodily from running off.

August's team wore embroidered blanket saddles that were worked into the harness system. The small energetic dogs looked like diminutive ponies underneath. Within minutes of our arrival, we shed our packs and snowshoes, and hopped onto the sleds for a spin on the lake. Eli and August prided themselves on their teams' strength and responsiveness, a subtle competitiveness underlying the journey across the lake ice.

At one point, when August intimated that I might be a bit heavy for the dogs to pull, Eli blandly offered to take both Marypat and me in his sled. From inside the toboggan, we watched the working backs of the dogs out ahead, the sled bottom thumping along the ice while the driver stood at the back, encouraging the animals with cryptic grunts and calls, barking commands that the dogs responded to by turning left or right.

At the shout "Whoa!" the dogs immediately stopped, panting heavily. If the break lasted more than a few seconds, they curled up in the snow in furry circles. Along the way Eli and August demonstrated the process of making trap sets—staking down the chain, priming trap jaws, and sprinkling snow over the metal—even though only two students had bothered to come for the lesson.

Many native youths had no interest in learning the old skills, saw no application of them in their lives. The children who were interested very likely didn't even attend the camp, for that very reason, and instead spent their time living on the trapline with their parents. For them, the lessons would have been a waste of time, basic skills one learns the first morning in the bush.

Most of the students viewed the camp-out simply as a break from settlement living, a chance to be out with their friends. Back at the wall tents, Angela and another woman were instructively pounding strips of caribou meat on rocks with the blunt side of a hatchet, but again, no schoolchildren observed. Unperturbed, the two women worked without fuss or hurry, pounding meat from a large mound and then hanging the thin strips inside a plastic tepee-style smokehouse. Meanwhile, the kids listened to Top 40 music on a tape player and hung about outside the tents, shoving each other around, laughing at jokes, the northern version of teens loitering outside the neighborhood hangout.

With the caribou meat curing over a smoldering fire, the native adults set about preparing dinner. August fried bannock in Crisco over a Coleman stove. "*Dene* doughnuts," he told us, with a gummy smile, using the general term natives employ to refer to themselves. Cigarette dangling from her mouth, Angela rethatched the spruce-bough floor, layering the woven boughs over the litter left behind on the previous level, her strong brown hands efficiently tucking and fitting branches until the entire floor had a fresh pungent covering.

In the main wall tent the adults sat cross-legged in a rough circle, mid-day meal before us on a sheet of plastic. The culinary entree sat in a large stewpot, brimming with greasy broth and loaded with assorted caribou bones and chunks of meat. The odd vegetable floating in the stew was largely ignored. Accepted etiquette involved fishing out a meaty morsel, landing it on your plate, and working it over with fingers and a knife, until the bone had been stripped clean.

The natives ate with graphic thoroughness and relish, downing gristle, marrow, sinew, spinal cord, everything but the hardest bones. Between main assaults on the meat, people reached for pieces of bannock to sop up broth on their plates. Marypat and I watched closely, and followed the example of our hosts as best we could. I thought I had managed a creditably complete job on my boney hunk of caribou, and added it to the glistening bone pile, only to see August pick it back out and finish it off properly. The older Chipewyan displayed an intimate familiarity with the animal they consumed, knowing the exact contours of each bone, where the most recessed and secretive bits of meat hid away, how to hold and maneuver each piece.

Inside the wall tent, a small airtight stove kept the temperature comfortable, and we reclined against bedrolls and duffles, the litter from our primitive repast scattered around us, conversation at low tide. By late afternoon the clear day turned bitter cold, and we helped haul in more firewood to ward off the chill. The sled dogs curled up by their stakes, noses tucked under tails like small, off-color mounds of snow.

People began making evening raids to the smoking rack, pulling off the long strips of "drymeat" that had been curing longest. The smokey meat had turned stringy but still had a moist pliable quality, a lean and faintly gamey flavor. Natives spread lard on the meat before eating it, just as if they were putting butter on toast. I tried it their way, and was surprised to find it very palatable.

We passed around bags of dried fruit that our hosts gobbled up like candy, and spent the evening in a lazy bi-cultural circle, sharing experiences, passing food, asking questions, feeling the cold gusts when people came and went through the tent flap.

Eli and August expressed curiosity over our equipment—sleeping bags, packs, coats, inflatable sleeping pads. They studied the gear with practiced eyes, men who had lived in conditions unfathomably harsh by our standards, and made do nicely without the aid of Gore-tex, Quallofill, and Thinsulate. While they peered at sleeping bag construction, we examined their canvas wraparound mukluks, worn over felt liners, comfortable in the coldest conditions.

They immediately saw the advantage of compact lightweight equipment for our kind of travel, and discussed aspects of our gear in fast-paced Chipewyan, but showed no envy, no interest in trading. They had spent a lifetime learning the best ways to dress, the most efficient way to pack a toboggan, pitch a tent, choose a campsite. More important, they could read the sky and the wind, tracks in the snow, thin ice. All the modern trappings money can buy couldn't allow me to approach the harmonious state in which they lived out of doors. Their level of comfort and competence in the wilderness resulted from a state of mind, a practiced inheritance that cannot be picked up at a store or learned by reading the latest manual. How many more generations would carry on that quality of grace?

Marypat and I laid out our sleeping bags between the natives' bedrolls, their bulky foam pads and layers of blankets next to our nylon mummy bags. As the fire died out, the cold intensified, outside temperatures at least -30°F. My summer bag kept me comfortable about half the night, and after that I kept waking, shivering, sleeping in short naps, deeply burrowed in my cocoon, waiting for first light and the sounds of someone stoking the stove. When I heard August stirring about, I dressed warmly and sidled up to within a foot of the stove, soaking up the pulsing heat. We made a pot of coffee and conversed in monosyllabic spurts that were separated by long coffee-sipping, stove-feeding silences, while the sleeping forms of our comrades procrastinated in the face of the frigid morning.

The late March sun came over the horizon by seven-thirty and arced more boldly across the southern sky. Even better, the rays actually had a discernible warming effect. On cold nights the temperature routinely dropped to -20° or -30°F, but by mid-day we could go about outside in light jackets or long-sleeved shirts, without wearing hats. By the time we returned to our cabin from the native camp, the exercise of snowshoeing had forced us to strip off our coats and hats, and reopening our home amounted to little more than building a fire to thaw things out.

2

We had received word that our Wisconsin friend, Grant Herman, would visit us at the end of March—the only acquaintance who took our invitation to come north seriously. His four-day journey to our cabin turned out to be a transportation medley, as if he consciously set out to experience every possible form of travel. It went like this: an eight-hour drive in a 1967 pickup truck from central Minnesota to Thunder Bay, Ontario; a discount-fare train ride to Regina, Saskatchewan, on the way missing his Winnipeg connection to Saskatoon, which necessitated a day's delay and an extra bus connection; a flight north to Stony Rapids, where Ed and Margy met him; and finally, a three-hour snowmobile ride behind Stan's assistant, Bill, across Lake Athabasca to Otherside Bay.

On the other end, we waited at the cabin for Grant's arrival, apprised only of the delay caused by his missed train connection. For the first time all winter, the weather turned surprisingly soggy, positively wet. On the day he arrived a sleety snow dripped out of heavy clouds and the deep drifts turned into a morass of white concrete.

Appalled and disheartened by the wet early-warming trend, Mary-pat and I had cooked dinner and left the door open, so we would hear the sound of approaching snowmobile. Late in the afternoon I swore I heard an engine, but when I stood on the porch, listening, I couldn't be sure. Perhaps it had been the stove draft moaning with the rush of air. I went back inside. Then it came again, a distant motor. My ear cocked, I heard my friend's emphatic voice, an unmistakable four-letter expletive floating clearly through the air. Grant had made it, almost.

When we snowshoed past the windsock, we saw that deep slushy snow in the bay had proved too much for Bill's snowmobile. The two men struggled with the mired vehicle, which was stuck as irrefutably as if the snow were mud. After the four of us freed Bill's machine from the hole and sent him off on his way, Grant's final half-mile, the cap to his heroic multi-vehicle journey, was made by ski.

He came as an emissary from the world we left behind the moment we slid away downstream from Jasper. All our other winter visitors were part of our adventure, acquaintances who embodied fresh chapters in the unfolding journey. Grant re-attached the umbilical cord we had severed, his presence a flesh and blood contact from the world we had, until then, touched only with letters and an occasional distant telephone voice.

With other visitors, we listened and learned and probed, mining them for information and assistance. With Grant, we were like third graders giving our parents a school tour, stumbling over each other to illustrate our northern experience. We fed him moose specialties, made him look down the four-foot ice well on the lake, proudly explained the shower rig, read him essays and showed him drawings, retold the bear story, and bit by bit, revealed the difficulties and joys of our winter internment.

Grant brought with him three complete sets of ski equipment—boots, poles, skis, and wax—to make up for the touring season we'd lost when the postal service wouldn't send our gear. Every day we explored our trail system and pioneered new areas, fell down the hills we'd snowshoed all winter.

The warm weather continued, turning the trails into icy bobsled runs and rendering the waxes wholly ineffective. Confident of cold weather, we had told Grant to leave behind the sticky klisters that would have at least made hill-climbing marginally workable. As it was, we took off our skis and ignobly walked up even short inclines.

The most absurd aspect of Grant's visit involved our attempts to manufacture klisterlike substances with the materials at hand. We turned to a series of experiments noteworthy for their creative ingenuity as well as their abysmal failures on the trail.

Our first foray married organic and synthetic ingredients. Five minutes' work in the spruce forest behind the cabin, scraping away at tree trunks with the edge of a tin can, yielded us a cup or more of sticky natural resin. Melted down over the stove, this metamorphosed into a promising-looking slurry of amber adhesive with a heady north woods fragrance.

"Hey, hey!" Grant raised his eyebrows at me. "Looks pretty sticky, but let's cut in some blue wax for color."

We spooned in a healthy dollop of special blue, and spread the glop onto our skis. The trial run produced a euphoric kick-and-glide for roughly twenty feet, at which point the brittle application peeled off.

The most successful concoction combined spruce resin, crystallized honey, Aunt Jemima pancake syrup, and red wax. Bubbling thickly in the saucepan, appearing like some multi-hued thermal mud pot, the stuff looked evil enough to do the trick. A brief turn in front of the cabin proved encouraging. Off we went, enjoying for the first time a real grip and reasonable glide. Five minutes out, I was rash enough to christen the situation "ideal Aunt Jemima conditions." About that time the home remedy wore off.

Grant had five days to spend with us before embarking on the ludicrously convoluted return journey. As with our few trips to town, the nature and particulars of his transportation back to Stony Rapids remained vague and foggy, but we ignored that as long as we could.

The demonstration of friendship Grant evidenced by his marathon travel north swept away any tendency to bog down in social nicety or frivolous etiquette. He had been a partner on earlier adventures, the other half of a canoeing team, a workmate, my best friend. And so we bathed him in an outpouring of insights and perceptions, conflicts and frustrations, fears and expectations. As if Grant were a sounding board, his visit a dress rehearsal, we lived the parts that had become ours but that we had not yet put to the test with our old friends.

He brought a series of treats with him, which he unveiled day by day at opportune moments. A bottle of peppermint schnapps one evening, a block of Wisconsin swiss cheese at lunch, a can of salsa and green chilies, artichoke hearts, chocolate Easter bunnies, tidbits of luxury from the south.

On Easter morning Grant introduced us to a Polish custom, a traditional toast to family and friends. Using dehydrated eggs and homemade bread as a substitute for whatever more ethnically appropriate food is normally utilized, we made small speeches commemorative of our relationships with each other, and then ate bits of food off a toothpick, a gastronomic seal on the statement.

Standing in a circle, no other human within twenty miles, the stove radiating its warmth, we looked each other in the eye and said things that otherwise somehow never get said. The cabin felt too small to contain the glow of feeling, the intensity of our interaction creating an energy too large for the shell around us. We clasped together in a triangular embrace and then laughed at our weepy tendencies.

Grant's departure, pending almost as soon as he had arrived, loomed too quickly before us. Arrangements for his return had to be worked out.

The warm weather complicated matters by making the dirt airstrip at Stony Rapids soft and muddy. Small planes could still take off and land, but the strip became too mushy to handle the larger planes that flew south. Ed called to tell us flights had been suspended. "Last year we went two weeks before big planes could land again!"

A teacher we had met at the Chipewyan camp offered to take Grant to town with him if we could meet him at the trail early in the morning. Timed perfectly to prove the truth of our stories about the deep cold, the thermometer fell to -45°F on Grant's final night, and I walked him out to the rendezvous in the familiar biting air. We said goodbye at the edge of the snowmobile trail, on the armored surface of the tremendous lake, embracing through the bulky mittened layers. Grant climbed onto the toboggan and waved once before gripping the handles for balance and then roaring eastward across the white vastness, a forty-five-mile journey that would take longer than his six-hundred-mile flight south.

3

On April 1 the bald eagles returned. I sighted one flying with a small flock of ravens, and thought at first it was a trick of perspective that made the one bird seem so dominant. But in the next days we saw several flying over the bay and circling up the river, perhaps the same birds we had last seen in the early gray days of November.

Upriver the eagles roosted above a fast open stretch of water, and we watched them surreptitiously for clues to their nesting site. They chose a jack pine with a view over the moving water and a high cradle of branches in which they secured their heavy platform nest. Sometimes we caught sight of the wide-winged birds bringing sticks and tufts of river grass to add to the nest, trailing housing material from their strong talons.

We even watched, astonished, while the eagles copulated one afternoon, the male descending in a slow hover to cover the squawking female. When they completed their ungainly tryst, the two birds perched next to each other on the windy branch, stroking and preening each other's white, fiercely beaked heads.

Drawn by the drama of ice breakup, our walks gravitated to the Otherside River. After the stark silent winter, the sound of opening burgeoning water pulled us toward it. Even at the cabin I listened for the new noise, the rush and combat of the season, the environmental excitement.

Eaten away from the bottom up by current, ice at the middle of the river slowly bowed down, at first a slight swayback, then a pronounced valley, and, finally, complete collapse, fracturing away from the thick ice on the banks to be gnawed and devoured by the resentful torrent.

Huge angular floes obstructed the current like white boulders, damming channels, creating short-lived rapids and ledges, resisting the hungering force of liquid, but swelling the river's volume as they succumbed. Even stints of cold weather couldn't hold back the new watery strength. The seasonal corner had been turned. As inexorably as the ice had tightened the vise in November, the river reasserted its voice and dominance in April and May.

We cheered the river spirit on, and took up floe-hopping as a form of sport, our way of participating in the spring celebration. Leaving the stable edge of ice still anchored to the banks, a solid bench five feet thick, we jumped onto ice dams and isolated bergs, leapt along strings of stranded cubes, and minced across ice bridges, the current sucking and pulling just below our feet. What wonderful sound, that pure swelling water—running, running, running—curling past the sharp-angled ice, tearing away softened hunks, wearing channels in the yellowed layers still clinging to the streambed. Like children, we lost whole afternoons to the play, our laughter in harmony with the river's.

But the lake ice remained solid and unmovable, as vast and unbroken and titanic as in January. Even at the mouth of the river, the steady battering current took days to make a dent in the bay ice. Our water hole made slow movements, not enough yet to keep ice from forming on it, but a slight agitation still, and bits of weed and grass came up in our buckets. One morning a dead whitefish surfaced, loosened from lake ice or carried down by the river, a winter casualty.

March and April were the windy months, turbulence at the flux of seasons, the combat zone. Wet snow piled into whopping drifts. The sled course from the water hole traversed a range of steep-fronted hills, precipitous declines down which we ran in front of our load—and more than once lost the entire supply in a sled capsize. Our hardened trail resisted the melting influence and became a low ridge along which we balanced on an icy rail; six inches to one side, we fell to our waists in the drifts.

Days at a time the wind blew, whipping up ground blizzards as thick and swirling as sandstorms in the desert, streams of hurrying snow six inches above the ground, spuming off the tops of cornices like white hair. The draft in the stovepipe sounded like a far-off barge or the howl of a lone wolf. Sometimes the rush of air damped the fire down and backed up the smoke so that sooty clouds billowed in our faces when we opened the stove door to add fuel.

Between wind and the still-daunting cold snaps, warm afternoons coaxed us outside, where we read books in pools of sun, threw snowballs for Bandit to chase, watched for new birds—sapsuckers and redpolls, crossbills and fox sparrows—porch sitting as if we lived in Georgia or North Carolina, soaking the sun in through our naked white skin.

The sun jumped into the sky in the mornings, and I found myself hopping out of bed to greet it, unable to stay prone, making up for months of darkness and sloth. We hardly bothered with lanterns by the end of April, and took long sauntering walks after dinner, still managing to return before dark.

Knowing that bear would come out from their winter dens soon, I began looking for tracks in the snow. And the wolves returned. We saw them first well up the river, on the far bank. Three phantom shadows in the wind-gusting snow, they trotted off at the sight of us, but we could make out their wide tracks along the edge of open water.

"Where's the fourth one?" I wondered.

"I'll bet it's the one Eli told us had been shot earlier in the winter," Marypat voiced my own thought. The attrition in the small pack, if indeed we were correct, made us feel as if a neighbor family had lost a child, leaving a sad gap in the local equilibrium that we were used to.

We caught quick glimpses of the wolves along the edge of the bay, creamy long-legged creatures with wariness in every step, not as bold as they had been earlier in the season. They didn't seem to howl as often as in the cold months, the impulse perhaps subdued during the denning time of the year. It seemed to me, also, that there was less need to voice one's mourning in spring. Wolf howls sound right in gray light, when life is difficult and bitter and hunger waits on the fringes of every day.

It takes opening water to bring the birds back in numbers, and then it happens with a staggering rush. One morning, from inside the cabin, I heard the unmistakable carrying honk of Canada geese. The noisy pair circled the small patch of open bay, then sedately slid out of the sky to land smack in the water.

Then, within what seemed a matter of hours, the sun-sparkled water exerted a magnetic force on other birds. The ubiquitous and assertive mallard, the whistling-winged goldeneye, opportunistic gulls, more geese, hovering hawks, shrill killdeer. The bedlam of arrival was cacophonous. I would never have expected to find such unbridled enjoyment in the raucous combat of herring gulls or the pedestrian barnyard plaint of mallards.

Binoculars lay close at hand on my work table, atop the field guide. Many times each day I grabbed them to discover what made the new noise or whether the quick-winged arrival might be the first yellowlegs. Snow buntings, nattily attired in summer plumage, twittered in hyperactive flocks across the ground, just as they had in October, making the long months in between feel like no more than a scene break onstage, time to change costumes.

The ptarmigan, our winter comrades, fled northward as if unable to cope with the loud crowds. They shunned the soft life, leaving as soon as things became easy again to move north in search of snow and cold. For weeks we had seen their white molting feathers caught in vegetation, and their bodies already looked mottled as they left for the tundra. They went ahead as our point scouts, and as I saw the last few of them around camp, I wondered if we might stumble across them again that summer while making a portage or setting up a camp.

At night I stood on the porch, smelling sunlight in the wind, listening to the swelling river. Even the northern lights looked warm, the green wreaths soft and pulsing, as if with heat. Recapturing the memories of winter's fierce somnolence took a rigorous act of imagination.

In April and May, with light and life and warmth returning, I wondered what all the fuss of winter had been about. I would think to myself that winter hadn't been so tough after all. Comfort glosses over hardship so quickly. I forgot the battles with sluggish propane, minimized the jarring daily drudgery of pounding open the water hole, discounted the pallid mocking eye of a December sun that barely glimmered above the southern earth rim, chuckled at the weeks of -40°F weather, and laid aside the frantic trapped upwellings that had filled my heart some mornings when I woke in the frosted silent cabin.

The snow melted, sucked up on warm days with astonishing quickness. Each day, new bedraggled bits of ground reappeared, shabbylooking, as if not yet prepared for the sudden shameless disrobing. Bandit scented the wind with renewed interest, and I tested the breezes as well, with less acuity but no less vigor. In the forest I could smell the running sap of pine, pungent and green, earthy. I recalled the warm damp smell of moss, the resiny tang of pine bark, the fishy whiffs of riverbanks. My pale skin accepted the caress of the sun. I took the soft winds in my face, drinking them down.

In the first week of May we found the bear tracks we had been looking for. A line of familiar pad imprints made a trail in the melting snow, heading downriver toward our camp. A day or two later I saw a lumbering, half-awake black bruin walking the opposite side of the bay.

The twelve-gauge had been shoved under our bed all winter, but once we found bear tracks it leaned in the corner by the window, loaded with slugs. I picked up the heavy weapon, opened the door, and stared across the stretch of ice. The bear walked in what looked like a hypnotic daze, head hanging near the ground, taking no notice of the surroundings, a cranky grandfather wakened too early on a Sunday morning.

I walked to the edge of the bay, the animal oblivious to my presence. The river current created an upbeat music in the background and the early feathered arrivals sang in the forest. But I aimed into the sky and smashed through the lively sounds with a shattering punch from the gun, set off by the small pressure of my finger against the trigger, the gun kicking into my shoulder like the blow from a fist.

The bear jerked up his head and swung around into the trees, the mood of the day blown away by the gun's report, forest life scared into a breath-held silence. More shaken by the physical impact of my shot than by the emergence of an old threat, I returned the gun to its case, a scent of explosion sifting out of the barrel, and stood for a long time at the window, looking across the empty bay.

On walks after that, the gun hung from its strap over my shoulder and our eyes roved with a defensive alertness through the shadowy aisles of trees, vulnerability a remembered tight spot in our chests. Bears coming into camp with nonchalance were startled off by the reception. Bandit welcomed them with booming non-stop fits of barking, and usually all we saw was the quick-turning black rump and powerful galloping shape slipping off between cabins.

Going to the outhouse or crossing the camp to get water, we checked down the gaps between cabins like city-dwellers peering down alleys late at night. One May afternoon after lunch, I was putting the washed dishes on the table and looked out the window at the same moment a large bear walked around the corner of the cabin using the exact trail we always walked, five feet from our shower spot. His nose and mine would have been two feet apart had he turned his head to the window.

"There's a bear!" I strode toward the gun.

"What?" Marypat's voice sounded skeptical, ready to be the butt of a practical joke. She went to the window.

Bandit lay under the cabin, completely oblivious to the danger. I tore open the door, gun primed, and shouted out an unintelligible stream at top volume: "Heybeargetthehellouttahere!!"

By the time I edged around the cabin, gun raised, the bear had soundlessly vanished into the forest, not even a shaking bush marking his exit. Bandit, roused by the outburst, had the abject, confused look of a sentry caught napping when an alarm went off.

"He was big!" Marypat joined me outside. "As soon as you yelled he ran off, but he was standing under the bird feeder and the platform rested on his back."

We inspected the feeder, which hung nearly four feet off the ground, and glanced into the still forest, half expecting to be stared back at by a set of impassive brown eyes.

The combination of a thawing bay and the threat of bears abroad in the country motivated us to get the canoe out of winter storage, to shift our attention from walking to water travel. We set the boat across stumps and cleaned it for summer use, oiling the gunwales and wood thwarts, touching up scrapes with paint, rubbing off old waterlines and mud blotches. The shined and buffed canoe rested in front of the cabin, while snow lay in big splotches around the camp. The only open water available ran in a blue line that worked steadily into the bay, methodically melting toward the wide lake, the path of restless water a navigational chart of the river channel.

Instead of tramping our well-known trails, we took a daily paddling lap, exploring the limits of water and watching for new wildlife. The bow person got to use the binoculars, and checked over the flocks of geese and ducks for new species, or glassed the shore for wolves or bear. At first we could hardly go past the windsock, held back by the soft pans of ice that soggily resisted our attempts at breaking through. We explored each bay and pond, new space available every afternoon, and noticed the thick ice firmly frozen to the silty bottom in the shallower part of the bay.

Paddling again felt joyous; like musicians who'd been isolated from their instruments, we felt a profound release that we had been deprived of all winter. Even short periods tired us out, the price of winter softness, but the sleek boat under our knees, the small turbulence of our strokes, the partnership of synchronized power, all of it was so evocative, such a sweet way to move. From out in the bay, imprisoned but for a tiny pond of water, I let out an echoing whoop, my welcome to spring.

We added new birds to the list every day—yellowlegs, pintails, green-winged teal, bufflehead, marsh hawk, and loons. The first loon of spring we heard before seeing, that wailing watery call.

"Loon, Marypat!" We stopped, the canoe coasting. Again, the sound as titillating and stirring as a wolf howl. The call of a loon means summer in the north, twilight-calm lakes, the heft of a wood paddle, rock-island camps. Then we saw them, sleek and low in the water, their necks sharply ringed, their dagger-shaped fish-catching bills. More than sunlight, more than moving water, more than exposed ground or emerging bears, the loons told us that we had done it, had come through the winter. The incontrovertible evidence of spring rang in our ears.

4

Over the winter I had often found our status as distanced members of the human antpile to be bizarre and unreal. We listened to events by radio, heard debates and political posturings broadcast from the floor of Parliament, did dishes while a call-in opinion program aired a spectrum of viewpoints from across the continent. Because we had the time, we were better informed and had more opportunity for reflection in northern Saskatchewan than we might have had in a more urban location. Yet we remained geographically aloof, emotionally distant. An objective curiosity took hold of us, as if we had no organic stake in what happened but instead listened to the machinations and bumblings of aliens.

The juxtaposition, once we shut off the radio, felt fantastic. Our minds still treadmilled with the grist of news, but we looked out the window over the thawing bay, heard the sounds of hesitant but insistent spring, watched gulls wheel over the blue water. Behind the subdued noises of budding season lay a magnificent silence.

Ironically, the thing we missed most in our isolation was society. Not the juggernaut of civilization but simple human contact—family, friends, acquaintances. As horrible and repugnant as the outside world sometimes sounded, we longed for a closer contact with our part of it.

Our isolation neared its end. Cliff threatened to return at any time. Craig and Beth would arrive in June, and from then on the doubled group size would alter the quality and tenor of travel experience profoundly. The challenge of May became our ability to deal with an expanding restlessness.

I felt a dearth of worthy trials to combat. Showers became so luxurious that we took them every few days, and by mid-May we hardly required a fire. The water hole stayed open for days at a time and, even when it froze over, required only a tap or two to break through. Plenty of food, a supply of propane, daylight from five in the morning to ten at night—life became so cushy it drove me stir crazy. I turned to pacing, creating work around camp—moving boats, cutting wood, chopping ice away from motors.

We walked up to spy on the eagles, the quiet but observant white head all that appeared over the top of the nest. The pair of birds kept close to each other, sharing parental duties, one off hunting while the other sat on the eggs and then an exchange of roles. To get a more direct vantage point, we climbed a nearby jack pine, coming level with the nest some twenty yards away. The majestic birds circled and dove around us, white tails and heads against the blue sky, spread wings filling the camera lens, the sound of wind through their feathers whirring past. Then one would return clattering into the nest, talons outstretched, wings swept far back, to settle onto the large eggs, a quality of resolute patience about their vigil that I might have learned from.

From the start of winter, I had held back impatience, too awed by the span of time and the rigor of the season to let my expectations for spring intrude. But in May I lost the grip I'd maintained for seven months. The exuberant spring fever malady hadn't fastened on me only, however. Pilots buzzed our cabin with dish-rattling vigor. Ivan and another bush pilot, Rob, went over in tandem, wingtip following wingtip, their small planes a comical, slow-motion facsimile of fighter jets. Ivan caught us out paddling one calm evening and lined up for a pass so low that Marypat and I slithered down to the bottom of the canoe in alarm.

The phone horn rang in mid-May and Ivan asked how we'd feel about a postal air drop. "Hell, yes!" Nine-thirty that evening, the sky pale and dusky, we heard his incoming plane and hustled onto the porch. Ivan circled once and then made two low crabwise passes, dropping water balloons to test the wind. At first we didn't understand his tactics and mistook the balloons for letter packets. We ran about in the tall grass with the confused air of retrievers who can't locate a fallen duck.

By the third pass we were ready. The plane droned in from across the river, heading for the field in front of the cabin. The door in the cockpit swung open and a heavy black bag spilled out into space. It plummeted like a rock, trailing a plastic tail, and landed with a tremendous smack in the fast icy river. Without thinking, I sprinted across the dangerously thin lake ice that we'd avoided for days and plunged straight into the numbing river current. The package had landed fortuitously on our side of the river and floated down toward me in knee-deep water. Not until I had splashed out of the river and triumphantly raised the mail package to signal success did I realize that both my rubber boots were brim full of 33°F water.

*   *

Four Chipewyan men arrived unexpectedly by snowmobile in late May. We had assumed that lake travel would be impossible. The river channel had melted a gash over a mile long into Lake Athabasca, and ice beyond that had turned gray and treacherous, despite the refrigerated air that blew across it. But they managed, staying near shore, driving over rocks and logs if necessary, coming to camp out and set nets in the open water.

The four visitors sat on our porch with us, hot sun pouring down, and drank the black tea we served them. One pointed across the bay to a low bluff, near where we had seen the first spring bear. "My mother died over there," he said. "We were fishing in the fall. Came back to camp and she was dead."

I helped the men chop a wooden skiff that had been left at the camp out of the ice. We turned the boat over to drain, and then skidded it across the snow to the river. Launched into the current, their locomotion aided with mixed success by two paddles, the men swung around the point in their leaky vessel, set for their camp-out.

About noon on the following day we took the canoe out to go visiting down the bay to where their skiff was pulled up. Landing there, we saw the boat full to the gunwales with fresh fish—whitefish, suckers, pike—a prodigious and still-flopping catch.

Their camp sat back from the shore in the woods, invisible from the boat, but we followed a trail through the brush and found the men reclined in the forest. Snowmobiles were parked incongruously on the snowless ground, a small wall tent was pitched nearby, sleeping bags and gear were strewn about.

Like Robin Hood's merry band, the men lay in the leaves and moss, circled around a trench fire eight feet long and two feet wide. Fish skewered on sticks sizzled above the coals, the natives reaching out to tear off hunks of cooked flesh from time to time. Half a barbecued grouse lay forgotten in the roots of a tree.

Propped up on their elbows or leaning comfortably against the trunk of a poplar, the dark-haired Chipewyans ribbed each other about losing at cards the night before or falling through the ice while hauling in the fish net. No alcohol tainted the cheerful relaxed scene, a group of grown men at their ease on a warm spring day. They had nowhere to go, nothing in particular to do. One man voiced their intentions succinctly. "We aren't doing anything," he chuckled. "We just like being out, getting away from town."

They planned to pull the fish-packed skiff back to Fond-du-Lac behind a snowmobile, a scheme certain to turn the already dubious boat into a wooden sieve. But that remained a far-off project. They were in no hurry to rush back. The feast continued, another lazy warm day flowed by, spring waxed in the woods while the smell of leaves and damp earth steamed up from the ground like faint incense.

When we went paddling that evening, the men were gone. We spotted a black bear lumbering around the point we had walked to dozens of times to look out beyond the confines of the bay, the point where we often found fox tracks in the snow. On the other side, at the back of a marshy cove, two wolves slipped through the willows in hopes of surprising an unwary mallard, but melted into the shadowy trees when we coasted near. With light nearly bled from the sky, we made out a brown shape under the windsock. "You think it's a bear?" I whispered.

We paddled silently, wooden blades making noiseless slices into the water, the gap closing in the calm cooling evening. Suddenly the animal scented us and raised its head—a calf moose, gawky and spindle-legged, with outsize ears, a comical knock-kneed distress in its demeanor. It plunged into the water and swam in front of us, directly to camp, where it shakily clambered out on the rocks and stumbled into the woods, water spraying from its coat like mist.

The first pioneering mosquitoes hovered in the twilight, tentative in their mission, but a foreboding signal nonetheless. We lit a mosquito coil in the cabin for the first time. "Spring and fall are the nicest times in the north, don't you think?" Marypat asked.

5

Only ten days remained before the first camp clients were due in early June. Cliff loitered anxiously in La Ronge, giving us periodic updates on the radio phone, waiting for the lake to thaw so he could take off in his float plane. Chipewyan guides called almost daily to find out if they were needed yet. We swung between restless anticipation and the desire to prolong our peaceful quarantine.

The end came without warning, exactly thirty-two weeks from the day it had started, completing the eight-month wintering sojourn. We saw the plane circle overhead from up the river where we were watching the eagles. "That's Cliff!" I called out. We jogged down the wet trail, hopping over puddles and teetering across logs in swampy spots, loping onto the dock just as Cliff taxied in.

Bandit recognized the plane and the summer drill of tying up to the floating dock. She leapt onto the float and nearly turned herself inside out greeting her owner. Cliff embraced us at the same time he fended off Bandit's affectionate attack. "Hello!" he boomed. "I finally made it!"

Rigorous as our commitment to winter discipline had been, we abandoned it without a second thought when Cliff arrived. My journal lay neglected, writing projects were stowed away, radio shows, shower schedule, beading projects, all forgotten. The pace of life changed drastically as well. Instead of stretching out tasks in order to make them last all day, we attacked a monstrous list of duties that had to be completed before the unbending deadline of the first guests' arrival.

Cliff stayed for two busy days. In his own camp, he played the part of guest to our host, soaking up the low-key, intimate atmosphere. He was indoctrinated into our shower routine and served moose specialties for dinner; in the evening we would all relax together in our cabin.

"This is the time I like best in camp," he worked a toothpick with his tongue and patted Bandit's head. "Only a few of us here, nice unhurried pace, no generator going all day. I can actually enjoy it."

I laughed. "After the winter, this pace seems like downtown Los Angeles in the rush hour! But I know what you mean."

Late into the evenings we discussed the adventures of winter, mapped our trails and told him of the wolf pack we'd adopted, estimated the cords of wood we'd burned and revealed the good stands of dead timber, recounted Don's uncomfortable request for money and Muglar's invitation for Christmas, joked about Bandit's lack of ice savvy and how she repeatedly fell through thin spots without learning her lesson. With pride of ownership, we relayed the lessons of winter in his camp.

In two days' time we had the water system working, the generator fired up, electricity checked, and the lodge primed to open. At dawn on the second day, Bandit padded to the front window, growling deeply, and went into a spasm of barking that levitated me out of bed. I made the window in time to see the hind end of a black bear trotting off in unhurried fashion.

Dressing quickly, I grabbed the twelve-gauge and went prowling to see if the intruder really had gone off. Sure enough, I found the bear just back of the lodge, looking around as if trying to decide what to explore next. He saw me and made that characteristic surprised little hop on his front paws, the movement so indelibly seared on my memory from the bear I had killed at the Grand Rapid. After only a momentary glance of confirmation, the pitch-black bear hurried off into the woods, and I went back to the cabin to brew coffee.

As abruptly as he had come, Cliff taxied away, promising to return soon with more workers, this time to stay. Cliff had ignited our enthusiasm, only to turn off the power once he got us really revved up. I couldn't force myself to regain the old occupations, the former levels of concentration. I adjusted by diving into fast-paced books, diverting the flowing juices of summer energy by escaping through the imaginations of others.

We kept up the after-dinner paddling exercise, excited at the swiftness with which the lake ice melted. Huge hunks of softened plating withered away every day, until our laps covered several miles. The paddling rhythm came back to us like a remembered instinct, the old calluses hardening up, specialized muscle groups growing firmer, the boat our tool and companion.

I couldn't avoid the absurd image of Lake Athabasca as a gigantic cocktail, held in a two-hundred-mile-long bedrock goblet, pure and fresh and blue, cooled by an ice cube of unimaginable mass. I wanted the cocktail straight-up, and wished the shrinking ice cube on its way. Almost June, and the whiteness stretched unbroken for miles. Cliff had told us that the aerial view had been distressing, even the smaller lakes still largely frozen in.

As if some telepathic signal had alerted them to opening water farther north, most of the transient birds had passed on. The flocks we saw landed briefly and then took off, or simply whistled by overhead.

Marypat and I prepared ourselves for the upcoming increase in camp population, the hectic pace and tension of deadlines, the looming loss of our home.

"As soon as possible," Marypat announced, "I'm going in to Stony. I don't want to get trapped here doing dishes and laundry all day!"

Cliff called to say he'd arrive before noon on May 28. He mentioned his plans to fly up Craig and Beth's canoe on a later flight. By eight-thirty that night he still hadn't come, and the new estimate had been pushed back to nine o'clock. The plane finally droned in from the south, circled the bay, and set down in the open water nearly twenty-four hours late. At that point, isolation and serenity came conclusively to an end.

Our cribbage guru, Bob, unbent from the cramped cockpit and descended to the dock, followed by Irv, an acquaintance of Cliff's whose friendship included the benefit of his expertise as an electrician. Bandit could hardly stand the leap in attention potential, her tail going like wind cups in a gale.

As if running a filmstrip backwards, we put all the fall chores into reverse—unstowing and tuning motors, flying off to attend to the outpost camps, fastening propane bottles, toting all manner of objects back and forth across camp on our backs or in the wheelbarrow. Many nights the water lines froze up, and cold sleety rain hampered our efforts. On the sunny days, mosquitoes and black flies made work conditions maddening.

Marypat and I began losing the cabin. First, the radio phone went to the lodge, then the cook stove; our large wood stove also moved up to the bigger building, replaced with a tinny airtight model. The side room we had used as our winter freezer and pantry metamorphosed into the cabin bathroom. Irv wired the building for electricity. Emotionally, we started to protect ourselves from the loss, withdrawing our attachments, taking down pictures from the walls as a symbolic cutting of ties.

The men Cliff brought with him to handle the many projects made me feel like an overeducated bumbler around the simplest mechanical tasks. They used tools with the grace and familiarity of musicians, judged torque and the sound of an engine with an experienced intuition, set about problem-solving with efficiency and simple logic, all the while clothing their work with easy badinage and good humor. I watched them rip apart and reassemble engines and appliances with stupefying abandon and speed. At the end of the day, they appreciated good company and a chance to laugh, a stiff drink before dinner, maybe a twilight foray onto the water to troll for trout.

The camp population grew by steady additions. Two cooks took up residence, relieving Marypat and me from our job as camp food preparers. Another of Cliff's friends, also named Bob, a man conveniently handy with motors, flew in to help restore mechanical health to the operation. The first native guides managed to dodge ice floes and follow open-water leads from Fond-du-Lac to camp, like Arctic explorers angling for the Pole through pack ice. Don McDonald amazed me by nonchalantly handing over a folded wad of Canadian twenties. Six months late, but he made good on a loan I had given up as an unfortunate lesson in northern business principles. The guides strung up their wall tents and pitched in on chores, preparatory to the first clients.

The initial group for the summer promised to strain every capacity of Athabasca Camps. The day they were due the weather turned wintry; rain lashed down, the winds drove the last herd of ice chunks off the big lake, creating the first hazardous waves of the season in the process. Two stranded groups of customers, one in Fond-du-Lac and the other in Stony Rapids, waited for eight hours while the float planes scheduled to pick them up held out for more hospitable landing conditions.

In camp, construction projects proceeded with down-to-the-wire haste. Bunk beds built during the day were slept in that night, a shower installed in the afternoon refreshed a customer two hours later, firewood was cut and split for use the same day.

The Stony Rapids contingent eventually arrived by late afternoon, and Marypat made good her threat to escape, hitching a ride back in the empty plane. Just before dark, nearly midnight, the Fond-du-Lac group came in. Every bed in camp had been assigned, our winter cabin packed with tourists. Kicking myself for not evacuating earlier, I asked the pilot if I could ride back to town with him. "Sure," he said, "but it will have to be tomorrow. Too dark to fly now."

He and I slept on foam mattresses on the floor at the back of the lodge, squeezed in between humming coolers, a sleep that began at two in the morning and ended at five-thirty, as the breakfast crew came on. By six I found myself at the griddle, frying eggs and flipping pancakes.

I fled at the first opportunity, on five minutes' notice, hopping into the Twin Otter next to the pilot and abandoning the bedlam that our winter haven had become. On the flight I studied the land and water to the north, eyes sharpened by the knowledge of our pending journey in that direction. First, I strained for the sight of ice-covered lakes, but couldn't find any on the immediate horizon. The country looked lush and fresh, rivers tumbling over bedrock on the way to the big lake, sun-dappled water, cliffs and ridges of bare rock—and to the north, a vast wealth of wilderness that we would paddle and walk across, on which we would stake our tents and build our cook fires.

6

Ivan dashed my romantic vision of summery landscape as soon as I set foot in town. He'd just returned from a flight several hundred miles to the north, where winter had hardly begun to relent. His trip had brought him to a lake near where we would pass, and he had seen a good section of our proposed route from the air.

"I couldn't believe it," he exclaimed. "It's still winter up there! I could have landed on the ice if I'd wanted to. Snowdrifts are as high as a cabin! Windy and cold like spring isn't even close!" He stopped long enough to wrestle a crate out of the plane he was unloading. "I sure hope it changes pretty soon, or you guys will have a tough go!"

"Thanks, Ivan, you're really helping my day. What about farther south? Aren't we clear for quite a while?"

"Well, for a ways," he conceded. "But Selwyn Lake has ice on it and Wholdaia has quite a lot still. You should be up there a week after you start!"

We knew that late ice on tundra lakes is the potential nemesis of northern paddlers. Trip reports we'd read recorded ice on the larger lakes up to the end of July in some years. Others found none at all, even early on. There were accounts of groups going to sleep one night with nothing but blue water in sight, only to wake up to a solid pack of entrapping floes, driven in by a wind change. Just when I'd exhausted my fund of expedition challenges to fret over, Ivan had presented me with a new one, a worry that I could work into suitable bulk as we inched northward.

I found Marypat still snoozing at mid-day, sleeping off the revelry of the previous night. While I'd been bunked down between coolers, she and Margy had been dancing until dawn at a party. "You made it out just in time," I told her. "I stayed half a day too long!"

Craig and Beth were due the following night. They were already driving north, a two-day trip. Leaving their car in La Ronge, they would board a plane for the final travel leg to Stony Rapids. I wondered how it would be to greet them, to show them the eagle nest or our cabin, to share our hopes and feelings about the summer. Our experiences of the past year had been so engulfing, so consuming, so foreign that I had difficulty conjuring up an image of my own brother and sister-in-law, as if the totality of our wilderness existence had blurred the focus of their features. But when their plane rumbled down the dirt strip and I saw them step tentatively down the three-step ramp, my reticence and shyness shrank away, blown offstage by the warmth of our reunion.

We could hardly have intersected from more opposite worlds. They had just finished a hectic teaching year, then strapped immediately into their vehicle, loaded to the roof with expedition gear, and driven non-stop to central Saskatchewan. They landed in Stony Rapids directly from a life diametrically counter to the one we had led for a year.

While we had experienced overabundant solitude, they had been swamped by human demands; while our human contacts had been the source of joy and spiritual sustenance, theirs had provided the single most consistent source of stress in the professional year. We had lived in intimate connection with a wild environment for twelve months; they had been lucky to claim a few weekends in the mountains. But at our meeting the gap was erased by our shared excitement and exuberance. The evening's events carried us along in a current of spontaneity that obliterated any opportunity for reflection or introspection.

Given the usual pattern of travel letdowns, we shot out of Stony Rapids with express-train efficiency. An hour after our companions arrived, we loaded into float planes along with another batch of camp guests and the inevitable overburden of duffles, fishing tackle, food, and camping supplies, and lifted off for Athabasca Camps.

I imagined how the lake below must have looked to Craig and Beth, that spread of water. "Now that's a big lake!" Craig turned to say.

"This is the narrow end of it," I replied, leaning forward to look west. "That's Pine Channel down there. We thought we might camp there on the paddle in to Stony."

Over the drone of the plane engine, we pointed to landmarks and recounted winter events, enthusiastically engulfing our new partners with welcoming tidbits. Fortunately, the first client group had vacated camp, and a smaller population made it possible for the four of us to reinhabit our old cabin.

The building seemed completely alien, so altered from the place in which we had endured and savored winter that we no longer felt the pangs of separation. It wasn't our home, but only served as a shelter for the few days before embarking.

For two days we did nothing but pack food, study maps, dip cheese in paraffin, stuff bags and packs, and jettison every extra ounce of weight we possibly could. With no realistic chance for a re-supply along our route (Ivan joked that he'd air drop a case of beer to us), we made every conceivable sacrifice to minimize the load. Even so, the mound of equipment looked elephantine.

Ivan and Diane popped in for a quick visit on a flight to Uranium. Diane mirrored our sentiments about the remodeled cabin when she looked around and announced, "I don't like it anymore. It isn't the same."

Ivan hefted a few of the packs and looked dubious. Putting it in terms of a weight he could relate to, he said, "Those packs are at least as heavy as full propane bottles."

The second expedition canoe languished in La Ronge, waiting for a ride north with Cliff. Meantime, we nailed down the trip logistics, escorted our partners down the trails we had pioneered, played rounds of four-handed cribbage, pointed out the eagle nest, still devoid of young. Craig and Beth visibly relaxed as time passed and we introduced them to camp routine. Eli took us out to the island where he tethered his dog team for the summer, the skinny animals raising a non-stop din of howling and barking while we slopped them out fish carcasses and refilled their water buckets.

The weather alternated between hot buggy days and Novemberlike misery. One day we'd wear headnets in camp and sweat over even minor exertions, the next we'd sidle up to wood stoves, drink coffee, and watch sleet drive into gray waves on the lake.

Cliff kept promising us that he had to fly out to La Ronge any day, and that the canoe would arrive in plenty of time, but we weren't reassured. Camp demands and a perpetual state of emergency kept him flying until midnight, running between crises and just barely treading water. Our scheduled departure was June 15, but on that day we sat in the lodge observing a wintry landscape, fidgeting over the lack of things to do. Cliff promised delivery for the next day.

June 16, another supposed paddling day. We stacked our packs and duffles and paddles on the porch, and waited. Lunchtime came and went, the afternoon droned past, a perfect travel day, but no boat to sit in. Every distant plane engine brought me to my feet, only to hear it pass by and diminish in the distance. Clients returned from their day of fishing and had dinner in the lodge. Marypat bantered with the guides.

At nine o'clock Cliff flew overhead, the seventeen-foot canoe strapped to one float, and set successfully down in the bay. "I had a hell of a time tying that canoe on right," he told us. "Technically, it's probably an illegal load, but I got her on. All the way up I had to fly with the rudder hard over to compensate for the wind drag!"

It didn't matter that we couldn't get off before late at night, we had so much reserved energy that we commenced packing the boats immediately. All of it came back: the old order of packing, the way the boat heeled over with the weight, the tie-down system, the same knots. Incredibly, we had so streamlined our packing technique that we were able to snap on the spraydeck, an accomplishment that hadn't occurred until a week into the previous summer. Insects were so thick we loaded up in full defensive gear, complete with headnets.

Leave-taking was anticlimactic. How could it have been otherwise? How could we adequately commemorate the significance of a departure from the place that had become such a peaceful and memory-laden home? Full of people, injected with summer intensity, the camp had been transformed.

Cliff had us up for a round of farewell drinks—Bob, Stella, Cliff, Bandit—the cadre of expedition companions we had never expected to encounter at the outset but who had given a human texture and depth to the journey, friendship with them all out of proportion to the length of contact. We toasted each other inadequately and talked superficially, understanding nonetheless what we really meant to say.

The four of us slid into the canoe seats by eleven o'clock, plenty of light still left, knowing the hour of day for the final time of the summer. Our gunwales cleared the water by a few meager inches. Friends lined along the dock, guides and guests watched from the hill. In my preoccupied state, I forgot to give Bandit a final pat on the head; she assumed, I imagined later, that we were off for our evening exercise.

The first two miles of the summer were as familiar to Marypat and me as the oft-trodden camp trail up the river. Turning past the windsock, I looked at camp, raised my paddle, felt a sting in my eyes. The night sky paled, clouds to the west lit to a flaming peach color, and a silent V of geese flew past, their strong wings dark silhouettes, a wild benediction.

PART VIII

OVER THE HEIGHT OF LAND

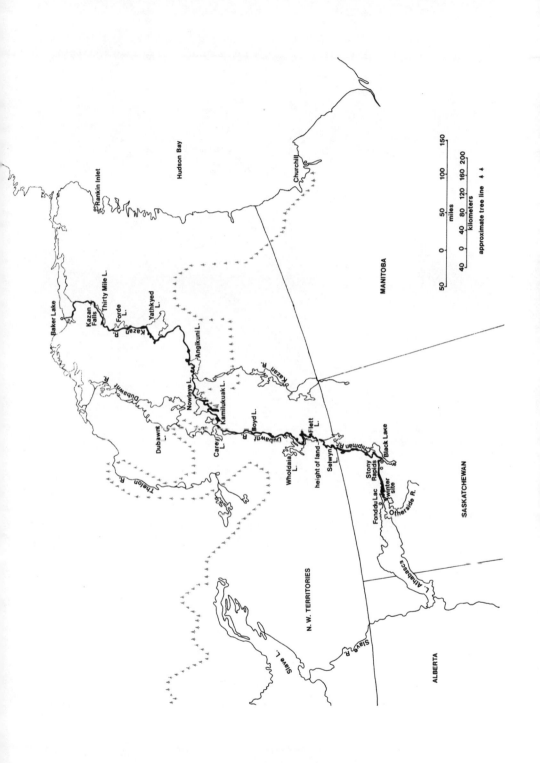

It would have been gratifying to shift gracefully into expedition gear, to slip into a wilderness travel mode as effortlessly as putting a truck into four-wheel drive. As it was, though, the mass of the canoe jolted me. Within three miles my hands felt tender and I sensed in my body the accumulation of winter softness, a burden as real as an extra pack in the boat.

We stopped after six miles, midnight dusk cloaking the sky, and camped on a boulder-strewn island. In from shore, an eagle nest seemed to squash flat the top branches of a jack pine, and the nesting adult circled for a time, calling, before settling back onto the sticks and matted grass that held its young.

Adequate tent sites were nonexistent. We hoisted bulging packs from the canoes and piled them in a heap just above the waveline. Our tents went up across patches of angular rock that were covered by lumpy mattresses of moss. In my sleeping bag, I writhed and contorted until I found a moderately acceptable position, rigidly confined by rock, and closed my eyes. I fell asleep negating the day, locking in a mental drawer the confusion and anxiety of departure, determined to begin the final expedition phase properly at sunup.

The sound of light rain pattering on the tent woke me. When it stopped I escaped from my uncomfortable bed to start breakfast. A fire I should have been able to start blindfolded took four matches to light, and I fumbled through three packs before I found all the breakfast food and cooking paraphernalia. We ate a marginal meal while studying the lake for signs of its mood. Dawn rain clouds dissipated in the sun's warmth, and a breeze that had sent a steady march of waves against the shore died away. We set up group photos, the before of a before-and-after sequence—clean-shaven, freshly clothed, like freshmen in the first week at college.

Marypat and I had traversed the eastern end of Lake Athabasca by plane, car, motorboat, dog sled, and foot. For the forty-five miles from camp to Stony Rapids, we hardly required the maps kept handy in each canoe's bow. Even so, paddling the well-known territory felt different, new. I expected to make faster time, but distances that had taken minutes to cover by plane or powerboat took half a day to paddle across.

Our paddles dipped into the calm, mirrorlike water of Lake Athabasca. Looking over at Craig and Beth, I could see their precise reflections in the water, distorted only by the disturbance of their wake and paddle strokes. We adjusted our speeds to coincide, talking as we traveled, the two canoes side by side.

Craig identified birds by fragments of their far-off calls or distinctive flight patterns, birds I had no idea were even in the area. My younger brother by two years, competent woodsman, natural history expert with an avid interest in birds, he had accompanied me on several earlier northern expeditions and had made others of his own. His ability to describe the natural history as we traveled added substantially to our environmental understanding. Beth had been one of Marypat's best friends since the third grade, and had also proven her wilderness mettle on remote northern journeys. Conversation helped the miles go by and distracted me from the ache in my shoulders and the warm red spots on my palms.

After we had made the cruise into Stony Rapids, the four of us would face the most daunting and remote traverse of northern wilderness any of us had ever attempted. For over eight hundred miles, we would strike north and east, toiling upstream for some of that distance, struggling over dozens of rugged portages, venturing across the unpopulated center of Barrenland tundra, and descending two dominant northern rivers, the Dubawnt and the Kazan. If successful, we would reach, in early August, the small Inuit settlement at Baker Lake, Northwest Territories, lying just south of the Arctic Circle.

For two days the lake blessed us with utter calm. Emboldened, we cut trails straight across bays and wide spots, bit off twenty miles and more at a whack, stripped to shorts under the hot sun, watched torpedo-shaped fish flick away from the oncoming shadows of canoes. As if roaming the back streets of a former neighborhood, Marypat and I shared scraps of local history and pointed to landmarks—trapping cabins, barge markers, a rounded hump of rock we'd grazed in a camp boat. We recognized Cliff, Ivan, and Rob in the plane traffic that droned over-head, and knew that they'd been watching the lake for our tiny boats. Ivan roared over our second camp in an ear-splitting gesture of Twin Otter friendship. The first barge of summer passed us headed out from Stony Rapids, going west, back to the country we'd put in our wake.

Owing to the weight of our supplies, meals became less an opportu-nity for nourishment than a chance to consume poundage. Entrees were assessed for their heft rather than their taste. Chipman portage, a series of seven carries out of Black Lake, beginning with a three-mile back-breaker, lay less than a week in the future. Horsing packs a few feet from the boats to camp and back was struggle enough; what would three miles of forest and muskeg be like?

The lessons of the first summer quickly returned for Marypat and me. Within a day or two, we regained the old packing order, knew where to find the saw or matches or dinner food, could trim the canoe's balance with quick shifts of the duffle. I watched Craig and Beth go through repeated searches for some item, asking each other six times a day, "Do you have the . . . in your pack?" I detected discomfort in the set of their backs as they paddled. Their disorientation recaptured the gawky period we had struggled through a year earlier, made me see how far we had come in managing wilderness existence.

Coping with the adjustment to a larger group required a new level of compromise. Marypat and I had been alone for a year, awash in silence, intimate to extremes, self-sufficient, a pair of closely orbiting planets in space. Abruptly, our focus expanded to include companions. I found myself gauging my paddling speed to stay abreast of the other boat; not competing but concentrating on their position and pace, an occupation that kept my thoughts from wandering. During the first summer I had indulged in fantasy, internal dialogue, and reflection, but with Craig and Beth I externalized thoughts and feelings.

In camp and in the canoes attention gravitated to the group, tending to create a social spotlight that demanded our involvement. Instead of sensing the pressure of environment encircling us, our humble presence in vast quiet, we exerted our own force outward, demanding a territory. The adjustment was subtle, but not minor.

Fresh from a fast-paced, tension-laced life, Craig and Beth talked, it seemed to me, incessantly. My own vocal cords hadn't had such a workout in months. I wondered if my reaction was similar to winter guests who had visited us to find themselves verbally bombarded by our blathering. At first the social stimulation was a welcome breeze, but I soon strove to minimize dialogue, hoping our friends would gain the same penchant for quiet that Marypat and I had acquired. Even at a hundred yards, I could hear the steady modulation of their voices.

For eleven hundred miles Marypat and I had paddled with river current or across slack lake water. In that entire stretch of Alberta and Saskatchewan, we had faced only one significant portage, at the Grand Rapid. The Fond-du-Lac River, feeding Lake Athabasca from the east, ended that downstream coast.

In Pine Channel, still as much lake as river, the current flowing against us was nearly imperceptible. Our pace slowed, but slightly, just enough to make me wonder whether my paddling strength had slackened. But the lake steadily narrows, until, in the five miles before Stony Rapids, we were clearly confronting the current of the Fond-du-Lac River.

The river fought our progress with a steady push that made us track along the banks where any eddy current would aid our progress, away from the main channel. All the way to the Dubawnt River, well over the Northwest Territories border, we would fight the current in a quest to gain the height of land. If we weren't directly battling it, we would be portaging around sections too strong to attempt.

Last summer, in over a thousand miles, we had had one carry; now, in the hundred miles or so following Black Lake, we'd have fifteen. The five miles of river into Stony Rapids was a minor hurdle, not worth mentioning, not compared to what lay ahead. Still, there were a few swift spots that momentarily held us at a standstill, where our paddling strength inched the canoe laboriously around a corner, leaving us winded and fatigued. None of us spoke of the future, but the subtly increasing level of combat quieted our bantering.

Stony Rapids hummed and buzzed with summer activity. Every fifteen minutes, float planes ferrying people, gas, and supplies around the lake roared in and out of the wide, current-jostled river. We stayed well away from the river runway and tied up at a vacant float dock.

Ivan leaned out the loading door of a nearby Beaver and took hold of a propane bottle on its way into the plane's interior. "Hey, you guys," he called out, "where are you staying in town?" He turned in time to catch a box of food his partner threw him from the dock. "Summertime," he spat the word out. "Hurry up and wait! Hurry up and wait!"

"Look," he continued, climbing down from the plane and shoving his hands into the deep pockets of green overalls, "I'm off flying for the night. Here's the key to my house. You stay there. Use whatever you need."

He climbed up past the freight and wormed into the cockpit. "I know your route. I'll see about flying up there this summer." The river caught the floats, powerless plane pivoting away from the dock. Ivan waved, checked his instruments, and cranked up the props as we backed away from the buffeting slipstream.

The first carry of the summer was more commute than portage. We used Cliff's bus to ferry packs, then Craig and I labored up the steep dirt road, each under eighty pounds of boat, to Ivan's house. I assumed the short haul would be like a fifty-yard dash, a little heavy breathing, and felt betrayed by my shortness of breath and the sharp pain across my neck vertebrae, where the canoe thwart bore down.

The two days on Lake Athabasca had been warm-up exercise, a shakedown cruise through known territory. I saw it as time to bid farewell to the body of water that had been a home environment for more than ten months, savoring memories as much as looking ahead. Stony

Rapids felt like the jumping-off point, the true start. We enjoyed final indulgences—hot showers, a beer at the White Water Inn, and another weighty dinner selection from our packs, cooked in a microwave.

In the morning, Margy offered to haul us by pickup truck to our put-in on Black Lake, an offer that proved too seductive to refuse. As the four of us loaded packs, paddles, and boats into the truck bed, I noticed the sky to the west was a dark roiling mass of cloud, an ominous portent that melted my resolve to be on our way. I caught my companions' eyes wandering west toward the oncoming blackness.

By the time we lashed the gear in place and crammed into the truck cab, large drops of rain fell, small water bombs splatting on the windshield. The rough road uncoiled behind the truck, and the prospect of cutting the final tie with comfort and security loomed ahead through the storm. In full rain gear, we unloaded, hurrying to cover everything under the spraydecks, while sheets of water beat on the lake surface like hail.

"I hate starting a trip wet!" I growled as I passed Marypat on my way to the truck for another pack. She just grunted. I couldn't tell if she even heard me, encapsulated as she was in her rain hood, pelted by the storm.

Margy easily convinced us to delay long enough for a cup of coffee at a nearby fishing lodge, and we left the two canoes covered up, bobbing gently alongside a low dock, yellow and red steeds obediently awaiting the order to begin. Without seeming to procrastinate, we stayed nearly an hour, glutting ourselves with coffee, and when we emerged the torrential part of the storm had passed, allowing us the dignity of setting out in a lull between conflicts.

We embraced Margy in the continuing drizzle and released her to run back to the shelter of the truck. She watched us slip into the protective spraydecks and pick up our paddles with hands already chilled from exposure. As we backed away from shore, I could see her waving behind the rhythmic flick of wipers, her face blurry and indistinct through the rain.

2

Black Lake, in my opinion, was aptly named. The water looked deep and dark, and we followed a bedrock shoreline that fell steeply into the lake from a ridge above us, a shoreline with few inviting harbors. As the rain tapered off, a gusty wind forced us into our first confrontation with waves. A day earlier I'd worn a T-shirt and shorts, and worried about sunburn. On Black Lake my hands were slow with cold, and I wished I had put on my wool hat.

Compared to Lake Athabasca, Black Lake is a bathtub in size, but we had no opportunity to enjoy the smaller scale. I watched the yellow canoe plunging into wave troughs and slamming into watery crests, splashing spray to the sides. Beth's face looked grim and tight with the strain. We slowed to a crawl, each of us withdrawn, conversation snuffed out by the struggle to move forward.

I had memorized much of our summer route, and could picture the string of major lakes that led north and east ahead of us, probably a dozen of them as big or bigger than Black Lake. Before long we would lose the trees that offered some shelter, and venture into the wide empty Barrenlands, a vast tundra of wind and ice and water, a land so naked and exposed that the last glaciers might have retreated only fifty years ago.

"This is crazy!" Beth shouted above the wind. "We're not getting anywhere." I could hear fatigue and worry in her voice. But the shoreline offered no place to pull in, nowhere to camp. Instead, we found a narrow overgrown nook in the cliff-face to park the canoes and scrambled up the slippery moss-covered rock with the lunch pack.

All day the wind blew, gusting erratically from different directions, setting up a confused welter of waves. Our soft unconditioned arms strained against the foe, powering the canoes ahead foot by exhausting foot. If we stopped, even momentarily, the wind shoved us backwards. We finally camped on a sandy breakwater that protruded into the lake, a popular native destination, judging by the profusion of cigarette cartons, Coke cans, and chopped-down trees.

Beth volunteered to get cooking water and, stripped to her underwear, waded into the breakers to collect water that was a blend of agitated sand and liquid. The wind died down after dinner, and we crawled into sleeping bags to recover from the fatigue of combat, to gather ourselves for the Chipman portage, only a dozen miles down the lake shore.

Marypat and I woke simultaneously in the middle of the night. The tent bowed in against my face, warped concave by a tremendous onslaught of air. "Jesus Christ!" I rolled toward the middle of the tent and sat up. Outside, I could see sand mixed with glowing embers from our dying fire whip by two feet above the beach. The lake boiled in response to the gale, surf licking toward our packs.

Marypat sat up next to me and we looked out the mesh door at the spectacle. A nearly full moon shed serene light across a clear translucent sky, while demonic winds swept down the lake in frothy gusts and tore at our camp. "You think it can last?" I looked at Marypat, her sleeping bag draped around her shoulders, disbelief in her expression.

"We better cover the fire and move the packs," she grabbed for some clothes.

"One of us has to hold down the tent. I'll stay here." I pushed my hand against the wall and a force leaned back, like a thing alive. "Better check on Craig and Beth," I yelled as she disappeared through the door.

With Marypat gone, the tent rose and flapped and shuddered before the attack, pinned down by my weight alone. I waited for the inevitable sound of snapping poles, the rip of material.

I caught glimpses of my partner through the door. Hair straight out in the wind, sand swirling around her legs, she scampered from pack to pack, hauling them to higher ground. Her conversation with Craig and Beth took place only a few yards away, but I didn't catch a word of it.

"The sky's completely clear!" Marypat burst out as she scrambled back into our flimsy shelter, bringing a cold blast of wind with her. "Where is this coming from?"

We sat, shoulder to shoulder, watching incredulously while we leaned our weight against the wind-bowed tent side. The gusts finally abated some, were separated by longer periods of time. We lay back nervously to try to sleep. The tent withstood the blow, but I thought bleakly about the windy land ahead and pictured us patching together tents shredded by the invisible tormentor.

We were windbound. The lull lasted only long enough for the meteorological forces to catch their breath. As soon as we crawled from the tents in the morning, we discovered the first project of the day. Without our weight holding them down, our shelters strained and snapped like hot-air balloons against their frail moorings. We had to move them to more protected ground.

Instead of dismantling the tents, we carried them as they stood, a four-person maneuver, three of us on the corners, blindly following the directions of the fourth. We negotiated the beach and lurched into a jack pine forest, giggling and stumbling, shouting like inebriated fools while wind turned the tents into sails and threatened to wrench them from our grasp. Once we had anchored the tents down again, in a small depression protected by trees, the gale might have been a remote sound effect, for it hardly grazed our new camp.

During the day's wait I began my summer-long affair with maps. I started calculating mileage and visually pioneering ahead. My eyes wandered away from our route, traveling on the upper Fond-du-Lac River, over to the Porcupine, and then back to our trail. The hodgepodge of water and land, place name and legend, mesmerized me. I studied the maps in the tent that evening until failing light forced me to stop.

I slept lightly, as if listening, and woke early. The air felt cool, the sky barely pink, and the lake appeared to be at least momentarily still. I snuggled against Marypat, trying to wake her slowly, but she ignored me. "MP," I said, quietly. "It's morning. Looks good outside." She grunted and hitched her bag sleepily over her head, but I knew she'd get up.

We were quickly on the water, dawn light the last we saw of the sun. A gray mat of cloud slid like a curtain overhead, and a light drizzle persuaded me to don the familiar yellow rain gear. I didn't mind, as long as the lake stayed calm. I'd take rain over wind any time. Relic swells like the broad backs of whales heaved the boats up and down gently, and we paddled steadily toward the Chipman River. The rapid-filled narrows would force us to make our first long portage of the summer. The low sky and approaching challenge kept us quiet, and from the bow I monitored our progress on the map.

Without the aid of sun, the day took on a timeless quality. I lost hold of my mental clock in the rhythmic dip and swing of paddles, the lift and drop of waves, the slow approach and passing of landmarks. Our boats slid along, just out from shore, tightly sealed against the rain. The menacing dark bulk of Black Lake spread to the east. By the time we coasted to land at the frothy mouth of the Chipman River, the start of the portage trail, I had lost any feel for time of day. We decided, since we'd come a dozen miles, that it must be the lunch hour and hunkered in the wet grass above the incoming river to eat.

"Too bad this portage doesn't come at the end of the summer!" I gave voice to my anxiety, looking around at the daunting loads we'd have to carry.

An old frame for a wall tent stood crookedly in an opening off the river, and we cast about on several false trails before finding the right one, which led off for several hundred yards at the lake's edge before cutting inland. I explored up the Chipman River, wondering if we might be able to wade and line upstream rather than carry around, but the small river tumbled and roared through a rock valley, with no easy alternative to portaging. I stopped and turned back at a healthy pile of bear turd, suddenly aware of the quiet woods.

Everything about the portage was burdensome. Because the rain continued, we worked inside cloying rain suits. Wet mud caked heavily on our shoes. Mosquitoes and black flies grew so ferocious that we reluctantly accepted a green-hazed view through headnets. Worst of all, the loads were killing. Fifty-five days of food and equipment, minus the few meals already consumed, ferried in two overwhelming trips.

Canoes weighing close to eighty pounds had additional paddles, life vests, the first aid kit, and spraydeck lashed to thwarts and seats. The packs might as well have been loaded with anvils, but we strapped the shotgun and other random gear onto their sides as well. In our free hands we carried ammo boxes.

Marypat sat down to shrug into the harness of a pack, and then rolled to her hands and knees, where she stayed, unable to lever herself upright. She disappeared beneath the pack, a tortoise under its shell; when she was helped to her feet she bent almost double under the oversized load. Once moving, she became a coolie who has to trot ahead to keep pace with each step's self-generating momentum.

Rather than take each load the entire, three-mile distance, we carried in poses—shorter, leap-frogging carries, lugging packs and canoes about half a mile and then returning for the rest. The trail had been maintained by winter snowmobile traffic, Chipewyans from Black Lake running traplines or traveling north to hunt caribou. We passed old oil cartons, pieces of rope, broken taillights, chunks of seat cushion, but at least the path maintained a wide alley clear of deadfall. Otherwise, it offered a miserable blend of muskeg and rock ridge.

I came to understand the subtle nuances of muskeg texture, to gauge whether a light brown patch would be good to the ankles, or a darker brown spot might take me down to the knees. In several bogs the only alternative to quicksand subsidence was to keep moving; stand still and you were mired.

On the second trip of each pose, Marypat and I shouldered a pair of tremendous packs while sharing a fifty-pound duffle between us. Normally, the second load should be a breather between strenuous first trips under the canoe, but the weighty packs and awkward duffle were brutal punishment. Within two hundred yards, my lower back knotted with spasms. We had to walk two abreast, slapped by wet vegetation, sucking through swamp, staggering over rocks. At the end of each pose our breaks lengthened until, by the third one, we lay prostrate on the wet ground to recover, motivated to move again only when the chill from damp sweaty clothes under our rain gear set us to shivering.

The trail stretched interminably, no end in sight; more rain, more muskeg, more undeterred insects. We took on faith the assurance that the path led to our destination, but felt swallowed up by the forest. On the fourth pose I surprised myself by becoming so exhausted that, at times, I couldn't lift the duffle over obstacles with one hand. Muddy inclines sent me slipping and falling. We both stumbled and tripped through the vegetation until we agreed to leave the duffle behind for a third trip. At the end we didn't decide to camp; we were forced to stop.

Stuck at an unknown point on the portage route, surrounded by muskeg, in the midst of well-marked bear territory, we plunked down for the night two feet off the trail. Nothing in the previous year approached my physical exhaustion. I shoveled my way through dinner, treating the meal as fuel, not food, and shambled off to bed as soon as dishes were cleaned. I slept in a coma, too tired to think.

In the morning the grueling routine began again. Dawn clouds slowly burned off, presenting us with a warm sunny day, but the loads were unchanged. One more haul brought us to the end of the three-mile portage. I realized, when I saw water ahead, that I had subconsciously wondered whether the trail might lead off endlessly through the wilderness, a canoeist's purgatory.

Our bodies bruised and sore from toil, we nonetheless enjoyed a short bout of self-congratulatory jubilation. Then the packs went into the boats, we took our seats, and paddled across the small lake, where the second, one-mile portage waited.

Sign of bear littered the country—fresh tracks in mud, seed- and hair-filled scat on the trail, and I had the prickly sense that we were being watched. On each portage trip we carried one of the two guns and went about our business making an excessive racket, but the larger group filled me with a new sense of security, a confidence I hadn't been able to muster the summer before, surrounded by bear on the Athabasca River.

Six more times land bridges between lakes required portages. Some consisted of little more than a lift-over, others led through the bush for half a mile or a mile. The two or three trips it took to ferry our mountain of equipment more than tripled the walking distance. A half-mile haul translated into at least one and a half miles of walking, two-thirds of it under crushing weight. The initial three-miler actually totaled nine or ten.

At the end of each successive portage, our repacking technique grew sloppier, until we simply heaped everything more or less in the middle of the canoes, tent poles and shotguns protruding at every angle, the next unloading site usually visible across the lake. The endless choreography of hefting packs, lashing paddles, grunting the canoe overhead, and trotting to another lake, only to start over again, proved as draining mentally as physically. I fastened determinedly on finishing the Chipman portage that day.

On the final half-miler we stumbled to the put-in, driven along by a mixture of obsessive adrenaline and numb determination, dumping the packs into our craft on an arm of Chipman Lake. Although I knew we had completed the requisite number of carries to avoid fast water on the river, I distrusted the truth. Back in the canoes, gear more trimly stowed, I paddled away from the string of seven body-punishing portages fully prepared for surprise. Had another carry confronted us, I would have grimly accepted it as one more wicked twist in the route we had inflicted upon ourselves.

It was Beth's birthday. We made a special dinner of her choosing and baked dessert to commemorate the occasion, toasting with wilderness cocktails the last of the Chipman portages. The sun torched the calm sky to a pastel peach, half the horizon on fire. Before us, in water colored a liquid rose-quartz by the reflection, two loons filled the night with their lonely wailing.

3

In terrain where a two-hundred-foot ridge is a striking eminence, the height of land is a subtle thing. On maps, the uppermost tendrils of drainages sometimes nearly touch, separated by narrow land dams a foot higher than the water. Yet the rivers those trickles feed capture entirely distinct watersheds and lead to oceans that can be the breadth of a continent apart. Several lakes in Canada actually straddle divides, feeding from either end into rivers that run to different oceans.

Coming from country in which the words Continental Divide evoke images of Tetonlike barriers, the low relief of the far north lured me to underestimate the work involved in making a crossing. The Chipman River and its associated lakes drain south to Lake Athabasca, and from there into the McKenzie River system and out to the Arctic Ocean near Alaska. The Dubawnt River, which lay nearly a week uphill from us, runs north and east, pouring eventually into Hudson Bay, off the North Atlantic. Even after the set of portages just behind us, another half-dozen carries and seventy-five paddling miles, upstream and across major lakes, stood between us and water that flowed our way.

Foul weather continued to plague the north. On nine of the first twelve days we had rain. T-shirts and shorts sifted lower and lower in the clothes bags, as we chose sweaters, long underwear, and wool hats instead.

In the evenings, dinner often simmered under the scanty protection of a small tarp. We had no choice but to gain expertise in kindling fires with wood that almost had to be wrung out. Rain gear became our second skin, always within reach, even during clear interludes. The necessity of maintaining dry clothing grew paramount. Every sunny break induced us to drape socks, underwear, shirts, and bits of gear across the canoe deck or around camp like cloth ornaments. Uncomfortable as the wet conditions made us, the thought of weathering it without dry clothes turned us compulsive.

On Bompas Lake, and again on Selwyn Lake, thunderclouds repeatedly hurled deluges of rain onto us so violently the drops hurt. Caught in the canoes, we gunwaled-up against shore and endured the beating. Rain drummed our heads, pocked the lake surface like buckshot, filled our spray skirts with gallon after gallon of cold water, ran off our arms in streams that turned our hands numb.

No rain gear exists that will keep you completely dry under those circumstances. Ours succumbed at armpit seams and along zippers, slowly turning the layers underneath to damp sponge. Eventually we grew so inured to torrential cloudbursts that we paddled through storms that would have driven us to shelter a week earlier.

As a group we transformed into a portaging machine. In a two-day span, including the final day on the Chipman, we managed ten portages. The drill for finding trails, strapping loose items to the correct spots on packs and boats, helping each other lift the heaviest burdens, following tricky pathways from underneath a canoe, dealing with deadfall, hills, marsh, and boulder fields, became as familiar and monotonous as assembly-line work. Except for finding the trail, we could have done it competently by feel.

Objects of interest or beauty sometimes drew us out of the toil and drudgery—a pair of courting solitary sandpipers who staked claim to a weedy pothole pond halfway across the portage to Selwyn Lake, a whiff of wild rose wafting in under the canoe, a butterfly convention crowded into a spot of sunlight. One by one the portages fell behind us, rungs on an uphill ladder.

Initially shocked by the pounding of the Chipman portages, I began to rebound. I took affront at the level of exhaustion I had been brought to and slowly asserted my ability to handle the physical demands. Winter had softened me. Despite the residual tone I had maintained by chopping and sawing wood, dredging up water daily, snowshoeing through the woods, I had lost the lean edge I'd honed coming across Lake Athabasca. The first ten days of summer brought it back with the unrefined vengeance of a hellish boot camp.

Except for the bout with abscesses, my body had served as an unfailing engine. I thought back on the miles my arms had propelled me like slow-working pistons: the glacial green water high on the Athabasca, the putrid pulp mill effluence, the wild turbulence of Boiler Rapid, the maze of delta channels, and the gaping plain of Lake Athabasca. Through the better part of Alberta, across the top of Saskatchewan, and into the Northwest Territories, my body powered me with thousands of paddle strokes and footsteps.

Lubricated by internal fluids, fueled with my intake of calories, restored by sleep, my body chugged along efficiently, responsive in a concerted complexity beyond comprehension. I demanded brute power, day-long endurance, the delicacy of steering strokes, spurts of all-out exertion, an endless stream of tasks both minuscule and all-encompassing, often under conditions far from ideal. What engine of metal and plastic could do more?

I came consciously to appreciate and care for the physical shell that carried me through life. Sleep and nourishment, for most of my years, had been little more than parts of repetitive daily routine, necessary but without direct connection to performance and ability. But on the trail, the requirements of sustenance and the restorative powers of sleep became imperative. My existence had been simplified, stripped to the basics of travel and shelter and food, and somehow also enriched by the simplicity.

By extension, my canoe and paddle was the vehicle driven by the power I generated. When I woke at night I could feel the pressure and twist of the paddle grip in my palm, found my fingers curved to hold the wooden shaft. During the day a minute communication of current and wind and wave traveled continuously through my arms and hands, fed with information resonating along the paddle.

The canoe was my packhorse. It had personality and character I could read in the way it rode, in its response to my strokes. I knew the boat's foibles and weaknesses, felt myself become alert at moments of vulnerability. I took pride and confidence in the craft's strengths, and pressed to the verge of danger when conditions were good.

When we reached the actual height of land crossing, a portage over a mile in length that separated the two watersheds, I finally felt physically prepared. Craig and I set off under the canoes, a wilderness overland convoy, a cocky swing to our stride. I kept up a steady banter, a kind of evangelical bush jive, as a warning to residents of the ursine persuasion and to distract our attention from the heavy cumbersome loads.

"Brother Craig!" I cried out. "Feel the power, brother! Put your hands on the paddles and feel the power!" The boats creaked and heaved on our shoulders, our quick steps a softly jarring rhythm. "Brother Bear. Do you hear me?" I shouted. "We bad, Mister Bear. Remember that. We bad. We have the power now, the power that makes us unafraid. Say Amen."

"Amen," Craig's response muffled and hollow. The path wound on through stands of stunted pine and fir. A Harris sparrow whistled off to the side. We began a long descent and, tipping the bow up, I glimpsed the water of Flett Lake in the distance.

"I see the promised land, brother!" I exulted. "The promised land," my voice quavered and rose. "All the toil and tribulation lies behind us. We have arrived!" My exhortation finished in a breathless bellow as I almost fell over a root in the trail.

We pressed north and the wilderness took on a feel of increasing vastness. The signs of people fell off and untamed country enveloped our small party. Trails became less and less obviously traveled as we removed ourselves from the circumference of snowmobile dominion. The paths were harder to find, narrower, less littered.

On Selwyn Lake, during a gray cold afternoon, we crossed the Northwest Territories border, for us an arbitrary boundary. What mattered was not whose political jurisdiction we'd entered but how many miles we'd done, when we'd eat next, whether a rain cloud down the lake would hit us.

Groves of tall jack pine gave way to stunted stands of black spruce, trees kept scrawny and close to the ground by cold and wind. In spite of the apparent surfeit of water, vegetation can make use of its nourishment only when temperatures stay above freezing. As we were learning, no living thing could count on frost-free conditions, even during the few summer months. In addition, plant life is subjected to cruelty by ice, battering winds, and temperature extremes that can fluctuate erratically over a one-hundred-twenty-degree span. Gnarled and twisted spruce hold grimly to cracks in unforgiving bedrock—trees several hundred years old only two or three inches in diameter. Vegetation clings to frail moorings, dormant during much of the year, flourishing desperately during ephemeral periods of grace. The dirt layer, what can scarcely be referred to as soil, is excessively thin, sometimes only a skin of lichen on bedrock; at best it makes up little more than a vegetable rind, covering the naked and bony ground. Plants that earn the right to exist under these savage circumstances have the stoic, weather-beaten look of hard-bitten farmers whose hands and faces testify to the relentless brutality of daily survival.

Signs of recent human visitation diminished in direct relation to our push north. Plane traffic, at first a frequent distraction, became uncommon enough to prompt a curious search of the sky when we heard the distant drone of a bush plane on some errand. Evidence of snowmobile traffic petered out. On later portage routes, an increasingly prevalent intertwining of caribou trails dominated the ground—parallel paths trampled through the vegetative mantle by a myriad of round cloven hooves, trails maintained by decades of repeated yearly migrations.

On Bompas and Selwyn lakes, we sighted a few uninhabited cabins, fishing outposts or old trapping shacks, including one or two that looked tidy enough to be in use. We chose not to investigate. On the northern end of Selwyn, a Christian gravesite stood near one of our camps. The plot had been marked out with a crude wooden crib, the cornerposts rounded off and fashioned as if by a primitive lathe. No nameplate identified the occupant. The wood, weathered gray and infiltrated by lichen, offered the only clue to date the structure. With cold drizzle falling, it was a lonely place to be buried—lonely but defiant.

Arriving at Flett Lake, finally over the height of land, we camped on an island made from an esker remnant. Sandy ridges that wind sinuously across the glaciated north, eskers were formed from sand and gravel deposited by melting glaciers; they provide a major form of topographic relief in a land otherwise predominantly flat.

As with the majority of esker campsites, we commanded a sweeping view of the country from the ridge top, had our pick of any number of comfortable sleeping platforms, and enjoyed the pleasing symmetry of the landform. For the first time, I felt poised at the verge of the far north. The openness, the feel of reindeer moss underfoot, the small patches of tundra we could see from our camp, all of it wove together into a fabric that whispered to me of northern land.

The camp so seduced us that we succumbed to temptation and awarded ourselves a rest day. The toilsome trail we'd struggled along for seven days gave us adequate justification. I relaxed enough to see how focused I'd been on the physical challenge. Waves of inclement weather, combined with the physical demands of portaging under our behemoth loads, had turned me combative, tunnel-visioned, goal-oriented, so that I had forgotten to enjoy my surroundings.

On the little island, I woke again to the thrill of the land, the overarching sky, listened with rejuvenated ears to the call of loons, the lapping of waves. Even the advent of rain showers inconvenienced me only enough to relocate clothes I'd hung out to dry, and the rainbows that followed were ample repayment. We lingered over coffee, baked desserts, talked with satisfaction about the obstacles already overcome.

It would be the last time all summer we'd allow ourselves the luxury of resting through a calm day. Even at dawn the next morning my sleep was disturbed by the sounds of a growing north wind, and by the time we packed to go we had to load the boats on the lee side of the island to avoid the pounding waves. We paid for our indulgence with twelve miles of constant, arm-wearying face-off with wind. White-capped waves forced us against the shore, increasing our travel distance, and the gale tended to isolate us from each other.

Conversation, if it took place at all, went on in a series of shouts, even within the same canoe. Wind filled our ears, opportunistic surf demanded our concentration, and the level of exertion forced us to husband our resources, focusing our energy on the slow pounding rhythm of paddle strokes and the struggle to keep balance in the wildly pitching water. Every so often I'd glance at the companion boat off to one side, and see the reflection of my own strain in the set tension on Craig's or Beth's face.

We crawled past rocky points inch by inch, and in stronger wind gusts, paddled ferociously just to keep from losing ground. I resented every extra detour around a rock and fixed my sights on the next bay or peninsula, landmarks that went past after the expense of thousands of heavy strokes.

About the only thing to be said in defense of wind was that it kept the bugs down just as effectively as it held us in check. When we stopped to eat on a tundra clearing, more as an excuse to end our exertion for a time than as a response to hunger, the bugs left us alone. They were there by the millions, but hid themselves by burrowing into the spongy ground cover or hanging onto the lee side of bushes. They restricted their activities to a calm zone no more than two inches above ground.

After eating we lay in the soft turf, our bodies indenting the yielding mosses. My face felt flushed, blasted by invisible particles, like I'd just finished a downhill ski run on a blustery day. Lying next to the earth, I could feel the warmth of the sun as the wind gusts whistled by in another dimension.

On ground level I had to gird myself against roaming hordes of black fly and mosquito. Pant legs went under my socks, I cinched in the waist and cuffs of my windshirt, drew up my hood until only a small opening allowed me to breathe, and shoved my hands into pockets. I found if I lay completely still, acting the part of a landform, that the swarming insects lost the edge in their intensity. We all lay, trussed up like mummies, putting off the return to the canoes, enjoying the halcyon world that would vanish abruptly when we sat up.

One last stumbling block lay between us and the Dubawnt River. Although we had entered the correct watershed, we could cut off some paddling miles by making a final half-mile portage to Wholdaia Lake. Exasperated as we were with the overland routine, saving ten miles of wind-slogging was clearly the lesser of two evils.

If the choice hadn't been obvious before we returned to our canoes, the final four miles of slow-motion progress rammed home the point. The portage trail began in a swampy bog and skirted the worst of a series of muskeg flats along a snaking route on moderately high ground. Dozens of caribou paths confused the process of trail-finding enough to warrant a scouting foray all the way across to Wholdaia.

Even after reconnoitering, I managed to take a wrong fork on the second trip, traipsing off, under the canoe, along a caribou path. A hundred yards later I realized my error, but was too stubborn to go back the way I'd come. I'll just angle across this opening to the right, I thought. Pick up the trail farther along.

Two steps into the clearing, I sank to my crotch in muskeg. One second I was hot-footing across some wet ground, the next I looked like a dwarf wearing a seventeen-foot red hat. "Son of a bitch!" I muttered, from under the boat. The cold muck held firmly to my lower half, and I stood on some indistinct surface that trembled underfoot, doing little to inspire me with confidence that I'd completed my descent. Unceremoniously, I wrenched the boat off my neck and slammed it down next to me in the ooze.

Now that I had committed myself to bushwhacking and could hardly get much wetter, I wallowed on across the quaking bog, using the canoe for balance and buoyancy, hauling the boat alongside as I half-swam, half-floundered through the fifty yards of waist-deep muskeg that separated me from the trail.

Looking up I saw Marypat, watching the spectacle, an expression of combined incredulity, horror, and barely suppressed mirth on her face as she took in my northern rendition of monster from the black lagoon.

"Jesus!" was all I could sputter, once I'd regained my full height on dry ground. A withering look at Marypat stopped the worst of her hysterical convulsions, but when I presented myself to the group at the end of the portage, looking like I'd lost a battle with a vat of chocolate fondue, even I had to admit the humor in the situation. The event was memorable enough to earn me the sobriquet Muskeg Mike.

4

I remember, as a boy, the excitement that ran like adrenaline through my body the first time I saw the Rocky Mountains and the sweeping roll of high plains. Motoring across North Dakota and into eastern Montana, I sat hunched up with my elbows on the car dash, my eyes watery from squinting for the first view of snow-covered ranges. Two hundred miles early, I had called distant cloud banks mountains, and smothered my father with questions about the particulars of ranching. I had visually devoured the wide sky, towering thunderheads, dirt lanes leading off over the horizon, little herds of startled pronghorn, speed limit signs with no maximum, as if, no matter how fast you drove, you couldn't gather up all the space.

In slightly subdued form, it was the way I felt drawing close to the Barrenlands in a canoe. The knowledge that that wide, mysterious, untamed region lay over the northern horizon, a few days off, charged me with the same eager lust, the same uncontainable exhilaration. Just as I'd mistaken clouds for mountains, I fastened onto the small patches of tundra that had encroached into the boreal forest and tried to imagine them spread over the land, imagined the trees gone and space yawning about us. The anticipation made me squirm in my seat as I paddled.

On Wholdaia Lake, splotches of tundra growth defiantly held off the surrounding forest. Rich in green and brown and rust, colors of earth and peat and moss and flower, the parks of tundra tendered the first hints of what lay to the north. Wholdaia is a large lake, but the Dubawnt River flows into and out of its waters. We were, even if paddling across more than twenty miles of slack water, finally on the Dubawnt River, finally over the height of land, pursuing waterways that drained north and east into Hudson Bay.

The day after our cold windy hardships on Flett Lake—and in testimony to the drastic meteorological swings possible in the north— we enjoyed absolute calm and temperatures warm enough to bring out T-shirts. My bare arms hadn't been exposed since Lake Athabasca. The importance of capitalizing on propitious conditions hadn't been lost on us. We were up at dawn and went across the smooth lake at a determined pace.

Craig kept pointing out new birds, some of which weren't supposed to be there at all. "Look at this range map," he showed me a page of his field guide. "Black scoters aren't supposed to be near here." As I studied the book, Craig glassed a bay with his ever-present binoculars. "I've seen flock after flock of them," he pointed out a covey of ducks. "I'll bet there haven't been enough people up here to report them."

Since our first portages, where sign had been everywhere, I'd hardly given a thought to the danger of black bears. I retained the practice of scrutinizing lunch spots and campsites, sniffing about for tracks or scat, but the old habit had the feel of reflexive routine, not anxious phobia. The shotgun had a full complement of slugs, and came with us into the tent every night. But the edge of fear had been dulled, the confidence gained by being part of a larger group, illusory or not, acting as an effective antidote to my tension. I knew also that black bears stuck to timber, and didn't wander onto the tundra of the Barrens. Ironic that I should welcome the crossing into grizzly country, but I did.

We were cautious enough to camp on islands whenever convenient, and on Wholdaia we found one that was more tundra than north woods. Forest ringed the site like the fringe of hair on Friar Tuck's head, while the interior was bare tundra. We set camp at the edge of trees, and after dinner Marypat and I walked up to the open crown of the island.

The evening temperature was comfortably warm. Wholdaia Lake stretched like satin under the pale blue sky. We brought the heavily used maps with us and oriented ourselves by landmarks visible from the high vantage point. Mosquitoes swarmed our exposed hands and faces, making us pivot around in search of a mitigating breeze that didn't exist. I stuffed my hands wrist-deep into my pants pockets, and drew up my hood, blowing away the nearest assailants with explosive puffs of breath.

Arctic terns called frantically overhead, diving toward us, protecting their ground nests. We had to walk carefully to avoid the eggs, camouflaged to look like round speckled rocks, laid directly into tiny scraped depressions in the dirt, hardly nests at all. We found a huge boulder, several tons of granite dropped carelessly on the landscape by retreating glaciers, and leaned against the warm surface, our shoulders touching.

"Sometimes I miss you," Marypat said, her foot scraping a groove in the ground. "I mean, I miss the way we were alone."

"I know we weren't going to compare summers, but I can't help thinking about how quiet and calm things were." She fanned mosquitoes off her face and returned her hand to her pocket.

I kept looking over the silent land, realizing how infrequent our close times together had become. "We knew it would be different, MP. There are benefits too, remember. We can't dwell on things we can't change."

"I know," she sighed, shifting her weight. "I know."

On the way back, we found beds of pink moss campion, tiny fragile flowers only an inch above the ground, and we knelt together looking at them. The mosquitoes grew fiercer, if anything, as the temperature dropped, and the terns finally settled back onto their exposed eggs.

Minor irritants within a group undergoing physical and environmental stress are inevitable. Major flareups are entirely likely. I'd been on one expedition where such problems were severe enough to turn the whole trip sour. Our group exhibited nothing remotely close to that.

The two tents went up within easy earshot of each other, our canoes traveled in close proximity, we ate the same food, shared the camp chores, followed each other across portage trails, debated the constantly changing subtleties of navigation, argued the safety of paddling in wind or making a crossing. In short, we negotiated and compromised on every aspect of travel and daily life.

In the same way that people who live together pick up on small annoying habits, we all contributed idiosyncratic foibles to the group milieu. Craig and Beth still hadn't thoroughly organized their packs, even after repeated attempts, and I finally realized that a tolerance for a certain level of disorganization was their style, and not likely to improve. But to hear them wondering for the fiftieth time where the Grape-Nuts were could be maddening.

More significantly, we all had different preferred paces, reservoirs of physical stamina, thresholds for risk, tendencies toward optimism or pessimism in the face of adversity. Discussions and conflicts usually arose over matters as mundane as when to stop for lunch, how quickly to get going in the morning, or whether another two miles of progress was worth passing up an attractive campsite. We had faced many of the same battles over personal style as a group of two.

Mostly, we found acceptable middle ground. In fact, irreconcilable differences were never allowed to persist. Over the weeks a new style of travel evolved, molded through hundreds of intuitive understandings, minor arguments, observations, and the nuances of body language.

For Marypat and me the experience was neither better nor worse than our isolated time had been, simply different. Besides, there were some decided benefits. Finally we could capitalize on the outside friendships we had so sorely missed during the winter. We were sharing this endeavor with people we cared about, people who appreciated the life as much as we.

As a result of the larger group size, we also felt more secure, less at risk. Dangers still lurked, we traveled through an impartial wilderness, an environment capable of meting out harsh consequences to those who made errors in judgment or were victimized by circumstance. But over the spectrum from bear phobia to whitewater nervousness, the increased numbers made me feel less vulnerable, more willing to push limits.

Marypat and I continued to develop as an efficient team. Our portaging technique had been fine-tuned to the point where I knew which hand would carry which object on which trip across the trail. We paddled in unthinking sync, mostly without the need for conversation, alive to the language of boat, paddle, and muscle. Even from the bow I could visualize the way Marypat would hold her paddle as she made the necessary strokes to avoid a rock, how she'd shift to balance herself on a lean, and could even picture the look on her face, the way her wrist tendons would stand out.

5

Day Seventeen. After a tricky crossing in three-foot waves, using islands as blockers, our canoes furrowed into the Dubawnt River, current going our way for the first time since early August of the previous summer, our last days on the Athabasca River. I noticed weeds straightened out beneath the boat, but could feel no pull. Then, as the channel narrowed, I sensed the first tugs, the joyous insistence that is a river going downhill. No longer did we struggle upstream, unlikely trout on a spawning run. No longer were we responsible for every bit of our forward momentum, helplessly prone to the fickle favors of wind. We rode the river!

"Wahooo!" I crowed, and laid my paddle across my thighs, watching the rocky bank slide past, the river bottom accelerate beneath us. "Hello, Dubawnt!"

The Dubawnt River is known for its shallow rocky character. The bed is a jumble of rounded boulders, often submerged under only a few inches of water. With all the early summer rain, I couldn't imagine the river being low, and the bank vegetation looked flooded, yet we had to wind our way through fields of rock, grating ignobly over moss-covered granite as we familiarized ourselves with the new watercourse.

During the afternoon a gusting tailwind sent us rocketing down a wide pool in the river. The canoes schussed down wavefronts as if they were surfboards. Spray blew off the wave tops, our decks repeatedly shed water. I glanced over my shoulder at the yellow boat and saw a scene out of a stormy ocean watercolor: minuscule boat on a heaving sea.

The inaugural camp on the Dubawnt was set on a wide plain of tundra. We gravitated to the lone stand of wind-twisted spruce, shelter from the gale and source of dead firewood. I cooked spaghetti for dinner, a favorite meal because we usually had enough to allow seconds and thirds. At one point, while tending the fire, I turned to see Craig at the crest of a low rise, binoculars affixed to his eyes. He was a dark silhouette against the gray sky, a lone figure in a prairielike space. Wind moaned through the nearby spruce. Stirring spoon in my hand, I shuddered with subdued excitement.

Craig and I had a pattern going in the mornings. The first to rise started the breakfast fire. When the sounds of snapping firewood and the smell of smoke wafted across camp, the other would crawl out through the mosquito-netting door, and we'd share a time together at dawn, sipping coffee, comparing impressions. At the tundra camp along the Dubawnt, we could as easily have been on the English moors.

Heavy mist, actually a light drizzle, limited our horizon to thirty feet, even shutting out the river. The overcast had the effect of amplifying our noises while closing out the rest of the world. Cotton grass, oversized Q-tips with stalks, bent over with the weight of moisture, and the carpet of vegetation led suggestively off into the mist.

The drizzle did nothing to dampen the ferocity of bug life, however. Mosquitoes and black flies continually made kamikaze flights into our hot coffee, and we faced into whatever breath of air blew past, using our height to escape the worst insect concentrations one or two feet off the ground.

"I was thinking . . ." Craig straightened after feeding a stick into the flames. "You start to understand how natives could believe in spirits in a place like this. The land has a power," he continued. "It feels stripped down, kind of basic. I can see how you'd deal with immediate forces like wind and animals and cold, how you'd interact directly with the environment, feel like you could communicate with inanimate objects."

I picked an insect suicide out of my coffee and swung to face the smoke from the fire, the lesser of evils. "I know what you mean," I agreed. "So much of what seems important in civilization has no meaning here. Time, money, career, getting ahead. And it's more than being reduced to dealing with elemental needs. There's a depth you experience once all that other stuff slips away, a peace. You get meditative serenity that doesn't require taking twenty minutes a day to say some hokey mantra."

Now that we had put the uphill toil behind us, I felt less driven to confront obstacles, more ready to soak up the environment. Craig's thoughts reminded me to be more receptive. The mist lifted slightly, so we could see a bit farther, but not much. Leaving camp, we startled a tundra swan. The magnificent white bird lifted itself heavily off the water, paddling with its webbed feet, a silent white phantom flying into the fog.

The river ran slowly through marshy countryside. The deadening of sounds that I'd noticed at dawn also must have limited the awareness of wildlife. We crept up on willets, dowitchers, phalarope, and more swans as we stole quietly downstream. I felt that we were in a nature preserve, except that the usual boundary markers, bird-watching blinds, and warnings against hunting didn't alert us. We were truly in a preserve, but not one set aside by man, walled off defensively against the insidious raids of humanity. The muffling fog and prevalence of wildlife turned off our conversational tendencies.

The Dubawnt was molten pewter in texture, flowing seamlessly, without sound, without haste. The canoes floated past an arctic tern that stood on a rock hidden just underwater. The bird watched us with its alert glittery eyes, sharp red bill contrasting with a black cap. The river split into tiny V's past its reptilian legs.

We surprised the first big game of summer, a bull moose feeding on a grassy island. The black bull raised his head, weed and muck dripping from the sides of his fleshy mouth, and then plunged across the river, knees high, spraying water, giving us wild-eyed glances before lunging up a gravel bank and disappearing soundlessly into the alder.

Little rips of fast water marked the end of marsh. The test of route-finding, reading moving water, learning the tricks and character of a new river, changed our perspective, narrowed our attention away from the land. More out of caution than necessity, we scouted a short rapid, Craig and I hopping down a bouldery shoreline and verbalizing a strategy, while Marypat and Beth held the boats. The fast run down a series of chutes impressed upon me the extent of my whitewater rustiness, skills I hadn't called upon since the Athabasca River. Even on an easy rapid, the boat several times stubbornly refused to cooperate, and we reached the bottom arguing about the failed maneuvers.

"What were you doing, drawing the bow into the wave?" I remonstrated with my partner.

"You had us broadside!" Marypat shot back, turning halfway around in her seat to face me. "I wasn't about to get dunked." And she gave me her back.

Selection of campsites had become a refined process. The island we chose on Hinde Lake had enough trees to protect the tents from wind, good mossy plots for beds, an exposed point on which to build the fire and catch some insect-controlling breezes, and the security offered by a moat of cold water.

Since benefiting from the river flow, the threat of being windbound had dimmed in my thoughts. Even with winds, we'd have current to aid us and smaller expanses of water to generate waves.

My assumption proved grievously mistaken.

6

The pleasant island turned into a prison, a cell we paced across, became familiar with against our wills, a foundered ship in rough seas.

The winds were such that it wouldn't have mattered where we had camped. Hinde Lake was no more than a wide length of river. Between islands, current rippled the water, but high winds humped up the surface so wildly we didn't even bother to speculate about leaving.

For a day, July 4, I accepted the delay with equanimity. In fact, I perversely enjoyed the wild weather, and spent most of the time hunkered on the rocky point where we'd put our fire, coffee cup in hand, watching the muddied black water boom against the smooth rock. Every wave wore a lather of whitecap, and the body punch concussions of their impact shuddered the rock. Sometimes a fleck of spray hit me in the face, and I imagined myself at the prow of an implacable veteran ship, head up into the wind.

Laundry we put out had to be knotted onto twigs; it flapped dry in the time it took to sip down a cup of coffee. We used a crude wind-measuring device to get a feel for our adversary. Craig stood on the point, visibly leaning into the wind, jacket hood snapping behind him, trying to assign a number to the blow. As best we could tell, the wind maintained a thirty-mile-an-hour clip and gusted significantly higher.

I held onto the hope that an afternoon or evening lull would allow us to spurt forward, but none materialized. Even the terns, who find sport in strong winds, stood forlornly on rocks, hunched over in groups like nattily attired businessmen at a bus stop, waiting it out. I gave up, and accepted the time as an enforced rest day. The evening—gray, cold, turbulent—reminded me of fall, not July.

On the second day, restlessness got the better of me. The same gray sky, the same whipping wind, the same angry surf. We had succeeded in entertaining ourselves for a day playing cards and exploring the island for small discoveries. On the ground I found an abandoned owl's nest, a platform of sticks and down feathers, littered with the cream-colored remains of the hatched egg. We found a mossy protected hollow for our card games. But by the second day I was pacing the rock, looking ahead at the many broad lakes in our path, studying the map, and noticing the paucity of trees signified by a predominant whiteness on the topographic sheets.

I began to see how groups could get disastrously delayed by inhospitable conditions, how wind and rain could hold you back until food ran short. If we ran into ice farther north, our progress would be critically curtailed. Already we had battled ahead on many days it would have been easier to stay in camp. Even at that our mileage average was significantly less than the fifteen a day that I had thought would be easy.

The wind became a presence I resented, a presence that never waned. In the midst of it I could hardly remember times when my ears hadn't been filled with air surf, my hands chilled, my lips dried and cracked. In the tent it chuffed and flapped at the nylon material, tugged at the stakes, and outside it wore me down mentally with unrelenting blows.

By mid-morning we talked ourselves into believing the wind had moderated a notch, that fewer waves were white-capped, that we might be able to escape. But gearing the craft for travel had the feel of saddling unbroken horses without halters in an open corral. Even in the lee of a rocky point, the boats bucked and turned and tipped as we lashed things in. As we emerged from the protection of the island, the unmitigated gale struck us full on, fought us to a stand-off.

The two boats heaved up three or four feet on the choppy water, then dove into the next mountainous wave. By angling just off from head on, we could escape shipping water with each attack, but barely moved forward. In the stern, the fight to maintain the canoe's angle took away from each stroke's forward power. In the bow, the tremendous effort made arm joints ache with the tendency to separate.

Marypat bent her head down in the front of the bucking canoe, concentrating with effort, too demoralized by the glacial forward momentum to watch, her top hand tucked inside her jacket sleeve for warmth, bottom hand soaked time after time by the cold lake.

In what felt like an endless series of plunging twists, spray-laden gusts, and shoulder-wrenching strokes, we put four miles behind our sterns. No matter how we maneuvered—hugging the shore, hiding behind islands, even in narrow channels—savage wind hounded us, making a folly of our puny assertions of strength. We admitted defeat and found the next windbound camp.

If the previous evening had the bite of fall, that night winter arrived. A light sleety drizzle added further insult to the day's trials. Hot lunch and a guttering fire only momentarily cheered us up. I returned to my glum reckoning with maps, hunched on the lee side of a boulder, layered in long underwear and sweaters. Ahead lay Boyd, Barlow, and Carey lakes, all major bodies of water, separated by narrow river sections that would put off the next open water crossing only briefly.

I consoled myself with the satisfaction of having tried. We could do nothing more. If the wind died, we might sprint down twenty miles of water. Wilderness fortunes sometimes swing from desperation to triumph in half a day. My penchant for imagining the most dire scenarios worked at full clip, but when I went to bed, listening to the trees creak and complain under the punishment, I fantasized a hot, utterly still day on which the canoes would skim across mile after mile of water.

My eyes opened cautiously in the gray light of dawn. I tried to will good conditions, but heard wind in the trees. The sound angered me, provoked me to get up and confront the day. The waves were clearly smaller, but the sky brooded overhead, the wind bit coldly at my face. "Let's go guys, before it gets worse." I collected twigs on my way past the tents, rubbed hands together to limber my fingers for striking a match.

The lake had calmed considerably. Even with a steady headwind, we would make progress. After the experience of the previous day, our concept of impossible paddling conditions had inflated several large notches. "It shows you," I said, "not to underestimate even a small lake. If someone had told us we'd be windbound on pissant Hinde Lake for two full days, I would have laughed."

Once again the river current aided our quest. Boulder-garden rapids actually provided a kind of entertainment, a relief from the ever-present wind. We cheerfully scouted a few runs, the four of us debating ledge drops and chutes and the whim of current, and then kneeling in the boats for the diversion of whitewater.

Marypat and I pumped each other up with compliments. The boat responded more readily to our combined teamwork, we accomplished maneuvers as planned. The old confidence returned, the canoe was a companion and ally again. During the brief descents, wind was forgotten. We concentrated instead on the velocity of river, the balance of the boats, the look of a drop, the accessibility of eddies. Just as I had physically and intuitively become intimate with the Athabasca, just as

I would become acquainted with the Kazan River in another week or two, I soaked up the sensation of the Dubawnt.

But as the day went on, wind reasserted its oppressive grip. Without the river current we couldn't have proceeded at all. With its help we strenuously crept ahead. I felt robbed. By all reason, the stretch of predominantly riverine channel should have been a coast, a good ride, a break from wind.

The land we paddled past looked almost arid. Sandy esker ridges flanked the river, wound off in the distance. Spruce and birch trees grew in thin stands, defiant concentrations where soil and moisture allowed them to endure. More and more the tundra dominated the countryside. Open land spread above the river in large expanses, scraped to bedrock by ice, littered with thousands of boulders dropped by retreating glaciers. Caribou paths stitched an erratic pattern across sand banks and mossy flats, and I found myself glancing over the open ridgelines for the profile of wolf or bear or caribou.

Wind absorbed most of my attention. Slamming upstream against the current, gusts built up tremendous rollers and created a kind of current of their own. I had to angle the boat both aerodynamically and hydraulically, sometimes able to find no compromise. Wind or river repeatedly took steerage completely out of my power, twisting the canoe in a half circle or blowing us across an entire channel.

Again and again we came to the brink of a decision to stop, to give up, but then continued on. If we can't paddle the river, I thought, how are we going to get past all the lakes? So we doggedly persisted, bend by endless bend. Wind blew the clouds out of the sky, so at least we enjoyed sunshine, but if anything, the gusts grew stronger. In a few protected places, around some tight bends, we got the feel of the river, caught agonizing intimations of what we might have enjoyed all day had it been calm.

At Boyd Lake the struggle, which up to then had been thick-headed and marginally reasonable, became unquestionably ridiculous. We had made eighteen miles, had actually gained on our average on a day that required every bit of our energy to move at all. Yet, I thought ruefully, it wouldn't be much fun if every day was as much a physical battle. The wind simply couldn't persist.

But I was wrong. In the far north the elements didn't conform to my standards of fair play. Early in the morning, wind only ruffled the water across Boyd Lake. I hoped fervently that the breezes would die and my calm-lake fantasy would be fulfilled. Two miles out it became clear that the meteorological mood would swing the other way, that the old interaction of lashing winds, heaving water, and bludgeoned muscles would characterize another day.

My turn in the bow. Rather than dwell on the depressing circumstances, I focused solely on route-finding, studying the map before me for the shortest distances, lee shores, the use of islands as potential wind blocks. Boyd Lake is crammed with islands, and I entertained myself by working out a complex strategy for minimizing wind and mileage.

During the mid-day break we inhaled our portions of food and lay down to rest, gathering energy for the next stage of the war for forward progress. I had begun to think that the rest of the summer would consist of an endless gusty beating. For four straight days we had been stopped altogether or severely hampered by wind. Day and night the currents of air had washed and whirled over the land, harrying every project, from pitching tents and building fires to paddling boats and staying warm.

By late afternoon we had crossed most of the lake, accomplishing an impressive twenty-one miles. We camped not because of encroaching darkness—daylight we had in abundance—but because we were exhausted. Nonetheless, I enjoyed a powerful satisfaction at bettering our mileage average on two straight days against strong winds. With a smug sense of conquest, I penciled in on the map our winding path through the many islands. We had won the day's skirmish, but faced an unpredictable foe capable of squelching our success at a whim. Even as I enjoyed the glow of victory, I dared not forecast a continuation.

A week's worth of exertion separated us from the last bathing indulgence. Reeking from layers of grime, we all four piled into an empty canoe and paddled to a pair of boulders well away from shore. A slight current flowed between the smooth rocks and wind swept insects away from our pale bodies.

I had thought Lake Athabasca in June felt about as cold as water could feel and still be liquid, but Boyd Lake was a heart-stopping temperature. The rinse cycle of our baths lasted two seconds at most. We stomped around on the rocks, bellowing with surprise like an alarmed herd of walrus, our skin peppered with gooseflesh. Ice, I thought. Ice has not been off this lake for long!

7

The other aspect of northern summer is an almost unbelievable contrast to the cold blustery conditions we lived through on Hinde and Boyd lakes. Overnight, the north can swing from wintry chill to the stultifying heat of the Oklahoma panhandle in August, from sleet to sweat—and from forty-mile-an-hour winds to utter calm, a transformation that occurred while we slept through the short night. The change came about as quickly as an adroitly switched stage set, cunningly transporting us to a different clime.

The final miles of Boyd Lake went under the boats while the perfect images of the canoes were reflected on its smooth surface. Black flies and mosquitoes, largely absent in the wind, followed whatever clues they employ across miles of open water to find us, compelling the use of protective netting jackets and even headnets from time to time. Not one of us complained. The memory of wind hovered too freshly in our minds to nitpick about the nuisance of bugs. The freedom to paddle unimpeded seemed a great wealth, a bequest not to be squandered. We made no boast of our good fortune, hardly even discussed it in fact, for superstitious fear of ruining the change in luck.

For the first time since Hinde Lake I could appreciate the land at leisure. Instead of being locked in a physical wrestling match with the environment, I glided through it, going long periods without paying conscious attention to the process, watching the last scraggly fingers of stunted trees peter out and the rolling ocean of tundra sweep away to the horizon. We were entering the Barrens.

I imagined explorers a century or two before me—men like Tyrrell and Hearne and Back—penetrating the vast engulfing openness without maps of any consequence, without modern equipment, feeling their way across the wide unknown as ants navigate a lawn.

I had read the accounts of Alexander Back, exploring the arctic river that now bears his name, and remembered his description of a calm day on a large lake, uncertain where the outlet for the river lay. He and his men had sat still on the water, quietly listening for the sound of a falls or rapid, some indication of the river's direction. They had put objects in the water to see if any tiny current might give away the watershed, and intently studied the waving bottom weeds for directional signals. Again and again those men had paddled up bays and inlets only to be turned back at dead ends. Their progress had pressed forward with an obstinate will, frustrated time after time each day, but dogged in the pursuit of larger goals.

We came equipped with faster boats, accurate maps, and the knowledge that our route had been done before. Yet the remoteness and sheer span of the land dwarfed our puny efforts. I felt the awe of Oregon Trail wagoneers in the face of the Great Plains, the humility of solo sailors in mid-ocean. At the same time that I felt minuscule, the horizon-expanding wilderness thrilled me, made me want to shout with excitement. I kept catching movement at the corners of my vision, kept picturing wolf or primitive man. We had come to the brink of the wild Barrens, land of ancient spirits.

Our own encounter with exploration unknowns waited several days ahead. The Dubawnt River runs roughly parallel to several other major Barrenland waterways. The Thelon drains off the land to the west. And the Kazan, having paralleled our route on the east almost from the start of the summer, runs south to north next to the Dubawnt. In the many map-studying sessions, we had isolated what looked like a relatively convenient traverse, connecting the Dubawnt and Kazan watersheds, a traverse we had not heard of anyone attempting before.

The proposed route looked reasonable on the maps, but maps only symbolize the landscape. Water-level fluctuations, swings in weather, the topography we had to portage across, all would combine to create the real experience. Three small inches on the map represents a dozen miles along unknown waterways and over land bridges. Slight cartographic inaccuracies or minor changes in landscape since the maps were made had the potential to create either an epic debacle or an easy triumph of our effort.

Like the Grand Rapid and Lake Athabasca during the first summer's journey, like the Chipman portage and the height of land a few weeks earlier, the watershed traverse stood out as the next expedition barrier. Anticipating the experience, I felt a distant kinship with the early explorers, and the prospect filled me with the same mixture of thrill and humility as the opening land that stretched away from the river.

Meantime I reveled in the joy of calm winds and the imponderable pull of river current. The Dubawnt, between Boyd and Barlow lakes, sped us north. A river still characterized by boulder-strewn channels, the Dubawnt had gained tremendous volume and power over the miles. Instead of bumping and scraping through fields of rock on slow current, we rode down chutes, ferried into powerful eddies twenty yards across, and shot along the strong deep channels between massive boulders.

Another bull moose, rack furred with summer velvet, welcomed us to the start of Barlow Lake. How many humans had that moose encountered? I sensed as much curiosity as alarm in the huge animal's gaze.

Marshy landscape and insistent black flies convinced us to lunch in the canoes. Arctic terns punctuated the air with their shrill conversation and harried the larger gulls like fighter planes harassing heavy bombers. A pair of tundra swans shepherded their cygnet in a marshy bay. Warm sunlight reflected off the water and we reclined in the boats, soaking up the warmth.

"Should we paddle by the swans for a picture?" I asked Marypat.

The sedate birds watched us more and more intently as we approached, and swam with their downy offspring deeper into the bay. Our paddle blades sliced soundlessly into the water, the canoe wake rippled symmetrically to the sides. Suddenly, the pair of adults took laboriously to the air, honking loudly in complaint, leaving the tiny flightless cygnet alone.

We hadn't intended to create such a disruption, and began backpaddling. But the sharp-eyed opportunistic gulls had quickly seen their chance. The small swan, hardly more than a feather ball, swam frantically for the protection of marsh grasses while gulls and terns dove out of the sky with murderous intent. The adult swans circled too far away to come to its aid.

We made haste to depart, feeling the shame of sandlot bullies who had taken their teasing of a runt a step too far, causing real pain. I kept glancing back at the scene, so tranquil a moment before. The baby swan ducked and feinted away from the lethal beaks of the larger birds and kept making for the safe grasses. Several attacks looked sure to succeed, the little bird taking direct hits, but miraculously the cygnet gained the thick weeds and disappeared into the undergrowth. Gulls and terns circled above, crying loudly over their missed chance to scavenge a meal, but soon appeared to lose interest in their quarry, now out of sight.

The swans still hadn't returned, but we paddled away, hoping our departure would right the balance we had so rudely disrupted in the selfish pursuit of a picture. For miles the vision of gulls diving on the little swan haunted me, and I imagined the cygnet being ripped apart by the avian scavengers, who were only acting out of their drive to survive. All for a goddamn picture!

On maps, Barlow Lake is where tree growth ends. Aberrant scruffy stands of ground-hugging trees show up here and there beyond that point, but tundra dominates. It was also the beginning of our daily search for driftwood and dead sticks, fuel for cook fires. Dead branches and driftwood were rarely more than an inch in diameter. The desiccated bleached wood burned to white ash in the time it took to find the next stick, requiring one of us to take up a seat next to the grill and feed in the small fuel almost continuously.

Insects welcomed us to the Barrens with a ferocity we hadn't yet experienced. When I bent over to stake the tent into the spongy ground, squadrons of black flies swarmed over my hands and pelted my face. I quickly pulled on mosquito netting, opting for sweat and a fuzzy view rather than insect attacks, but black flies were insistent. Even when I thought every part of my body had been armored, I'd discover oozing blood spots where a fly had found a tiny aperture and done its demonic business, completing its life's work at my expense.

Not yet acclimatized to dealing with bug stress, we piled en masse into a tent for cocktails and a game of cribbage. A horde of flies came in with us, and the first five minutes were devoted to squashing the predators, until puréed insects littered the floor. Outside, the pinging of black flies on the tent fabric sounded like steady drizzle. We stripped to the skin, but kept sweating. The still heat odoriferously exposed the cursory nature of our Boyd Lake baths. Days of all-out exertion and the effects of intense sunlight combined with cocktails to turn us into limp dishrags, barely capable of playing cards.

No one complained about insects, about heat, about the lack of wood. The weather stayed calm, gift enough for us. My fantasy had been realized, at least for a day.

A large snowdrift on shore glaringly testified to the ephemeral nature of heat on the Barrens. Well into July, and snow still lingered. I knew of expeditions that had encountered ice at the north end of Barlow Lake in July. Carey Lake, one more to the north, often held late ice, and Dubawnt Lake, the next in line, was notorious for being locked in ice, even into August. Part of our rationale for traversing east to the Kazan was to miss Dubawnt, the largest lake in the Barrenlands.

It seemed pessimistic to worry about ice-locked lakes while basking in eighty-degree temperatures, but most of the summer had been cold and rainy. My real hope lay in the strong winds we'd experienced. Wind, even more than heat, is often the most effective agent in clearing ice from lakes. Like a belligerent bulldozer, it slams floes back and forth from shore to shore, jostles chunks against each other, literally disintegrating the frozen plating.

But northern Barlow Lake gave a clear passage, and we paddled the river section between it and Carey Lake on the most beautiful day of the trip. Winds were again calm, the temperature had moderated to a comfortable level, the sky and river competed against each other for the deepest, most brilliant blue. I had fallen back into the timeless rhythm of travel.

The summer's events stretched behind me in an unbroken series of memories: physical aches, hardening muscles, a string of lake names, portage trails, campfires, loon calls. Beyond that, the many months of winter: sweeping northern lights, crackling cold, the faces of new friends, my view out the cabin window, our network of trails. And before that, the first summer: Sunday dinner in Vega, lonely trappers' cabins, the feel of the muscular Athabasca River, the unnerving presence of bear, smooth bedrock camps on Lake Athabasca.

My paddle slid smoothly into the water, a sensation as familiar as walking, another bite out of the continent. I could tell from the easy swing of Marypat's arms, the smooth fluid look of her back, that she enjoyed the same confidence and ease. It no longer struck me as remarkable that we paddled in wordless coordinated synchrony; that the paddles, the boat, my body, my partner were a meshed unit. I could have been convinced it was what we had always done.

Without thought for time of day, we stopped along the shore to enjoy the land. Craig unpacked fishing gear for a trial cast or two. Our menu plans included a week's worth of fish meals. The expedition supply load had been substantially diminished as a result, but we had had little luck catching fish. Often, by the end of a day, we were too tired to fish. In the few instances we had really tried, we'd been unsuccessful. I began suspecting that we had overestimated our angling prowess.

"Got one!" Craig shouted, bringing the rest of us scrambling over in time to see a healthy grayling leap clear of the water.

Beth flung a lure into the river and had a heavy trout on by the second cast. Marypat reeled in another grayling. I joined in the excitement and soon had a ten-pound trout on shore. While one fish flopped on the ground, the next struck at a lure.

"Hey, we better stop," Beth admonished. "I don't think we can eat any more."

"Maybe so, let's find out!" I shot back from the canoe, as I unpacked the cook grill.

In short order we demolished the two biggest trout, but still had plenty for dinner and tomorrow's breakfast. I remembered the group of feasting Chipewyan men who had come over to camp that spring to net fish. Bellies distended with the abnormally large meal, we lay about on the ground just as they had, fish skeletons burning in the fire, our fingers greasy from the repast. My stomach hadn't bulged that way in weeks. Our diet had been calculated down to a tablespoon of rice in the interest of minimizing the load, and I rarely finished a meal feeling completely full.

"What a day!" I shouted to the other boat, once we recovered enough to continue. "Trapped on Hinde Lake, I didn't think we'd ever have days like this."

Carey Lake spread blue and clear of ice as far as I could see. We stroked on toward the bay we'd picked out as the starting point for our traverse. Even the development of an afternoon breeze didn't dampen our good spirits. At another tundra camp we again gorged on fish, bounty from the cold water, and I anticipated the next day's challenge with a confidence fed by the many obstacles we had already overcome, the string of daily accomplishments and major difficulties behind us.

Near camp a willow ptarmigan made strange guttural noises, the breeding calls of summer. I listened to it clucking in the calm unruffled voice we'd become so emotionally dependent on during the winter. The ptarmigan's mottled brown-and-white plumage camouflaged it so effectively that we almost stepped on it before it flushed in a startling burst of whirring wings. Hearing the bird nearby in the arctic night comforted me, like finding an old friend in unfamiliar territory.

PART IX

LAND OF THE CARIBOU INUIT

Early portents for an easy traverse were inauspicious. Cool solid overcast clung close to the ground and spattered drizzle from time to time—the fifteenth rainy day out of twenty-five. A shallow rocky landing forced us to wade the canoes to shore for the first, half-mile portage. Open tundra gave a clear view of our route, but the uneven ground, punctuated by hard slippery tussocks of grass, made walking under heavy loads an ankle-twisting ordeal. Freshening winds caught hold of the canoe hulls, insistently twisting them sideways, so that we had to walk with our torsos wrenched halfway around, the boats acting as weather vanes.

The first lake, no more than three miles across at its widest point, had been scoured by winds so that wicked steep waves slapped and pitched the canoes dangerously. It seemed to be our destiny this trip to slip across the big lakes unbothered, then get hammered on the small expanses of water we took for granted.

At the far end of the lake, another bouldery shoal held us fifteen yards away from solid ground. The map showed a thin stream connecting to the next lake, a stream we hoped to descend. We searched the rocky end of the lake assiduously, but to no avail. If any flow of water existed, it seeped off under the boulders. We had to carry our load of unwieldy packs over a slick and often tippy series of stepping-stones just to attain dry land where we could start the second carry.

Once over it and across another small lake, disappointment struck again. Not only did no connecting stream to the next lake exist, but the view looked decidedly different from the one on the map. I hadn't been so optimistic as to assume that every squiggly blue line would be a stream we could float down, but I had expected the landscape to conform generally to the one represented on our charts.

We huddled on a rocky outcrop, passing the map around, trying to make sense of our location. Our bright wind jackets and rain gear contrasted sharply with the dull greens and browns of the tundra, the unbroken gray of sky. Had we gotten lost?

"I'll say one thing," I interjected during the debate. "I'm not going back the way we came!"

"Maybe the water's just really low here." Craig pointed out what might have been a shoreline that would roughly match the lake on the map if the water had been several feet higher.

"I don't see where we could have gone wrong." Marypat's lips were bluish-purple with cold as she spoke. She jogged to stay warm. "The water level has changed since they made the map. That's all there is to it. Let's go!"

Ironically, I was feeling as excited by the haunting new land as I was discouraged by the shortcomings of our exploration. Low bedrock ridges, scraped and smoothed by glaciers, the rock cracked by frost action, lent an undulating quality to the wide views. Dozens of erratic caribou paths wove across our portage routes. We used them when they went in our direction, following the hundreds of hoof prints pressed into the thin dirt. A ptarmigan flushed from a ground nest as we passed. The overcast sky lent the scene an ancient, ponderous quality.

To solidify our resolve, we boiled water for tea and hot soup after the third carry. I collected a small pile of driftwood from among the rocks, and we set the grill on a granite platform protected from wind. The next portage lay clearly in view, so close it seemed an extra burden to paddle there; but the warm liquids bucked us up, turning the group mood to a stoical acceptance of our lot, resigned to the task ahead.

The water was very low. Even in the middle of marked lakes we had to lift over or portage around rock dams and shoals. Our packs had lightened over the miles, our bodies had hardened, but the day's demands sapped all of our energy. At every possible turn we faced portages. Where water floated the canoes, our paddles could barely dig in enough for a good stroke.

I hoped for just one break. A final blue line connected our string of ponds to Big Rocky Lake, ending the first section of the traverse. If that line represented a navigable stream, we'd avoid a tundra portage two miles long. But when we came to the marked outlet and searched the surrounding area, the streamlike trickle wouldn't allow the passage of bathtub toys, much less our heavy craft. From the top of a rounded knoll nearby, we could see Big Rocky Lake in the distance, a long walk away. The spot suddenly looked like a nice campsite, a good place to end the day's travail, even if we'd come only eight miles. The progress had exacted a tremendous toll on our energies.

As we prepared dinner, the clouds lifted, exposing the vast rolling expanse around us. A huge red sun slid across the horizon, heading slowly toward its brief nap under the rim of the earth. I looked at my partners and remembered I hadn't seen myself in a mirror for nearly a month. Craig's face had thinned noticeably, his chin covered with a patchy black beard. All our faces were brown and wind-chafed, our lips dry and peeling. I rubbed my short beard, my cheekbones. My hands, chapped, cracked, and calloused, were lined with black from fire soot. Our clothes were stained and coated with the soil from weeks of exertion, grubbing for wood, moving rocks from tent sites. As a group we looked hardy and weather-beaten, a little wild.

Our campsite commanded a wide view over the undulating quiet land. From all that distance, lake and ridgeline, river and tundra plain, I knew with near certainty that no other human being populated the country. I could go to the top of the farthest hill visible and be faced with the same curving space, the same uncultivated roll of territory. Since Black Lake we had not seen another human. We had crossed no road, no rail track, no fence line, and the only planes we saw overhead were high-altitude jets, flying, I imagined, the polar route to and from Europe.

Pointing a camera lens at the landscape, the red fireball of sun, I felt disappointed, stymied. The square view cut out the peripheral spaciousness, turned the enduring untouched land into a paltry framed fragment, one severed piece of a tapestry that flowed endlessly out from our small gathering, from that little spark of fire burning on top of a hill.

It occurred to me that this might be the most remote spot I'd ever stand on. If we were right in thinking that few, if any, people had made the same traverse, we might be the first humans, more certainly the first whites, to enjoy the vista. The long, purpling twilight flowed across the Barrens like a slow wave. Silence engulfed us so completely as to have discernible depth. I acknowledged a need to walk softly, to speak gently, a show of reverence.

We found in the morning how variable the tundra landscape can be. From a distance the country appeared monotonous, unchanging. But from the standpoint of portaging, the close-up perspective, the tundra gave us options, choices that ranged from easy going to unmitigated misery. Once off the knoll we lost sight of Big Rocky Lake and oriented ourselves by compass for the first time all summer. Some ground lay dry underfoot, relatively smooth going, while other spots grew thickets of low entangling willow, a knee-high interlacing of tough sinewy branches. Marshy areas often didn't correlate with topographic low spots, making route-finding a matter of intuition, and we'd find ourselves unexpectedly mired in wet mud on a ridgeline. The most nightmarish combination interspersed high grassy tussock and calf-deep muck—a formula formidable under the best conditions, but hellish under the awkward weight of a seventeen-foot, eighty-pound boat.

Center thwart grinding against my neck, sweat streaming down my face, bugs enjoying a feast while my hands maintained the canoe's balance, I alternately hopped and stumbled from dry tussock to dry tussock, or gave up the acrobatics to march glumly through the shoe-sucking mud. At Big Rocky Lake, I threw down the canoe in disgust and took a long pause to reassert my presence of mind before returning for the second load.

Big Rocky Lake deserved its name. We waded twenty yards from shore before the water was deep enough for us to climb into the boats. Time and again, shoals and rock-choked channels turned us away, or allowed passage only through narrow and tortuous courses. Closely following each other, our two canoes slowly probed a way, like submarines tenderly navigating a minefield—bow person standing up for a better view, stern person stroking ahead in slow-motion, following hand signals for direction. When the lead boat ground to a halt on top of an unseen boulder, thereby identifying the correct route, the second canoe took its turn in front.

Since arriving on the tundra, we had found judging the scale of distant objects a difficult task. On Barlow Lake, a small island sported two isolated trees. "Look at the size of those trees!" I'd exclaimed. "We haven't seen spruce that big in fifty miles." I thought the two spruce towered like sequoias out of the island, but as we drew nearer they turned increasingly diminutive, increasingly scraggly, until, at a range of a hundred feet, we realized they were five feet tall at best.

Boulders across Big Rocky Lake stood out gigantically, the size of four-bedroom houses. When we reached them they were closer to outhouse size. With no familiar objects to establish relative scale, brightly colored, distinctive variations in the landscape took on disproportionate prominence. I joked that the Volkswagen-size rock with a grizzly bear leaning on it was actually a pebble next to a lemming.

Without even a thin blue line on the map to give us hope, certain portage lurked at the end of Big Rocky. When we drew up on shore, it looked like a short carry up a steep, boulder-strewn incline, followed by a precipitous descent. Scouting out the best route, I noticed a small cut in the hillside and walked that way. The closer I came, the deeper the little valley appeared. Then, when I reached a vantage point, I was surprised to see a small fast stream flowing around a bend. Excited by the potential change in fortune, I followed the bank down and found that the crystal-clear stream gave an easy passage to the next lake.

I found myself the recipient of an environmental beneficence, a free bonus where none had been expected. Spared the untying, unloading, carrying, reloading, retying drudgery, we whipped joyfully down one hundred yards of crystalline stream—a brief and simple pleasure, but one that inflated our spirits like a win for an underdog team.

At the next narrows, a pinch on the map that I assumed would entail a portage, we found instead a shallow fast rapid to run, and discovered, along a ridge at the bottom, a mysterious line of upright stones. Sitting in the canoes, alone in an untraveled corner of a wide and lonely land, we looked up at what was obviously a manmade construction. I knew that precious few white people had been to that spot, tucked away between major drainages. And I suspected that it had been decades since Inuit had been active that far inland.

The ridgeline revealed a confusing forest of propped-up rocks, either raised in short piles or simply stood up on end. Obviously they had been left by the primitive Inuit, and we had no inkling as to their meaning. With the feeling of stumbling across a remote miniature Stonehenge, I walked from marker to marker, trying to make sense of it.

The elation of finding runnable water instead of a portage paled in the light of the new eerie mystery. The line of stones may have marked a caribou crossing or served as a hunting ruse—or may have been nothing more than the product of child's play, Barrenland sand castles. The find made us thoughtful and silent, as if we'd come across a long-forgotten overgrown cemetery. At the same time, I experienced an infusion of excitement, the Eureka! sensation of an archaeologist at a new dig.

Our luck continued its positive trend. The next blue line on the map translated into a rocky but negotiable piece of water, another portage avoided. We stopped early for Craig and Beth to sew a replacement zipper on their tent, an equipment casualty from wind and grit and long use with the potential to turn the remainder of the summer into a buggy Hitchcockian horror.

I practiced the art of managing mental calm in the face of bug stress while I cooked dinner. Black flies rose out of the ground in uncountable masses, covering my body, searching for chinks in my defenses. Under the headnet, I suffered from heat and subdued claustrophobia. Every time I wanted a sip of tea, I had to lift the netting, allowing small-scale invasions of flies an avenue to my face. My eyes crossed studying the netting, two inches away, trying to distinguish flies crawling on the inside of the headnet from the more harmless variety crawling on the outside.

Finally I stowed the head gear and lathered my hands and face in strong repellent, but flies steadily pinged off my face, frequently dive-bombing into my eyes. Inadvertently, we preyed on the flies as well, for they expired in our food and drink in large numbers, so prolifically it proved futile to pick them out as they collected. We ate quickly instead, limiting the volume of insect protein supplement by our speed of consumption. Our tents were the only true haven for relaxation, the only place where we could strip down without fear of losing blood. I would have given up a meal a day rather than lose that comforting meshed door.

More good fortune on the traverse. I climbed a ridge to compare the countryside to the map, satisfying myself that we were navigating accurately, and saw numerous shallow sections ahead, places where smooth paddling looked doubtful. Time after time, though, we came to rock-strewn narrows and found canoe-width chutes an inch deeper than the draft of the boats. A scrape here, an extra shove there, and we were through.

Mid-morning, Kamilukuak Lake came into view at the base of a short rapid. A thin surface-hugging fog spread across the open water. As we slipped down the last few chutes, the final filaments of current, I felt a breeze blowing off the lake. The wind instantly reminded me of the breezes we'd felt on Lake Athabasca last spring, the feel of air coming across an expanse of ice. Refrigerated air.

2

"You feel that air?" I shouted over my shoulder. Even before we'd finished with the last current, my eyes were preoccupied with the lake ahead, my mind churned with images of a jostling icepack.

"You've got ice on the brain," Beth chided. But we all felt the new chilling breeze, and I noticed that she studied the vista ahead as intently as the rest of us.

Through binoculars the blue lake disappeared into a white haze, either a dense fog created by vaporized air lying next to super-cooled water, or maybe a layer of resistant ice. When we'd found Carey Lake to be clear, we'd assumed that our safety from that nemesis was assured. But Kamilukuak had the feel of winter. Just over the northern horizon lay Dubawnt Lake, a body of water I felt sure would still be locked up. We were granted open water for the moment, but masses of floes might be lurking around the corner, might be shoved against the northern shore, waiting for a change of wind to charge down upon us.

Around the first point we saw the largest snowdrift yet, a huge wind-blown ridge of packed snow that covered the better part of a small island, its brilliant glittery bulk visible for miles. I entertained visions of keel-hauling our boats across expanses of rotten ice, flirting with the danger of falling in, or waiting on the whim of wind to remove an imprisoning pack of floes.

I mentally totaled the summer's progress and realized we'd come roughly half the distance to Baker Lake, close to four hundred miles in twenty-eight days. Since the windbound days on Hinde Lake, we hadn't allowed ourselves a rest. Kamilukuak Lake marked the re-entry into more frequently traveled territory. Another forty miles of paddling and portaging stood between us and the Kazan, but we knew the route had been pioneered before. The landscape ahead on the map looked uncomplicated and without mystery by comparison to the traverse we'd already completed.

Marypat and I had a bad day together. We ran morning rapids while debating contentiously. The truth was, good routes usually didn't exist through the bouldery riffles, but each of us was convinced that our choice would have been the better, and we took the graceless grinding over rocks personally. Our usual choreography of teamwork was shattered, brought to a level of discordant bickering.

On the lake we were haunted by fear of ice, pestered by a gathering sidewind; our conversation, when it occurred at all, went on monosyllabically. I couldn't refrain from questioning Marypat's steering strategy, wondering out loud whether we were heading into waves at the right angle or were aiming for the best side of an island. Marypat struggled against the wind. When she paddled on the right side, she had to J stroke heavily to keep straight. On the left, she was forced to C stroke constantly, fighting both the wind and my power, and never getting a break. The canoe obstinately fought her, and I communicated doubt even in the way I paddled.

A rare southerly wind made progress increasingly difficult. On any number of previous lakes it would have been a sailing wind, a godsend, but on Kamilukuak it came from the side, making us hug shore, turning short crossings into pitched battles. To capsize in that water would be fatal in minutes, I kept thinking. Not a good day to lose our teamwork.

At lunch, after a particularly tense open-water crossing, Marypat and I confronted each other on top of a gravelly wind-blown island.

"What the hell's the matter with you today?" I blurted, self-right-eously.

"You act like you don't trust me in the stern," she accused. "You question me all the time."

"Well, sometimes I can't figure out why you're doing things. I'm supposed to be calling the route from the bow, anyway. You ignore me half the time!"

"I'm just keeping the damn boat straight. I can't even make a forward stroke in this wind. My shoulder's killing me."

"You want me to stern?"

"No!" her voice vehement. She turned into the wind, shoulders hunched, arms crossed in front of her.

"I'm sorry, Marypat. I guess I'm tired too." I walked in front of her, acted as windbreak. Incredibly, three or four black flies hovered in the calm between our heads, materialized out of still air. "I'm sorry," I repeated and took hold of her tight shoulders, felt her strong arms, still tense. She reluctantly came up against me, and I felt the wind plaster my coat against my back as I held her.

"There are days I wish we were alone," she sighed after a minute. "I get tired of dealing with more people. Little things get to me. I know it's not fair, but we aren't as close as we were when we were alone. We don't read to each other at night."

A twinge of tension passed through me. Dammit, there's nothing to be done about that, I thought. "It's a different summer," I said. "Lots of nights we're too tired to read anyway."

While I had buried any doubts about the larger group, accepted the change as irreversible in any event and not worth thinking about, Marypat came out with her feelings. She enjoyed company, and had good talks with Beth frequently. Our group interaction had been remarkably stress-free considering the potential for strain, but Marypat still allowed her disappointments to surface. It made me realize that I had let my attention to her fade, let the challenges of travel and the demands of the group blunt the interaction with my partner.

That night, camped in deep tundra moss along a rocky shore, we zipped our sleeping bags together, a conscious reconciliation. Through the night we held onto each other, and in the morning, hearing rain on the tent, we cozied up languidly, not caring if we canoed that day or not.

Craig and Beth shared our lethargy. At one point in the morning, between showers, we reluctantly started to pack, but a renewed downpour provided the excuse to stay put. We needed a break. In dry intervals, we emerged from the tents to build quick fires and arrange our soaked boots near the flames to dry. The trip had been an unending series of soakings and dryings. Boots that had been new a month earlier were rotten and tattered and worn through.

Driven by Spartan compunction or desperation, we bathed in the icy lake—baths shorter than any we'd ever sputtered through, in water that felt, if possible, more frigid than any we'd experienced.

In an effort to augment lunch, Craig fished from the shoreline. While I watched, his rod suddenly snapped down with tension. "Hey, I've either got one helluva fish or a snag!" he called. Just then the line whirred out against the drag and he almost lost his footing on the loose rock. Ten minutes later he landed the largest trout of the journey, a monster we assessed in the twenty-pound range. The fish scale in the tackle box went to a mere eight pounds, only useful for weighing arctic grayling.

"Yup, another eight-pound trout," Craig grinned, after he wrestled the behemoth to shore and held it up by the ridiculously dwarfed scale. Keen-eyed gulls hawked from the shallow water and fought over fish entrails, while we hungrily watched fillets two inches thick sizzle on the grill.

By the next morning Marypat and I had recovered from our outburst of tension, and the group wore a rejuvenated outlook, the day off proving as effective as a prescribed drug for expedition stress. Although rain had stopped falling, fog thick as the split-pea soup we'd eaten for dinner cloaked the lake. I expected to hear the boom of a New England fog horn from across the water.

Craggy rock, wind-twisted shrubs, mossy tundra hove up through the mist, while land we'd just slipped past disappeared into the maw of fog behind us. A pair of mergansers flew suddenly into sight, passing close overhead; their wings whooshed through the dense air and faded quickly from view. I had to imagine the wider surroundings, the large lake, the rolling topography, because the two boats proceeded ahead in a world limited to one hundred feet.

How far had we come? Was the rocky finger ahead the big point we looked for or just a false jutting of stone? We scrutinized the map, tried to decipher the puzzle of landscape by looking intently at the one isolated piece visible to us. We waffled over a decision to cross two miles of open water to avoid five miles of shore-hugging around the contours of a bay. The far shore lay hidden in mist. We would have to cross by compass bearing.

Trusting the compass was nerve-wracking business. Given the intense fog, our initial location remained problematic. The fluctuation of magnetic declination was extreme so close to the magnetic north pole, and the normal risks involved in making an open crossing added the usual air of tension. But we decided to try.

Three of us took compass bearings to check against each other, and we aimed well down the point of land to account for error. I lay the compass on the floor between my feet, and our boat led off. Ten strokes later I looked back and could see nothing. We paddled in a world of fog and lake. The floor of water provided the only plane of orientation in an environment gone vertiginous.

I kept my eyes on the compass needle, correcting the boat's angle in response to the wavering magnetic arrow, looking up only to check that the second canoe clung to our wake. I wondered if I experienced what a pilot feels in a cloud bank or whiteout, the vulnerability of depending on instruments instead of senses. If we missed the far point, miles of open lake lay beyond, open lake covered by a quilt of fog. I thought about the suppressed panic of a Great Plains homesteader groping for a cabin in a blizzard.

"There it is," Marypat's relieved voice sang out from the bow.

I straightened from my hunched position, smiled broadly at the hazy sight of fog-shrouded land ahead. If I experienced such excitement after two miles of tense compass reckoning, what an ineffable gush of emotion early sailors must have enjoyed at the dim sight of land after an ocean crossing.

A mile farther on the fog began to lift and, with it, the winds rose. Once across another bay, we forgot the fog and slammed through four-foot surf. "We're going in," I called over to Craig, and turned the bow toward shore, corkscrewing in the waves as we momentarily went broadside. The yellow boat followed, making an exhilarating surfing landing next to us on another cobbly shore.

We didn't set up camp, hoping for a later reprieve, but unpacked our wet things to flap and dry in the wind. We took up our vigil, striving for the patient calm of animals taking shelter from a blizzard. The sun crossed the sky, the waves beat on the shore, and we huddled, five feet out of the reach of spray, waiting for a break.

It came that evening, a lessening in the blow, and we shoved the canoes out again. When we next stopped, we'd gained the portage to Nowleye Lake. The sun teetered on the horizon, huge and blood-colored.

Wind had become as familiar a part of the daily routine as pitching the tents or building a rock windscreen behind the cook grill. Air billowed and gusted through the dim night, and swept across the land under gray skies while we portaged the next morning. I had become accustomed to seeing the yellow canoe torqued awkwardly on Craig's shoulders during a carry, to Marypat's and Beth's hair flying about their heads, to taking soft shoves of air at my back like an insistent, bullying companion.

For four miles the canoes slammed and wallowed on Nowleye Lake, white-capped waves an expedition experience so common as to no longer stir feelings of fright, the shore going by at the usual excruciating pace. It took most of the morning to make that distance, most of the morning and more than all the energy we'd stored at breakfast.

We took up the shorebound wait once more, parked in a bay with a pair of Canada geese and their pintsize young. The canoes rested calmly, tied to shrubs. Wool hats on our heads in the middle of July, we played card games and ate lunch with half-numb hands, drawn up tightly together in a knot of humanity.

Wind lull and another afternoon clearing trend allowed us to take up the paddles, to scoot over open water, to pass points and bays. We traveled toward an orange beacon on the crest of a ridge, visible from miles away, until the sun sank low into the northwestern sky. The marker looked manmade, as if sprayed with neon paint or wrapped with surveying tape, an unnatural fluorescence. Curious, we portaged above the boggy lowlands to camp on a bench halfway up the hill.

Marypat hiked to the ridgeline and stayed there for a time, looking over the land. "It's a rock," she stated flatly when she returned. "A rock covered with unbelievably orange lichen. And somebody put it there. It's stood up on end and propped from behind, like a signal."

"Well, look what I found," I called. I had stumbled across several circles of stones, circles that I felt certain were Inuit tent rings. Traditional Inuit, in their summer camps, lived in caribou-skin tents weighed down around the edges with heavy stones. When they abandoned camp the stone rings stayed behind. These rocks had been in place for some time, long enough to sink into the ground several inches, becoming incorporated into the pattern of vegetation around them. Partly because the circles demarcated the flattest ground available, and partly because we wanted to share the same sleeping spot as the Inuits, we raised our modern shelters within the circles of stone.

After dinner I sat by the ashes of our cook fire. The sun had long disappeared, and a half-moon laid a path of cool light across the calm lake. A willow ptarmigan burbled nearby. I thought about the primitive, competent, mysterious people who had lain on the same bit of flat tundra, perhaps sharing a laugh or talking quietly about their fishing strategy for the next day. People who marked their summer camp with a rock that shone brilliantly in the sun, people who contentedly took their living from this wide harsh land. Perhaps, I thought, they had been imbued with the same sense of peace as I on that still, moon-illuminated evening.

The campsite must have had the power of a good omen, for two perfect paddling days followed. On the first, we pushed ourselves twenty-six miles and gained Angikuni Lake, a large lake on the Kazan River drainage. Mild winds and rare warm temperatures motivated us across miles of open water, down the final rapid-filled narrows of the traverse, and onto the trail of our next watershed.

During the second day our canoes slid over another twenty miles, until we were arrested by the beauty of a campsite on an island just a few miles away from the first river section we would paddle on the Kazan. What's a trip for if we can't stop at a place like this, we agreed. Accepting the risk of being windbound, we stopped anyway. Craig and I caught trout for dinner off the bedrock ledges of the island. Our tents commanded another panoramic view from a rounded high point.

I was awakened during the night by a pair of sandhill cranes. The two birds landed not twenty feet away. The heavy workings of their wings made a flapping sound like a canvas tent come loose from its moorings in a wind. I peeked around the corner of the door to see the tall long-legged cranes hop and dance with each other in the moonlight, their wings coming away from their bodies like aboriginal arms. While they danced their voices croaked rustily, creaking and guttural, a lamenting sound uttered without passion or grief. The cranes stayed on the island a long time, ignoring our presence, asserting their own.

3

Our gamble backfired. Winds woke me again before dawn, bowing in the exposed tent sides, hurling loud surf against the shore, pinning us down. To escape the full fury of air, we once again effected the comical four-person tent carry, except this time no friendly sheltering forest stood by to grant sanctuary. A narrow hummocky hollow, a bit more protected from wind, had to suffice, and the two tents brushed against each other in the confined space. Rocks weighed down guyline stakes, and we tossed packs inside to hold the shelters in place while we stayed out in the weather.

All during the gray blustery day, thoughts of the Caribou Inuit preoccupied me. Craig had found an old piece of driftwood that obviously had been fashioned to some purpose—part of a tool or weapon, or maybe a handicraft or a toy. Ever since I'd slept inside the tent ring and we began seeing signs of primitive occupation, I had been increasingly aware that we passed through a land, now essentially deserted, that not long ago had been home to hundreds of hardy Inuit people.

The traditional Inuit of the Canadian arctic had survived in a land unbelievably harsh by modern standards. The moderate times of year were difficult enough, as we were finding out, but the winter, a season eight or nine months long, begat frightful conditions that were unimaginably brutal. While most Inuit settled along the ocean coasts, taking their sustenance from the sea, a small minority had adapted to make their home in the interior. For the inland settlers life was an even more marginal affair.

While coastal groups lived off the varied harvest of the ocean, utilizing fish, walrus, seal, and whale for food and materials, Caribou (or Inland) Inuit based their survival almost exclusively on the vast herds of northern deer. During a period between the early 1700s and the mid-1900s, Caribou Inuit flourished in the Barrenlands, and the Kazan drainage had been a focal point for a large number of these people.

Though they lived on the Barrenlands continuously for more than two hundred years, they left little mark on the country. That fact is as much a testimony to the austere, basic lifestyle they were reduced to as it is to any cultural fastidiousness. They lived and traveled light by necessity, and most of what they left behind has decomposed, or is in the process of decaying naturally, completing a cycle.

On Angikuni Lake we began seeing a great number of inukshuks, the rock cairns erected to identify trails, camps, burial sites, caribou crossings, the points of reference in a land otherwise featureless. The builders of inukshuks took pains to create enduring landmarks, constructing sturdy edifices to withstand wind and frost. Many were built from stones that matched in color, or were put together in whimsical, almost artistic fashion, much more evocative than a crude pile of rocks. *Inukshuk* means "something resembling a person," and I had once or twice experienced the unnerving sensation of being watched while paddling. When I looked over my shoulder at such times, I'd often discover a distant profile, disarmingly human-looking, standing lonely watch from a neighboring ridgeline.

While we found the Barrenland summer a tempestuous season, it was a time of relaxation and relative ease for the Inuit. The storms and winds were mild compared with winter weather, and the insects provided the only real environmental stress. Inuit bands camped at favorite fishing spots, killed ptarmigan and waterfowl for additional food, and made their preparations for winter.

Fall was the critical time of year. The caribou, fat from grazing on tundra vegetation, moved south toward their wintering territory, and Inuit hunted them along the way. If the fall hunt was successful, winter camps had food and supplies for the long season. If the hunt fell short, the grim specter of starvation and hardship haunted the small nomadic settlements, and famine held the camps in an icy death grip.

Before rifles were introduced to the Inuit, they hunted caribou at the narrows in lakes and rivers where the deer crossed. Inuit men ambushed swimming caribou, spearing helpless animals from kayaks or killing them as they emerged from the water. Women butchered the extra meat into thin strips and dried them in the sun for preservation and storage. Extra stores were protected under piles of rock. These meat caches were food deposits that, for the Inuit, represented the equivalent of savings accounts, tangible security that could mean the difference between comfort and devastation, life and death.

Besides meat, caribou provided skins for tents and clothing, bones that were fashioned into tools and weapons, sinew for thread, fat for oil, most of the necessities for successful existence on the Barrens. Through the long winters these people lived in igloos, enduring the dark bitter season. In times of starvation women were forced to fish through thick ice on lakes, and men ventured far afield hunting for rabbit or fox, hoping desperately to find larger quarry like musk ox or stray caribou.

Their winter homes were dimly lit by crude oil lamps—reservoirs carved from soft soapstone, filled with animal oil, with a flame flickering at the end of a moss or hair wick. That tiny flame provided the only light for much of the dark season, while the sun shone on the southern latitudes. No generator night indulgences offered relief for those primitive people.

Thick walls made out of snow blocks insulated the igloos and acted as effective windbreaks, but the interior temperature usually hovered between 30°F and 40°F, largely as a result of body heat. Even so, Inuit became so inured to bitter cold that they shed most of their clothes when inside. So long as a supply of meat staved off the threat of famine, the bleak winter season posed more a test of mental and emotional endurance than a struggle for survival. In response to the lack of stimulation and the long sedentary periods, Inuit achieved a state almost akin to hibernation.

When spring returned and sun lengthened the days, the igloos melted away and Inuit bands shrugged off the hardships for a short season of ease and comfort, a brief but languid few months, with the certainty of another long winter lurking at the end.

I had more time than I wanted to ponder the lives of the Inuit. For three nights and two days wind held us hostage. In the hollow, gusts reached only ten or fifteen miles an hour, but beyond our small snug camp, thirty- and forty-mile-an-hour winds remained the norm. We wore every layer of clothing available in our packs, yet barely managed to keep warm, aided by hot drinks and food. Cold sleet whipped us periodically, and I found solid ice left over from winter under boulders around the island.

Scarcity of wood forced us to use the gas stove for some meals. We built elaborate wind shields around the tiny wood fires we scrounged fuel for, or lay ourselves in a tight ring around the stove, using our bodies to block air from extinguishing our matches. Several times each day we foraged the island surface, prying under rocks for tiny dried out drift-wood twigs, pruning the dead branches off willow shrubs. The sinewy willow, even when dead, put up a grim struggle, and our dry chapped hands bled from the contest. I noticed bushes with dead branches that had been twisted and tugged. Had an Inuit woman, hunched over and intent, finally quit fighting them, just as I had on other willows nearby?

My mind played old games. Would the wind ever stop? Was summer over? Might we never get off the island? In twelve hours, overnight, the island camp had metamorphosed from idyllic wilderness outpost to forlorn Alcatraz, a lonely lump of weather-beaten rock. Five miles away, not half a morning's paddle, the Kazan River flowed out of the lake, a confined channel less susceptible to wind, a strong helpful current. But it might as well have been in South America for all the chance we had to get there.

I retired, on the third night, with my mental alarm set to ring. Hopeful of a break, I was ready to charge across the lake at the slightest change. In the darkest time of night I awoke to calm. For the first time in nearly three days the tent didn't flap, the wind didn't tug audibly across the tundra, the waves weren't battering the shore. I closed my eyes for a short nap, and woke again almost immediately to the sound of rustling air. Not a wind yet, hardly a breeze, but atmospheric stirring.

"What do you think, guys?" I woke my companions. "The wind died for a while, but I hear it again now. Should we try?" I pulled on cold grimy pants.

The sun, still below the northern horizon, lit a dense matting of cloud to purple fire, an unbelievable color. I felt breezes on my face, and climbed to the high point for a view of dark lake. Heaving swells but few whitecaps.

The well-rehearsed packing drill took only minutes. Tents dropped, boats loaded, decks fastened. We shoved off without breakfast, without ceremony, without talk, all hopeful that a crossing could be made, all afraid that around the corner of the island conditions would force us back, our escape foiled.

We never saw the sunrise. The midnight flames in the sky were the day's flash of light. The sky returned to a sullen dense overcast. The two canoes, a yellow and red splotch of brightness in a landscape of drab muted tones, ran down the broad backs of gray waves, climbed the steep watery fronts. We stayed humbly quiet, grimly goal-oriented. The water hissed and snarled under the gathering whip of wind, whitecaps breaking angrily, the lake surface wide, forbidding, powerful beyond description.

I saw an inukshuk on a ridge—a hard motionless silhouette—and felt comforted to feel the ancient company of mankind. We crossed to a shoreline that ran raggedly in and out of small bays, past headlands where surf slammed into rock. The two boats stayed abreast of each other, fighting waves as big as anything we'd been afloat in, and I felt a renewed fear of water. More than once, perched at the crest of a wave, my paddle grabbed air from the next trough. Other times, a pursuing mountain of water caught the canoe and soaked my arm halfway to the elbow. Thank God for spraydecks, I thought, as time after time the bow crashed underwater and waves from the side washed over a gunwale, slurping cold liquid across the deck, giving the boat a sickening twist.

But after an eternity of intense struggle, the Kazan River beckoned at the back of a long bay, a protected, less vulnerable channel, a river. We ran the boats to shore and hopped about on the rocks like schoolchildren at recess, free from tyranny, congratulating each other giddily. A hot breakfast and steaming coffee fired internal engines to combat the numbing chill air and loosen the stiffness in our limbs. The breakfast fire flickered in a rocky crevice, flames guttering, our pots set inches above the ground to capture heat before wind snatched it away.

The Kazan reversed the day's mood. Clouds held down a gray lid overhead, rain spattered on us for the twenty-first day out of thirty-five, a statistic hardly worth keeping anymore. And we wore most of our clothes, even while working hard. But the river took hold of our canoes and pulled impetuously downstream, the channel gradient a ramp leading us north. Mile after mile of Barrens sped past, the river's urgency matching our own happiness at being released from the implacable wind.

I warmed to the character of the Kazan from the beginning. It would be the final river I'd paddle in nearly two thousand miles of travel. I sensed it would be the best as well—cleaner than the Athabasca, less rocky than the Dubawnt, flowing through country of magisterial scope. I heard myself laughing down the first fast miles.

The Dubawnt had been shallow and littered with obstacles, while the Kazan ran along a deep channel, through scoured bedrock country where the powerful current apparently had shoved aside all but the largest rocks. Carefully running near the banks for the first miles, we discovered the challenges of the new river in ledge drops and heavy hydraulic action—broad sets of standing waves, deep swirling whirlpools, strong holes below ledges and huge boulders. Rather than pick our way through a maze of rock, always fearful of broaching or wrapping a boat around a boulder, we plunged down the deep fast channels, bucketing through waves, hardly paddling, while the austere country slid past in fast motion.

An astonishing twenty-seven miles accomplished by lunch, counting the slow lake miles. Somewhere along the river I calculated that it was Day Four Hundred. I remembered the awe I'd felt more than a year earlier, saying to myself, Day One, and feeling defeated by the prospect of the future. Feeling awestruck and incapable. If all went as planned, we were down to twenty days or less. Only twenty days, less than one lunar cycle, fewer days than it took to build our winter cabin. In the first twenty days of the trip we hadn't even gotten to the ferry crossing at Vega, had hardly broken in our expedition clothes, had just managed to snap the spraydeck over our bulky load.

I blocked off thinking about the end, refused the temptation to reminisce. Too much lay before us still, too much lay right around us in great hunks of wilderness. A large drift of dirty snow hunkered in a gully along a cool protected bank. The first set of falls and rapids, a triple portage, waited downstream, and the river pooled behind the tremendous drop, its pace slackened for miles behind the natural dam.

"Look!" Marypat called in a hushed shout. "Caribou!" She pointed to a steep tundra-blanketed bank. A large adult caribou, sporting an impressive rack, heard her call as well, and responded with a quick trotting ascent of the hillside. At the ridge the magnificent deer turned in profile, rear legs splayed out, acute tension in its stance, antlers stark against the cold gray sky. We sat in our boats and drank in the sight, struck mute by its power.

Sidling up to the first thundering rapids of the lower Kazan, with the lone caribou fresh in my memory, the prospect of the expedition's end faded from my thoughts. At the first portage, as much waterfall as rapid, we parked well upstream, cowed by the vibrating roar of cascading river. I climbed far out onto the bedrock dam the torrent pounded over, and felt the shivering impact of water just ten feet away, saw jagged rock clearly through the clean slick tongue of river falling serenely toward white concussion, shattering chaos. All that wide deep channel funneled down the narrow face of enduring rock, a shocking, thrilling drop, all the more exhilarating because we had worked for weeks to get there.

Turning away finally, I had to shout to my companions next to me. "And that's the rapid! The falls are down there." I jerked my thumb downstream where the river channel fell away, dropping out of sight over a sheer break.

Although the first portage came at the end of a record-breaking thirty-eight-mile day, I went across as though it were nothing. The packs had lightened measurably, my body felt leaner, more sinewy than I ever remembered it, and I was drunk on the wildness of the Kazan.

I watched Beth toil into camp under her second load, pack and duffle dwarfing her bent figure—roiling dark clouds above her, moist tundra for miles behind her, the crescendo of river hanging like primitive music in the air—and I thought of the Inuit moving camp, surviving without notice in the same awesome land.

4

The Inuit who lived in the Kazan Valley were known as the Harvaqtormuit people, a name that translates as "where rapids abound." We spent a full day discovering how aptly that name applied. Over the course of eighteen miles the river never let up its headlong descent. If it didn't drop dramatically over ledges and small falls or cascade through whitewater, it galloped along a sloping chute.

The land looked just barely freed from the grasp of winter. Shelves of shorefast ice two or three feet thick often bordered the river, wide patches of snow adorned the canyon section where we portaged the falls. When I walked to shore to scout rapids, pans of ice on the rock made footing treacherous, and the willows along the river's edge had been shredded and torn during repeated breakups. Fresh mud lay alongside the river, fresh enough to make me wonder how long it had been since the last ice had washed downstream.

Breakup along that stretch must be a wonderful, terrifying thing. An enormity of water with a head of steam like a locomotive on a downgrade, herding an imponderable pack of thick bulldozing ice. The banks even looked bulldozed. Uniform ridges of large round rocks rose as much as twenty feet above the river level heavy rocks, by the thousands, shoved aside by water and ice, creating a tunnel effect.

We dawdled all morning on the portage at the falls, enjoying the tumultuous grandeur. But during the afternoon we couldn't stop ourselves from running rapid after exciting rapid, becoming suffused with the river's energy, anticipating the next challenge just downstream.

The whitewater ran together all day, with hardly a distinguishable break, but the last section took a step up in severity. While we scouted along the tortured shoreline, hands tucked inside our life vests for warmth, the challenge of the rapid sobered our elated spirits. "It feels like the last ski run of the day," Marypat said, looking at the stretch of dark frothing river. "I really want to do it, but I'm tired. I know I might blow it." Blowing it would be followed by a long life-threatening swim, I thought.

Looking down at the hole below the first ledge, a hole we had no choice but to go through, I felt my bowels tighten in anticipation. "Let's go!" I clapped my hands and turned away, jogging to the waiting canoe.

Craig and Beth remained on shore to watch us navigate the difficult section. We backpaddled up to the first ledge, slowing the action, picking our spot, and I saw that the hole loomed bigger than I had thought, a dark curling basket of water, three feet deep at least. Remember to brace, I kept repeating to myself, shifting my knees apart, lowering my center of gravity, forgetting my cold hands, forgetting that Craig and Beth stood almost directly above us on a low cliff.

Up to the edge, the canoe as serene and unaware as water going over the lip of a falls—poised, committed—and then down, fast, smooth, a collision, cold water washing down the boat, into our laps. But we had no time to relax and reposition. The long rapid came up on us, the complicated maneuvering we had mapped for ourselves demanded constant adjustments, the next challenge rushed toward us with unstoppable velocity.

"We're good," I called. "We're where we want to be." The boat, the Kazan, our teamwork, began to mesh, a concert. As we had planned, we slid alongside the largest waves, ferried into eddies, ran down the slick V's of deep water, and aimed for the last and largest set of waves, waves we hadn't been able to assess from shore.

Again, the slow-motion, the nervous jockeying for best position, best angle, straightest shot. I craned for a final judging look. Then the quickening, plummeting, crescendoing ride, the water dousing us both. Finally, quiet water, a widening pool, the returned sensation of numb hands, whoops and self-congratulatory jubilation under a twilight arctic sky. We watched while Craig and Beth piloted their canoe through the wild water, their paddling grace together a satisfying sight.

Gray light, cooling temperatures, and fatigue forced us to halt at the foot of the heavy mile-long rapid that crowned our efforts. As we paddled to an island camp, the second caribou of the summer ran along the rim of land, dark against the sky, hooves thudding the earth. Scrounging for tiny driftwood for the fire, I walked a littered high-water line, easily fifteen feet above the murmuring river.

Life on the river had become simple, routinized, a repeated pattern. Searching for cooking fuel, interpreting the shape of topography from maps, erecting shelters, assessing the sky and the wind, guiding a boat down powerful water—it had become a way of life. For more than a year I had lived in profound simplicity but had hardly ever experienced boredom. Heading back to camp with my load of driftwood twigs, the land under evening shadow, I recognized the quality of wilderness existence as an empowering serenity.

As the miles clicked by under our keels, the long days flowed past. I understood the attachment the Inuit had had to the Kazan Valley. Broad sweeping tundra rolled away from the river in a green carpet, ridges and rounded hillsides providing relief. I imagined the empty land furred with thousands of caribou, teeming with herds, the clicking grunting mass of animals that meant life and wealth. The river itself ran past craggy cliffs with nesting peregrine falcons, down smooth ramps, fast rapids, small falls—a joyous invigorating flow of water. If I had been Inuit I would have chosen to live there too.

Along one stretch of river, near shore, I caught a movement on the bank and saw a tiny arctic fox—sharp eyes, motionless stance, curiosity and fear in its look. And then a disappearing act, gone. Overhead, a high-altitude jet flew past, leaving its white wake in the air.

In terms of direct distance, the people in that plane were the closest humans to us, separated by a few miles of atmosphere. Businessmen in three-piece suits, tourist families returning from Europe, people eating snacks off plastic trays, drinking martinis, distracted by a movie, glancing out the porthole at the vast empty blue and green tapestry below. Were they awed? Did they shudder at the thought of crashing in such a hopeless wilderness? They were my kind, my people. I had flown in those jets. But I could summon no sense of communion, no emotional spark, as I floated down the back of one of the blue ribbons they peered at.

The Kazan hurried toward Yathkyed Lake, a tremendous open sweep of water arguably the most intimidating in the Barrens, next to Dubawnt. To circumnavigate its border we would have to sneak along nearly forty unprotected miles of shoreline. We had penetrated to the heart of Barrenland country. Inukshuk markers crouched at the edges of our peripheral vision, and tent rings from old camps often affirmed our selection of choice campsites. The fishing came so easily it made us feel guilty, but it underscored the rich bounty of northern waters.

At the bottom of a set of ledgy rapids, we spent an afternoon luxuriating in rare sunlight, bathing in clear numbing pools, and hauling in twenty-pound trout from the frothy depths at the base of whitewater. None of us professed to be anglers of even moderate skill. We fished for dinner, period. Our reels were of the kind you might buy a thirteen-year-old nephew just starting out, wound with eight-pound test line. Our lures tended to be small flashy spoons and spinners, grabbed out of the box without plan or strategy. Aluminum foil with a hook would have worked equally well.

One- and two-pound arctic grayling struck lures at the edges of fast water, along the strong eddy lines, and fought with a leaping ferocity all out of proportion to their size. Trout we christened Sons of Jaws struggled at the end of our lines in deeper pools.

"Oh, my God," Craig moaned for the second time in five casts. "Look at the size of that damn thing!" He fought a monstrous trout, a log of a fish, easily twenty pounds, much more than we could hope to eat. Time and again we released big fish and cast lures to new holes in hopes of bringing in a prize more reasonably a meal's size, something in the ten-pound range.

That afternoon, bathing in the river, relishing the thought of trout for dinner, I realized I'd worked into a new physique, a foreign body. Never one to be called skinny, I was finding out what it's like to have a bony butt with no padding to sit on, to take a pinch of skin on my belly and get only that. Craig watched me return to camp and shook his head. "I don't want to alarm you by using words like emaciated," he began, "but you have gotten pretty damned skinny!"

We ate well, but in sparing amounts. A bowl of cereal, some dried fruit, and coffee made up a common breakfast. Lunch usually consisted of a few handfuls of nuts, a piece of bannock with cheese, and more dried fruit. Dinner amounts normally allowed for seconds, but rarely more. Dessert nights were hailed as special events, anticipated from a time shortly after lunch, a sweet extra portion of fuel. Clearly, my caloric intake didn't come close to matching the daily output of energy, the constant paddling regimen, with frequent bursts of exertion on portages or against headwinds. My body devoured its fat layer steadily, and though I often wished we had a bit more food, I reveled in my substantially reduced silhouette.

My concern over our mileage average began to wane. On the Kazan, we easily made up for time lost earlier on portages and by wind delays. Unless we were held up dramatically by weather, we had a good chance to make Baker Lake before our food ran low. Where, a week earlier, I would have pushed for extra miles, always concerned about wind, now I succumbed to the temptation of naps after lunch, lobbied for attractive campsites where we could relax with plenty of day left. If I probed more deeply for my rationale, I understood that my willingness to dawdle revealed an unwillingness to end our journey.

At the start of Yathkyed Lake, a proliferation of inukshuks coaxed us to shore to investigate. The small peninsula must have been a consistent hunting spot, a narrow crossing at the base of the lake. Tent rings and rock cairns lay about by the dozen, and Beth found an old meat cache, a small manmade cave excavated in a natural rock hollow, lined with stones and tundra moss—a cool safe place to stash caribou meat against the starving times.

When Inuit who relied on that meat had come to resupply their winter camp, the land would have lain monotonously white under a dark sky, the snow packed and sculpted by merciless wind, the lake a desert of ice crystals. Finding the cache, digging it out, seeing the meat unpillaged, must have brought out smiles and sighs of relief. Discovering otherwise would have forecast a grim confrontation with survival.

For the day and a half it took us to stroke around the expansive periphery of Yathkyed Lake, the winds gave us the gift of their absence. Nearly into August, fear of ice had left our thoughts. In another month it would be time to think about new ice forming, time to be off the Barrens. Along several pieces of lake shore, remnants of the last winter's ice stolidly resisted the season, fastening firmly to the rocks underwater, a good six feet thick from lake bottom to exposed surface.

On the second day we were emboldened enough to hazard mileage-reducing shortcuts across long bays, straying miles from shore, glancing nervously out across the bulk of satiny lake that met with the horizon. Only once, on a long open crossing, did a breeze ruffle the surface. A tiny breeze, but enough to almost instantly build small waves. This is it, I thought. We blew it. We're going to get caught this time. The closest shore stood miles away. But the breeze vanished, my heart regained its regular pace, and we coasted across twenty-seven miles of slack water to the lake's outlet.

5

I suspected that the Barrenlands had been named by people who knew nothing of the country firsthand. Barren of trees it certainly is, and it remains barren of humanity to an extent almost unheard of anywhere else on the globe. But the tundra world that was scraped nearly bare by glaciers, that boasts a climate harsh enough to demand adaptation and acquiescence, is a world that teems with life.

Inching mile by mile across the watery landscape, exploring pieces of land, I grew aware of myself as an outsider. The birds and mammals and insects have developed a complex web of interactions and survival strategies that allows them to thrive and perpetuate their kind. We were the foreigners, the visiting animals who had to carry a cumbersome load of buffering supplies to cope with environmental stress, the creatures who arrived briefly from another world and then escaped.

During the ephemeral tentative summer, life burgeoned and blossomed around us everywhere. Insects by the billions hatched on the tundra ponds and rivers, and I wondered, when they descended on us in zealous predatory droves, if they had some devious way of communicating to their peers that succulent unfurred visitors had wandered haplessly into their camp.

Cotton grass, fireweed, Indian paintbrush, harebells, and campion adorned the tundra like delicate jewelry, tiny daubs of indescribable color and fragile beauty—flowers that flourished with desperate energy and then died away, lying dormant and patient most of the year. Dozens of bird species flew thousands of miles north to establish territories here, to court and nest and brood their young on the verdant tundra. Golden plover, pectoral sandpipers, sandhill cranes, peregrine falcons, snow geese, rough-legged hawks, willow ptarmigan, arctic terns, yellow-billed loons—birds that perched watchfully on cliff faces, sat motionless on ground nests, raided the insect populations for food, circled on updrafts overhead, and rode on the pure water.

The water swam with huge fish, the air swarmed with insects and birds, and the land gave up thrilling glimpses of mammal life. In the misty rain, across from the last camp on Yathkyed Lake, a lone bull caribou appeared, trotting along shore, then lying down in the soft groundcover. Catching wind of us, he jerked to his feet and hesitantly continued on toward camp, curious, perturbed, visibly torn between fear and interest.

"We must be right on a trail," I whispered. Caribou trails wove so densely over the area that we couldn't have set up a tent anywhere without covering two or three.

The caribou kept coming, prancing with agitation, finally giving our camp a looping detour, and then stopping to study us. Thirty feet away, the bull stood trembling, pawing, pacing back and forth, at a loss as to how to react to such interlopers. He finally trotted on down the shore, stopping to glance back every few yards.

One day farther on we scouted a campsite from a rocky ridge along a fast section of river and saw several calves and adults grazing serenely on reindeer lichen. Suddenly, out of a gully forty yards away, I saw a brown face appear from behind a willow, an alert face aimed right at us.

"Grizzly," I said. "There's a grizzly!"

My companions couldn't see the bear, took issue with my statement, came over to look for themselves. I grabbed the telephoto lens from around Marypat's neck and focused in on the brown head. Unmistakable. The zoomed-in grizzly stared intently back into the lens, aware of our presence, unafraid. The closeness of the image unsettled me so much I forgot to click the shutter.

"Yup, it's a bear." Craig turned toward the canoes. "I think I have energy to paddle a few more miles," he called over his shoulder as the rest of us clambered after him over the rocks, watching our backs, accelerating to a run on the way.

More caribou came into view downstream, strings of them swimming the current. Another herd crowded on an island and were sent into a thundering confusion of antlers and legs and muscular bodies by our silent passage a few feet away. We watched them plunge into a fast channel, swim to the mainland, and rise out of the river again.

Approaching Forde Lake it was obvious that we had come into a concentration of wildlife—not just stragglers or lone animals but milling herds. One hundred at a time, three hundred, two thousand. We stood next to a lone inukshuk on a high island and estimated a herd of three thousand caribou visible on the tundra around us. Caribou resting in sunlight, feeding on lush growth, moving in groups along the many trails; caribou that never crossed pavement, never confronted barbed wire, never hazarded railroad crossings. No wildlife boundary, no arbitrary manmade line confined these animals. We were the intruders.

"This is like 'Wild Kingdom,' " I laughed when we resumed paddling.

"What's that?" Marypat pointed to a dark spot on a shoreline over a mile away.

Bear, I thought with certainty, the grizzly face a fresh mental imprint as we paddled in that direction to see. Craig raised his ever-present binoculars and held them to his eyes a long moment. "I can't believe it," he looked over at us, whispering even though we stood a mile off shore. "It's a musk ox! A goddamn musk ox!"

Cameras nestled in the hands of bow people while still half a mile from shore. The lone shaggy mammal, like a prehistoric throwback, a contemporary of the woolly mammoth, munched away calmly in a clump of willow. Our strokes were as soundless as we could make them, even our breathing hushed. Closer and closer, each stroke gliding the boats across another ten feet of calm water. The musk ox hadn't even raised his head.

CRUNCH! CRUNCH! The canoe bows slid up on shore, the sounds a startling exclamation. Finally our quarry looked up, turned to face us, so close I could see the insects swarming over his body, the broad rough plate of horn across his forehead, the bloodshot buffalo eyes peering nearsightedly at us. Long gold-tinged hair hung like velvet armor from the massive shoulders. The beast stood before us for a long quiet time, assessing. Humming insects the only sound.

Slowly, he turned, moved toward the vegetation, headed off, unhurried. A ptarmigan burst from cover next to his hooves, a sudden flurry of sound and motion. The huge animal lumbered into a gallop, drumming away up a gentle dry hill—golden hair shimmering in the sunlight, great prehistoric head shaking insects off in the wind.

The tense hush we'd maintained broke down completely. "Well, I can die now," Marypat laughed, summing up the power of the moment.

"I hoped for caribou," Craig added. "I knew we'd see plenty of birds. But I never let myself even consider a musk ox!"

I became the group wildlife tour guide, narrating fantastic wilderness events, rattling off possibilities for upcoming sights on the Barrenground safari. Already, caribou were old hat, and I promised candid views of wolf families, herds of musk oxen, and a variety of boggling wildlife encounters climaxed by a caribou stampede through camp.

Three miles down Forde Lake my predictions proved true. More musk oxen, this time eighteen animals—calves and assorted adults, dominated by a large bull. The herd browsed lazily along a sandy beach, some lying in the sunlight, others munching on willow, the calves staying close to protective females. Our boats coasted up stealthily, again drawing near before the herd grew skittish and nervous.

When we stopped just off shore, the lead bull heaved himself up onto his feet and the herd spooked, galloping over the tundra, wide sky behind them. With white towering thunderheads as a backdrop, the musk oxen became a muscular flow of brown and gold, their hooves a wild drumroll. Several times the animals pulled up, blowing and snorting, and watched us, until some signal sent them rolling off again across the endless sweep of land.

The next day we saw the same herd. This time the dominant bull stared us down, as if to communicate his waning patience with our pestering reappearance. Wind swept long hair from his side like a skirt, and the golden coat along his back glistened in the sun. We stared at each other, four aliens in odd craft facing the herd patriarch. The bull took several steps toward the lake, gave us a final stare, then trundled off at a disdainful pace, followed closely by his herd.

※　※

The next wildlife chapter unfolded the following morning. We had fought another whipping wind across lake and river to camp at a strong rapid upstream of Thirty-Mile Lake. Inukshuks marked the point of land we camped on as a haunt of the Inuits, and the Kazan ran wide and wild past the campsite, looking as big as the Colorado River, but untampered with and immeasurably pure by comparison.

Early in the morning Marypat and I hiked to a low ridge to inspect artifacts, and I gazed off across the river to the hills and bedrock outcrops. Something looked different, dynamic. I looked through binoculars and remembered to shut my mouth only when a black fly flew into it. "Look, Marypat." I handed her the glasses, unable to explain.

Her reaction mimicked mine in all essential details. "It's solid caribou!" she finally breathed.

The night before, an empty landscape had lain across the river; by morning the view in all directions consisted almost entirely of caribou. The herds pushed steadily along the valley, moving south, trotting after one another, stopping briefly to graze, but always heading briskly along again, prodded by instinct, goaded by the fear of being left behind. I swept the binoculars across the land, and everywhere masses of deer pulsed over the tundra, majestic antlers standing out against the sky.

We raced back to the tents to roust our partners. Thousands of deer swarmed down hillsides, coming into view as quickly as they disappeared to the south, running along the riverbank, collecting in moist vegetation to graze, a river of wildlife, the current running opposite to the Kazan. Every variation in color and size and stature passed by. Chocolate-brown animals contrasted with others almost white; calves ran to keep pace with hurrying cows; young and feisty caribou cavorted past the old and lame, who managed to stay abreast of the main herd only with great effort.

We forgot entirely about moving on downstream. Film rolled through our cameras by the case, the immediate panorama always a bit different or more dramatic than the last. This was how it felt to see buffalo on the Great Plains, I kept thinking, before people shot them all, before we'd tamed and cultivated and cut up the land, relegating whatever vestigial wildlife populations remained to postage-stamp wilderness areas. All day long the caribou moved by, always south, a restless milling energy fueling their march, an endless supply of animals pressuring from the north.

In late afternoon, mostly as a means to diffuse our excitement and energy, we paddled on against a stiff wind, crossing to the far side to be close to the caribou. We continued downstream a few miles to a campsite fifty yards away from the migrating herd. By evening the migration had thinned to a trickle, but lines of caribou kept passing behind the tents. A short-tailed weasel flirted curiously with our camp from the protection of boulders, a wildlife sighting that hardly merited comment, considering the past few days.

By morning, another misty dawn, the caribou had gone by, and only scraggly bunches dotted the tundra. One herd of twenty or thirty grazed just downstream of our camp while we ate breakfast. Craig and I stood idly watching them as we chewed cereal, when the deer suddenly scattered in a chaotic panic. A small terrified calf galloped recklessly toward the river, literally catapulting with a crash into the fast current and striking off for the distant shore. Right on its heels an imperturbable wolf loped down the riverbank and began swimming after the calf.

Craig and I pointed, speechless, rooted to the spot, cereal bowls in hand. The caribou lost ground to the river, got swept downstream through a set of waves, and swam frantically back toward the original shore, back toward the herd, now scattered and out of sight. The wolf followed every move, swam the same waves, maintained its calm deadly attack. Back on shore, the spindly legged calf shook spray from its coat and ran down the bank. The wolf, as if pantomiming, did the same, pursuing the calf at an easy run, exuding confidence. They ran out of sight, victim and killer.

In short order we packed up camp and paddled downstream, riding through the waves the caribou and wolf had just negotiated, and parked around the corner to look for clues to the drama's conclusion. The calf had barely made two hundred yards. In the time it had taken us to finish breakfast and load up, the lone wolf had killed the caribou and devoured nearly half the small animal. The torn eviscerated carcass testified to the unequivocal laws of the wild, an unedited confrontation with life and death in the ongoing struggle for survival.

We had witnessed the most dramatic form of struggle, but had seen other versions along the way. I remembered the abandoned cygnet that had very nearly lost its life as a result of our avarice for a photograph. And, earlier in the journey, we'd watched a pair of herring gulls lure one of their own kind off its nest long enough for a third bird to swoop in and steal the egg.

Although the wolf exhibited a chilling calm in ending the life of the small caribou, there had been nothing demonic or rabid in its action. Gulls stealing each other's eggs or diving at a vulnerable swan acted out of the overwhelming drive to exist. How different were we, hauling fish out of the lakes and rivers to fry over our fires?

6

A mile downriver another herd of caribou moved along the far shore. A huge inukshuk, six or eight feet tall, marked an upcoming river narrows. Might this be a crossing where Inuit traditionally hunted? As if on cue, the lead animals brought the herd down to the river and plunged into the dark current. We quickly paddled to shore and ran into a field of boulders, hunkering behind them.

The deer swam for a long time, even in the narrows, before reaching our side. Light cold drizzle fell on the misty river, a row of antlers and heads moved purposefully across the flow, and we crouched motionless among the weathered rocks, shooting caribou with our camera lenses. In businesslike fashion the herd reached shore, clambered out of the river, shook off a spray of water, and heaved up the steep sandy bank. On the tundra again, the compact herd moved on without a backward glance, unwavering and confident in their instincts. I shared the excitement of an Inuit hunting party, crouched behind rocks, waiting to ambush the caribou that would sustain them. Below Forde Lake we had come across a group of tent rings, the rocks overgrown with moss and lichen. Bleached dried-out caribou bones littered the ground there, decaying evidence of an ebullient primitive feast.

The burgeoning wildlife coincided with a noticeable increase of Inuit artifacts. Given the sights we'd seen, it wasn't difficult to comprehend the concentration of traditional people in the same area. Yathkyed and Forde and Thirty-Mile lakes had been favorite haunts of the Inuit, both for caribou hunting and summer camps.

Inukshuk cairns crowded the shores and islands on Thirty-Mile Lake, covering entire ridges, making the presence of the Inuit a lingering aura. The largest inukshuk we'd seen drew us to a small island, where the carefully crafted pile of round rock towered over ten feet high, a good five feet in diameter at the base, constructed without mortar or chinking.

Strange piles of rock and small circles of stone dotted the ground every few feet. Walking among them, wondering what their purpose might be, I suddenly found myself staring into the eye sockets of a human skull. Grave sites. We had stumbled onto an Inuit cemetery. The piles of rock protected human skeletons, and some had been uncovered, exposed to the bleaching of summer sun and the unrelenting winds of winter.

The skull had subsided into the tundra moss, and gray lichen grew on the dome of bone. How had these people died? Who had buried them? Were they remembered? Had they left life content or desperate, willing to give up or struggling against starvation? We pondered the Inuit remains, walking carefully from site to site, studying the cracked and weathered bones of fellow humans. A tiny caribou calf walked by not thirty feet away, completely alone, as if to ask if we could help find the rest of the herd. Alongside one grave a blue enamel teapot, chipped and rusted, had been left on the ground. Offering or careless mistake?

Wind stopped us halfway down Thirty-Mile Lake, and we chose to camp next to a pair of striking inukshuks. Just out of reach of the waves, a single grave lay on the gravel, a small pile of rocks with a human rib cage visible through gaps between stones.

Inuit lived in their traditional way on the Barrens until the mid-1900s, finally driven off the land by starvation, to resettle in towns like Baker Lake or Eskimo Point. Nobody knows how many Inuit flourished on the Barrens when times were good, but by the 1950s only anemic relics of once-healthy bands remained.

The demise of the traditional Inuit came as the result of their interaction with white culture. Two salient developments, the rifle and the fur trade, initially brought improvement to their lives but ultimately proved disastrous. The decline of their culture may have come about in any event. Life in such a harsh land, predicated solely and precariously on a single animal, would never be easy, but the collapse of traditional ways was unquestionably hastened by the representatives of white society.

Away from the coastlines, Caribou Inuit escaped early contact with whalers, fur traders, and missionaries, but by the closing decades of the nineteenth century, trade goods, rifles, and the introduction of a fur trade economy began making irreversible inroads into the old way of life.

Rifles made hunting far easier, and Inuit killed caribou in comparatively vast numbers. This, combined with the reduction of caribou wintering grounds in the far south, dramatically diminished the size of herds. Slowly, Inuit bands switched to an economy based on trapping of arctic fox. Pelts destined for the fashion mills of western society were traded in the far north for ammunition, flour, tea, and tobacco. Suddenly caribou were not the only source of food and life-giving materials. Where once the fall hunt had been the critical time of year, the yearly trip to the trading post with fox pelts assumed dominance. Inexorably, the Inuit were weaned away from their old routine, becoming linked to market forces that they had no way of understanding or impacting.

When global depression, war, or the fickle moods of fashion dried up fur markets, the Inuit would arrive at a trading post with their pelts, only to find the buying power of their goods drastically diminished or nonexistent. During several tragic years, some traders actually abandoned their posts, leaving Inuit bands struggling to make do, trying vainly to revert to the old ways, weathering agonizing winters during which starvation pounced on the isolated camps.

Traditionally, northern deer had flourished in such numbers that bands could depend on successful hunts, but by the mid-1900s hunters played a high-stakes guessing game on the vast tundra, hoping the shrunken caribou herds would come near enough to kill. Sometimes years passed without a good hunt. When those periods coincided with depressed cycles in the fur trade, death ravaged the Inuit.

The last scattered and emaciated people, final remains of a healthy population, succumbed to their fate and resettled in towns during the 1950s. There, they were forced to adapt again, to adopt the laws and cultural expectations of twentieth-century civilization. Within two generations the Inuit passed from a Stone Age existence to life with snowmobiles, video recorders, airplanes, and drugs. Small wonder that there have been some difficulties.

The stark exposed Inuit skull hovered in my thoughts as I tried to sleep, and I lay a few paces away from another simple grave. The transition those people had been forced to make, leaving behind their land and their efficient survival strategies to cope with the laws and customs and complexities of a foreign society, beggared my imagination. In a few days I faced my own jarring transition, but it shrunk in importance next to theirs. Profound as my experiences and insights had been, prolonged and extreme as my travels had been, the adjustment required of me would be superficial and fleeting, just one adaptation of dozens in a life full of choices and disruptions.

I woke to the moan of wind through the gaps in the nearby inukshuk, the crash of surf, and thought of the exposed grave almost in reach of the waves. Nothing new: we were windbound. To distract ourselves from agitation, we packed a picnic lunch and hiked off across the tundra to a set of low bedrock ridges. Marypat collected musk ox hair caught in the branches of willow and dwarf birch—fine filaments of startling softness. I had read that musk ox fur so effectively insulates the animals that snow on their backs never melts from escaping body heat.

Knock-kneed with curiosity, another caribou calf, alone in a landscape across which we could look for miles, came within thirty feet of us and circled around for ten minutes while we played a game of euchre and snacked on bannock. Feeling the smooth ancient rock beneath me and looking across the broad countryside, back to the lake where our canoes waited, I recognized that I was gathering in a memory, consciously branding the essence of scent and feel and view, taking a sensory grip on the Barrens.

By evening the lake calmed and we continued for eleven miles under the inanimate supervision of inukshuks, guardians of an extinct way of life. I looked back at the yellow canoe once, and saw behind it a cairn made from a spall of granite—a thin curved blade of rock stood improbably on end, delicately balanced but sturdy enough to withstand the onslaught of wind and ice and drifting snow. A metaphor for life in the Barrens.

Wind again challenged us the next day. Lake crossings through substantial waves, a tundra portage around a difficult pounding rapid, whitewater whose strong current we rode like a horse. Miles flowed past in gulps or came in grudging inches. We stopped repeatedly to collect driftwood for fuel, and black flies competed for our blood. All familiar, all flowing together.

We felt the vibrations of Kazan Falls as much as we heard the roar. Well upstream of the whitewater, an art gallery of inukshuks crowded a bedrock knoll, whimsical structures vying for the ultimate in delicacy and balance: low archways, leaning piles that seemed in need of guywires, rocks wearing rakish hats. But the falls preoccupied me. I stayed in the boat, eager to see the challenge, while my comrades walked among the small monuments.

Kazan Falls drops sheer into a narrow boiling canyon, at least a mile long, a shadowed rocky chasm full of sucking whirling river. Upstream, rapids precede the actual falls for two miles—significant rapids, white-water in which a mistake in midchannel would almost certainly commit one to the most breathtaking ride of a shortened life.

Not at all enticed by the thrill of suicide by water, we nevertheless begrudged any additional distance in an already lengthy portage around the gorge. For the better part of an afternoon our two canoes inched down the two miles of whitewater to the lip of the falls. Carefully lining through water we would have run without a second thought but for the falls below, we scouted the route in fifty-yard bites. The four of us jockeyed our craft along shore, the roar of tons of falling water in the background so overwhelming we had to shout at each other.

No one said as much, but Kazan Falls marked the end of our remote days. Already, frequent low-flying planes had disrupted the silence. For more than forty days, we had traveled alone, out of sight of the human race. But Kazan Falls represented the final unnegotiable obstacle to up-stream travel from Baker Lake. Only a few days from town, we would surely encounter other people downriver.

The rest day we awarded ourselves at the gorge was, for me, a day to say goodbye. Marypat discovered a calm pool next to the falls, a pond we might ferry across in a canoe to explore the rock buttress in the center of the drop, around which the river split. For most of the morning we hopped from one vantage point to another in the midst of a wild unknown Niagara, engulfed in torrential sound, dampened by falling mist, the rock under our feet shuddering with the conflict. The sensations urged my heartbeat into a gallop.

Scouting the mile-and-a-half portage, the final one of thirty carries, we collected armloads of driftwood for cooking. Climbing down the rock walls of the gorge, scolded at and dived on by a pair of fearless peregrine falcons, we fished for grayling in current that tugged and ripped at our lures with inestimable strength.

The falls was a fine wild place, a place to exult in. Marypat and I had paddled nearly two thousand miles to reach it, had prepared ourselves by living alone in wild places for more than a year. As on the night before we put into the Athabasca River, when we had listened to the sounds of rain and wind and thought nervously about the unknown river running by, my partner and I lay next to each other at Kazan Falls. Without need of speech, we held each other before sleeping, knowing the thoughts that ran in a fast current through each other's minds.

PART X

RE-ENTRY

Almost immediately below Kazan Falls signs of present-day culture cropped up in the form of garish litter. Back in June oil cans, snowmobile parts, and discarded Pampers had marked the entry to our summer of solitude, and the same trash forecast our emergence. Lengths of nylon lashing rope, chunks of foam from snowmobile seats, a stripped and abandoned three-wheeler mixed together with more primitive remains—more inukshuks, rock hunting blinds, cairn fences that would have coaxed unsuspecting caribou to a crossing where hunters hid.

The Kazan ran as strong and pure as ever, through country as vast and powerful as any we'd seen, but the human detritus, the knowledge that people were certainly nearby, blunted the wild edge of the experience. I paddled along realizing that I had already removed myself emotionally by a notch, that I had submitted to the first stage of re-entry.

At lunch we heard a far-off powerboat. Later we paddled in a headwind past a summer fishing camp, boats bellied up on shore. At least a dozen Inuit stood on an island watching us—children, elders, dogs—a wall tent behind them. A few of them waved and even beckoned us to come over to visit, but we were shy. I wasn't ready to visit, to socialize, even with the descendants of the people with whom I'd come to feel a vague sense of kinship. An image of a traditional camp flashed through my mind—skin tents, kayaks, drying racks draped with fish.

The Kazan hurried to reach the lake. In the final ten miles, the river descends over one hundred feet in a smooth sloping coast. Half a dozen powerboats, wide high-sided freighters, rammed full throttle against the flow, skipping over waves, slowly breasting the swift section. People aboard watched us pass without comment. We held back, lingering without paddling while the river pulled insistently forward.

A substantial knoll, 513 feet high, according to the map, stood out ahead, well back from the river—an eminence we decided might be worth climbing, an excuse to stop the headlong rush toward the journey's end. An Inuit family cruised up as we unpacked, the driver expertly throttling back as he nosed into the slack water near shore, hefting the prop smoothly out of the river and poling in to where I caught hold of the high gunwale.

He settled back on the seat, fished out a cigarette from inside his jacket, and gave us a shy grin. "Hello," he said, "where you coming from?"

"Stony Rapids," I answered. "Saskatchewan."

"Ah," he blew a plume of smoke, paused reflectively. "Long ways."

"Good country between here and there," I responded.

The man's wife sat quietly on the middle seat, her smooth face young-looking as a teenager's. In the broad hood of her jacket an infant slept. A small boy, probably her son, fiddled with an oarlock. A grandmother made herself comfortable between seats, cushioned by flannel sleeping bags, cigarette stub hanging from her drawn-up lips, a scarf over her black hair. From time to time she shifted position, drew on her cigarette, but never looked up at us. If she wore a heavy coat in early August, when was the last time she'd been outside without it?

I squatted on my heels, noting that our faces were nearly as brown as theirs. The warm sun on my shoulders made me drowsy.

"Caribou around here," the man said, gesturing with a sweep of his arm. "Everybody waiting for them."

"We've seen lots of them upriver," I told him. "Above the falls."

"Kaminuriak herd passing through. Pilots told us they're coming. Good winter meat." He tossed his cigarette butt into the river and worked another out of the pack. "Well, see you." He abruptly brought the visit to a close as he drew in the first breath of smoke, stood up to maneuver away from shore, lowered the outboard into the river.

"They leave with about as much dilly-dallying as the Chipewyan," I laughed, straightening up and waving to the roaring boat.

The strong current of the Kazan had helped put us several days ahead of schedule, granting the luxury of extra food. For the first time in weeks I ate until I couldn't anymore, my shrunken stomach disappointing me with its reduced capacity. At twilight the sounds of distant rifle shots cracked through the air, small pops sounding harmless as little firecrackers. When we scrambled to a vantage point, we saw a stampeding line of caribou racing in front of the high hill, and heard the staccato fusillade of modern Inuit continuing an ancient tradition. The caribou had come.

Despite feeling that we had returned to civilization, despite sighting one bear all summer, I slung the shotgun over my shoulder when we struck off to climb the hill in the warm morning. Fresh caribou tracks were deeply embedded in the mud, the tracks of running animals. The hill stood farther away than we thought, an illusion created by the clarity of air. A good many boggy stretches of ground tested our resolve along the way, but we reached the glacially rounded knob of quartzite and ascended its cracked and riven surface to the top.

A pair of rough-legged hawks soared overhead, then set off in a long glide, heading south on motionless wings. A peregrine hovered nearby, watching for prey, and circled the hill. All around, the tundra land stretched to the limits of vision, cut by meandering rivers, dotted with pure lakes. Baker Lake consumed the northern horizon, and the Kazan ran into it, adding its prodigious flow. Back the way we'd come, the river wound from sight, the green land and gray rock surged off under the pale blue sky in a limitless span, a space I filled with intimate memories.

Behind the hill, hidden from hunters, another herd of caribou worked its way south. Seeing them and soaking up the broad wilderness, I had to breathe deeply to keep my throat from constricting. The next view I'd get across such a mass of tundra would come through the small window of a plane.

The Kazan flushed us into Baker Lake that afternoon, running past wall-tent camps stocked with fly-covered quarters of caribou, animals alive and vital less than a day earlier. I paddled only when we had to steer or slow down. The current slid us downhill like a toboggan run, tumbled over the final set of stair-step ledges, gave us a carnival ride. We got cocky, scouting ahead by standing in the bow to take a quick read of the water, and paid for our lack of caution by getting caught on the wrong side of the river and dropping unprepared over a good-sized ledge, scrambling for balance in the waves below. Shot by the Kazan into the calm of Baker Lake, I took what felt like my first breath in miles.

Baker, our last large lake, was as still as a park pond. Emotionally, I'd emerged from the deep wilderness. Kazan Falls, the throat-catching view off the hill, the last farewell sluice down the Kazan, that had been the emotional end for me. Baker Lake was an afterthought, the paperwork at the end of an assignment.

Marypat hadn't so ruthlessly blocked the process of transition. The summer hadn't ended. She would have staunchly held out in some lakeside camp until all supplies ran dry before confronting the wrenching step back to civilization.

She resented Craig's and Beth's talk about getting home, preparing for another year of teaching, seeing friends. For them it was the end of a summer's adventure, a powerful but relatively short interlude in the pattern of their lives. For Marypat and me, reaching the settlement on Baker Lake signaled the conclusion of an odyssey, an occupation so fulfilling, so compelling, as to have become a lifestyle.

Our partners for the summer had no way of sharing that emotional shock, but their exuberance over nearing the end grated on Marypat. She let up in her paddling efforts in order to slip back, out of earshot, to be alone with her thoughts. "I don't want to hear about going home," she responded when I asked why she wasn't paddling hard. We stroked on silently, the droning of powerboats like huge insects in the distance.

But the Barrens couldn't let us slip in without a final test, a blustery memento. Wind, drizzle, and overcast sky greeted us the next morning. So much wind, in fact, that we gave up the forward battle after several miles to hunker in another windbound bivouac, canoes loaded and ready for a break. Beth and Marypat sat next to each other in the beached canoes and talked, while Craig and I each strove to fit indescribable emotions onto the pages of our journals.

For once, we had plenty of food with which to divert ourselves. Snacks led smoothly into a hot lunch, then it seemed a shame to waste the leftover coals, so we baked a dessert. Not long after we cleaned the dutch oven, dinner became the logical order of business.

By the time the wind abated, twilight colored the clouds a dark purple, and we managed to overcome our bloated lethargy enough to paddle. The calm lasted just long enough for us to cross two wide bays. When we camped on a thin sandy spit, waves again humped up the lake and real darkness underscored the waning summer season.

Baker Lake, modern Inuit town, sat incongruously on the rolling tundra not two miles away. The Thelon River, final trip obstacle, ran between our camp and the sprawling settlement. Construction machinery, at work on a new dirt runway, roared and beeped well into the night. I lay awake, unable to block out the noisome background. When the machines eventually shut down for the night, I heard sled dogs howling their fretful lament and the throaty whine of a three-wheeler.

2

Marypat bitterly fought against our arrival. She argued for a rest day on the sandy pit, said the wind was too strong, marshaled every delaying strategy she could think of. But we had already arrived, I kept thinking. To sit in the sandy camp, civilization noise all around us, and pretend we were still in wilderness was pointless. She didn't agree.

Winds were indeed a force to be reckoned with. The current of the Thelon ran smack into an east gale, and the conflict produced waves of sobering proportions. Marypat didn't talk, mechanically went through the motions of paddling.

"Marypat!" I shouted. "You better do up your spraydeck."

No response, her body language saying that she didn't care one way or the other. Waves crested up to the gunwales, the bow plunged and corkscrewed through deep troughs.

"Dammit, MP, I didn't come all this way to die two hundred yards from the end!" My bellow went unheeded. A wave slurped water over the bow plate. "I don't want the trip to end either, but we're here. Do up the deck!"

Sullenly, without acknowledging my words, she snapped the fabric

over the gunwales, pulled the nylon skirt over her head, made the canoe
seaworthy. We paddled the final tumultuous yards in silence, my partner bitter and angry, myself unable to help.

Day Four-Hundred-Sixteen. The red canoe touched shore near the
end of the dirt runway. We climbed out of the boat whose every nick and
contour we knew, stood on shore next to the faithful craft as we had
thousands of times before. Then Marypat walked off to be alone.

Quickly, events wrested control from our hands, sped up the pace,
swept us along. The construction foreman insisted on giving us a lift to
the little airport building, our final portage made by pickup truck.
Within hours a freight plane landed and then whooshed off, carrying our
boats in its belly to Churchill, Manitoba. We would follow in two days.

Beth approached me on the runway. "What's wrong with Marypat?"
she asked. "She's starting to get to me."

"I know. I can't say I understand it. Mainly she's sad." I slapped black
flies away from my face. "She didn't want to come in. I think she's more
afraid than anything. She has a hard time with transitions."

I looked off at the nearby hillside and saw Marypat coming back,
walking slowly, head down. When she drew closer I could see that she'd
made a reconciliation, enough so that I felt free to embrace her,
physically trying to smooth the rough edges of our arrival.

As we negotiated arrangements at the airport building, I noticed an
older Inuit woman who swept the floors and emptied the ashtrays. She
wore an unbecoming janitor's uniform of cheap brown fabric, presenting
an unremarkable figure as she quietly worked at her duties. Although she
spoke little English, we found that she knew the Barrens, was familiar
with the Kazan River. In fact, until she was sixteen she had lived in the
same country we had paddled through, when her family had been driven
off the land by starvation. This woman's life symbolized the adjustment
of her entire culture. Within her lifetime she had lived the primitive
simple round on the Barrens, and then made the monstrous leap to cope
with the complexity and confusion of modern society.

When we talked about Thirty-Mile Lake, Yathkyed, the herds of
caribou and musk oxen we had seen, her eyes sparkled with recognition,
her creased face spread into a knowing smile. The bones of her people

may have lain in graves we'd seen. Her father might have collected meat from the cache on Yathkyed Lake. Her family may have slept on the same ground we had, inside a skin tent.

Our own routine collapsed in Baker Lake. None of it applied anymore. Cold rain fell almost the entire time we stayed in town, and we pitched our tents on soggy ground next to the runway. Suddenly I felt grubby and unkempt, at loose ends, adrift from my moorings. The expedition seemed distant, an experience that had taken place in another dimension, without connection to the present.

On August 7 we waited in the building for our flight south. Cigarette smoke hung in the close warm air. I pushed thoughts of the future from my mind. No job waited for me, we had no house or apartment, no financial security; but, oddly, I felt little concern over future challenges. Instead, I escaped the present by running reel after mental reel of Barrenland sensations—remembering the spring of tundra underfoot, the lightness of the canoe plunging over a ledge, river mist at dawn, the fathomless chasm of silence, the pounce of unimpeded wind, the electric moment of contact with a pair of grizzly bear eyes.

I knew that already the sharp edge of experience had dulled, the lights in my memory had dimmed. But I also knew that if I returned in a week I'd be surprised and invigorated all over again by the spacious breadth of tundra and the fresh breezes on my face. Though I returned, buoyed by success, to the security and known comfort of familiar society, I understood that I left something vital behind: a life force that had flamed fiercely in the lonely lands, a flame I would tend and nourish until I returned.